Cultures of Border Control

Cultures of Border Control

Schengen and the Evolution of
European Frontiers

RUBEN ZAIOTTI

The University of Chicago Press
Chicago and London

Ruben Zaiotti is assistant professor of political science at Dalhousie University. He has published in *Review of International Studies, Millennium, Journal of European Integration,* and *International Journal of Refugee Law.*

The University of Chicago Press, Chicago 60637
The University of Chicago Press, Ltd., London
© 2011 by The University of Chicago
All rights reserved. Published 2011.
Printed in the United States of America

20 19 18 17 16 15 14 13 12 11   1 2 3 4 5

ISBN-13: 978-0-226-97786-7 (cloth)
ISBN-13: 978-0-226-97787-4 (paper)

ISBN-10: 0-226-97786-2 (cloth)
ISBN-10: 0-226-97787-0 (paper)

Library of Congress Cataloging-in-Publication Data

Zaiotti, Ruben.
    Cultures of border control : Schengen and the evolution of European
frontiers / Ruben Zaiotti.
        p. cm.
    Includes bibliographical references and index.
    ISBN-13: 978-0-226-97786-7 (cloth : alk. paper)
    ISBN-10: 0-226-97786-2 (cloth : alk. paper)
    ISBN-13: 978-0-226-97787-4 (pbk. : alk. paper)
    ISBN-10: 0-226-97787-0 (pbk. : alk. paper)   1. Schengen Agreement
(1985) 2. Europe—Boundaries—History—20th century. 3. Border security—
Europe—History—20th century. 4. Europe—Politics and government—
1945–   I. Title.
    KZ3684.5.E85Z35 2011
    [D1058]
    363.28'5094—dc22

                                                              2010032033

CONTENTS

ILLUSTRATIONS

FIGURES

TABLES

This book is about the enduring yet ever-evolving nature of territorial borders in contemporary European and world politics. King Solomon once quipped, "Boundaries are the beginning and end of everything." Borders, the political boundaries par excellence, conform to this precept. After all, they are an essential feature of all the major territorial arrangements that, since antiquity, have dotted the political landscape of the Western world and beyond, from the ancient empires to the medieval city-states and the modern nation-state. Recent discussions about a "borderless world" brought about by globalization have turned out to be premature. Events such as the terrorist attacks of September 11, 2001, in the United States, and long-term trends such as the growth in "unmanaged" flows of people and goods worldwide, have drawn attention to the vulnerability of the current international system based on territorially defined political units (i.e., states), but also highlighted the lasting relevance of borders in the system's management and protection. Even talk of the *rebordering* of world affairs—as recent attempts to build new "security walls" around states have been called—can be misleading, for they imply that borders have (at least temporarily and in some areas) disappeared from the political map. But clearly they have not. While globalizing processes might have rendered them less visible and politically salient, borders have maintained a pivotal role in defining who can move what, where, and when around the world.

Borders thus still matter. Yet borders are not static entities; they continuously change as a result of human endeavor and novel social, economic, and political circumstances. Their current characteristics and functions therefore differ from those of, say, the ancient empires' frontiers or the medieval city-states' walls. Their shape has mutated over time (e.g., from the irregular and "elastic" imperial frontiers to the linear and relatively stable boundaries of the modern state) and so has the pace of their evolution, ranging from the dawdling and imperceptible to the rapid and groundbreaking. Recent policy developments in Europe and in other parts of the world indicate that a phase of unprecedented transformation in the modern, statecentric conception of territoriality is under way, a conception that for a long time has defined the international system and its dynamics. New and oftentimes conflicting demands on states—on the one hand, more economic openness to be competitive in a globalized market and, on the other, tighter security to keep up with ever more dangerous domestic and international threats—have increased the pressure on the current system and encouraged the formulation of alternative models of territorial governance. The dawn of a postnational era for border control might therefore be in the offing.

The argument advanced in this book is that, in order to fully understand the origins, meaning, and implications of these developments, it is necessary to foreground the underlying features and dynamics constituting border control as a distinctive policy domain. For any given time and geographical location, this domain is characterized by a discrete set of assumptions that inform and guide policymakers in the everyday management of borders and that policymakers reproduce—and possibly change—through their activities over time (e.g., debating and drafting political and legal documents, implementing and evaluating policies). The upshot of this line of inquiry is that recent developments in the border control domain are not the result of purely technocratic policy exercises involving carefully crafted compromises among rational policymakers, nor are they the direct consequence of sudden geopolitical shifts affecting a given region or country. These developments are instead due to the fundamental transformations that border control *practices*—understood as a relatively stable pattern of social activities performed by a group over time—have undergone in recent years, transformations that have affected these practices' location (e.g., the spread of border controls beyond a state's national boundaries) and internal dynamics (from governmental relations among state officials to *trans*governmental interactions involving both national and supranational actors). Taken together, these transformations signal that the nationalist approaches that policymakers have traditionally relied upon to manage their countries' frontiers are progressively giving way to new types of postnational border practices that policymakers are performing around the world today.

Although these trends have a global reach, there are evident geographical differences in terms of their significance, content, and timing. Europe has historically been one of the most fecund milieus for political innovation. Indeed, some of the most daring experiments in border control are currently taking place in the region, situating Europe once again at the forefront of global political transformations. It is for this reason that the book focuses on Europe and, more specifically, on events occurring since the 1980s. But while Europe has undeniably been a policy groundbreaker with regard to border control, important changes in this policy domain have occurred elsewhere as well. The argument elaborated in this work used to make sense of recent policy developments in Europe can therefore be applied beyond the Old Continent. The book will explore this possibility, paying special attention to current policy experiments involving North American borders.

Before I proceed further, I wish to acknowledge the support of the many fellow travelers who have accompanied me on this intellectual journey. Emanuel Adler ignited the spark that pushed me to explore new theoretical horizons, and over the years, he has given a sense of direction to my wandering ruminations and encouraged me to continue on my path even in the face of what I thought were insurmountable roadblocks. It is because of him that I have made it thus far. Steven Bernstein and Randall Hansen have provided invaluable feedback throughout. Graduate students and faculty at the University of Toronto's Department of Political Science and the Munk Centre for International Studies have created a vibrant intellectual environment that stimulated my creativity and rendered more bearable what is typically a rather solitary endeavor. This journey has taken me to various places in Europe and North America. I am particularly thankful to the Secretariat of the European Council in Brussels for giving me the opportunity to spend three months as an intern at the Secretariat's Legal Service (Unit 5—Justice and Home Affairs), and to the council's Schengen and Justice and Home Affairs Libraries for allowing access to precious primary sources. The present book would not have seen the light of day if not for the University of Chicago Press and especially David Pervin, who has believed in this project from the very beginning and who has provided helpful suggestions throughout the editorial process. I am also indebted to Sarah Hipworth and Maia Rigas for proofreading the manuscript and rendering it less abstruse, and the *Journal of European Integration* and *Perspectives on European Politics and Society* for kindly granting me permission to reproduce excerpts from the author's previously published material.

Any traveler knows that even a well-planned trip cannot be realized without generous financial support. For this I am particularly grateful to the Joint Initiative in German and European Studies at the University of Toronto and the Canadian Social Science Research Council. Last, but certainly not least, a heartfelt thank-you to those who have always been close to me in this journey's ups and downs. Nancy, Ari, Luca, Chiara, Mom, and Dad: this book is dedicated to you.

ONE

Introduction

Of course, we want to make it easier for goods to pass through frontiers. Of course, we must make it easier for people to travel throughout the Community. But it is a matter of plain common sense that we cannot totally abolish frontier controls if we are also to protect our citizens from crime and stop the movement of drugs, of terrorists and of illegal immigrants.[1]

Anxious to strengthen the solidarity between their peoples by removing the obstacles to free movement . . . the Parties shall endeavour to abolish checks at common borders and transfer them to their external borders.

—1985 Schengen Agreement, preamble and article 17

Europe, Border Control, and the Emergence of a New Common Sense

Margaret Thatcher's 1988 "Bruges Speech" is considered the political manifesto of British skepticism toward Europe. In her notoriously trenchant language, the then prime minister traces an indissoluble link between borders and security and argues that *national* governments (as opposed to supranational institutions) should be in charge of this issue. She also contends that the triad of borders/security/national governments is so ingrained in our collective understanding of what border control means as to not require further explanation ("a matter of plain common sense").

What is interesting (and generally overlooked) in this speech is that, in order to make the case for a "nationalist" reading of border control in front

---

1. Margaret Thatcher, speech delivered at the College of Europe, Bruges, September 20, 1988.

of her Continental partners, the Iron Lady couches her argument in collective terms (hence the references to "we" and "our citizens" in the text). The aim is to present this interpretation not just as the latest expression of British golden isolationism, but as part of a *sensus communis* also shared by the United Kingdom's partners across the Channel. This rhetorical move seemed well founded. Indeed, it was in Continental Europe that the modern "national" conception of borders first emerged (Anderson 1996). According to this conception (which has its roots in the early phases of the modern state-system in seventeenth-century Europe), borders are continuous territorial lines marking the outer limits of a state's authority and a key foundation around which the principle of sovereignty in the international system is built. Borders represent the very essence of statehood (delimiting its authority in the international system) and one of its most visible embodiments (its "skin," according to an often used biological metaphor). At the same time, borders are a powerful symbol of identity and historical continuity, both for the state as institution and for the peoples they contain. Their protection is therefore a matter of "national security" and the exclusive responsibility of central governments.

This perspective has long imbued official arguments and practices in the border control domain in Europe (and elsewhere), and it has been widely accepted by both decision makers and the population at large. Thatcher's take on border control should have resonated well with a European audience. But it didn't. On the contrary, while she was delivering her speech, something extraordinary was under way in the heart of Europe. Since the mid-1980s, a group of European countries (France, Germany, the Netherlands, Belgium, and Luxembourg) had been taking the first steps toward the abolition of controls over their shared frontiers. The goal of the emerging border control regime (which would be known as "Schengen," from the name of the Luxembourg town where the founding agreement was originally signed) was the creation of a common space where not only goods and capital but also individuals would be free to circulate. Schengen did not imply that borders were to completely disappear or lose importance. In order to compensate for the perceived security deficit stemming from the elimination of controls at common frontiers, the regime envisaged the relocation of controls to the external perimeter of the Schengen area, while other, more diffuse types of controls would be undertaken both within and beyond this area.

Borders thus have remained a central feature of Europe's political landscape. Yet the premises upon which the Schengen regime is based clearly clash with Thatcher's vision and with what was, until the 1980s, the dominant nationalist approach to border control across the Continent. First, by joining the regime, a national government has to renounce its absolute power to control the movement of people across what used to be national borders and now are Europe's "internal" frontiers. These controls can only be reinstated in exceptional circumstances, and other partners should be informed of the decision and give their consent. Second, Europe's external borders, while maintaining the function of barrier from potential threats, are no longer purely "national" as had been the case before Schengen. All members share the now-common perimeter defining the Schengen area, even if they do not physically contain it. An individual entering Italy through its sea frontier with North Africa can move freely to Belgium, for example. Hence, the border s/he has crossed is not just Italy's, but de facto also Belgium's.[2] Third, since the external borders are shared, new questions regarding their governance have arisen, questions that were relatively unproblematic when borders were the sole responsibility of individual countries. Who should now be in charge of Europe's external borders? Only governments of countries whose territory includes them? Or should others be involved? The solution envisaged in the Schengen regime is a hybrid system of governance consisting of a mix of supranational and intergovernmental features. Issues of border control have become a matter of multilateral negotiation. These negotiations now involve all countries in the Schengen area and, to a minor extent, future members. The system also entails the partial relocation of the locus of decision-making power over borders. Key decisions in this domain are taken within regional institutions composed of both governmental and supranational actors.[3] Finally, Schengen involves a redistribution of responsibilities among national governments with regard to policy implementation. Each Schengen member must transfer part of its prerogatives related to border control to other partners, while at the same time assuming new undertakings on their behalf. Overall, such a governance system

2. The present is not a legal argument. Formally, borders in the Schengen area are still under each European country's domestic jurisdiction (Müller-Graff 1998). There are nonetheless some interesting exceptions to this rule. For example, articles 109(4) and (5) of the Dutch 1999 Aliens Act provides that the Netherlands' borders, for the purpose of admission of aliens, shall be found at *the edge of the frontiers of all the Schengen states* and that in this context Dutch "national security" means *the national security of all the Schengen states* (Guild 2001: 2).

3. In the early stages of the regime, the key decision-making body was the Schengen Executive Committee. The committee was composed of representatives from each member state's government. The regime's incorporation into the European Union's institutional framework in the late 1990s (see more on this point below) added a more marked supranational flavor to the system. The Council of the European Union and the European Commission now share decision-making power over border-related issues.

could be described as a kind of "intensive transgovernmentalism" (Wallace 2000: 33).

From this brief sketch it is apparent that the creation of the Schengen regime represents more than a mere policy shift, as unprecedented as it might have been. It signals instead a fundamental break from the traditional nationalist approach to border control that had characterized European politics for centuries.[4] As one participant in the initiative put it, "Talking about freedom of movement (in the 1980s) was considered by many as a profession of faith" (Hreblay 1998: 16). Indeed, just contemplating the idea of a postnational approach to border control while the Berlin Wall was still standing was a courageous act. The same argument, however, could be applied to the post-1989 period. The material and symbolic importance of borders is as great today as it was in the past when borders were the object of contention and, periodically, of overt conflict. While they have lost control of other key policy domains (e.g., trade), national governments still consider border management one of the last bastions of their autonomy in the international system. The same could be said for increasingly anxious domestic constituencies who are worried about the negative fallouts of globalization and who still consider well-protected national borders a reassuring presence against external threats. From this perspective, the U.S. government's decision to create *ex novo* a department of homeland security, and to increase the resources and personnel to patrol the country's territorial frontiers in the aftermath of the terrorist attacks of September 11, 2001, can be read as a spirited attempt to reassert both the country's violated sovereignty and the government's own authority (Andreas and Biersteker 2003). The idea of national governments divesting control, even partial, over their borders is therefore controversial and politically risky, more so than in other issue areas where questions of state autonomy are involved. This is also true in Europe, even if some relevant state prerogatives, such as trade and monetary policy, have already been delegated to a supranational institution such as the European Union.

Not surprisingly, Schengen had to endure a long and tortuous gestation before it established itself as the new official approach to border control in

---

4. This was clearly recognized by Schengen's original proponents. The agreement that established the foundations of the regime was signed aboard the *Princesse Marie-Astrid*. The cruise ship operates along the river Moselle, not far from the town of Schengen. That section of the river is legally under the joint sovereignty (what in international law is called a *condominium*) of three countries: Germany, Luxembourg, and France. The choice of the location for the ceremony was therefore highly symbolic of the new "postnational" approach to border control that Schengen represents.

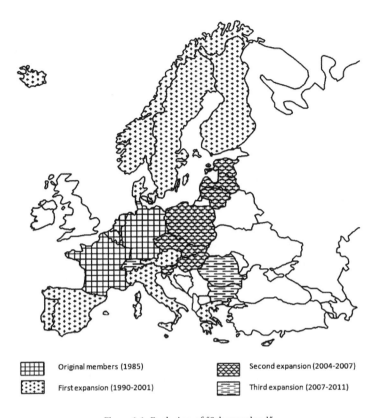

Original members (1985)

First expansion (1990-2001)

Second expansion (2004-2007)

Third expansion (2007-2011)

Figure 1.1 Evolution of "Schengenland"

Europe. The regime began as an intergovernmental initiative elaborated by a small group of countries outside the institutional framework of the European Community (later the "European Union"). This situation changed in the late 1990s. With the entry into force of the Amsterdam Treaty in 1999, the Schengen regime was incorporated into the EU. By then the number of participants had increased from the five original proponents. Today the regime includes all EU members—with the notable exceptions of Great Britain and Ireland—plus non-EU countries such as Norway, Iceland, and Switzerland (see figure 1.1).[5]

5. Unless otherwise specified, future EU members are automatically included in the regime upon accession, although a transitional period is generally required before the regime can be fully operational.

Thanks to the regime's institutionalization and expansion, the term "Schengen" has entered the everyday vocabulary of European politics. Although not free from periodic challenges, its underlying assumptions are broadly accepted by European policy makers. More and more European citizens are also becoming accustomed to the new approach to borders, thanks, above all, to the newly acquired freedom to travel across the Continent without the hassle of passport checks. Schengen has thus become the symbol not only of a sui generis entity on the region's political map (sometimes referred to as "Schengenland"), but also of a new way of thinking about and practically managing Europe's borders.[6] In other words, Schengen is today—*pace* the Iron Lady—the new common sense across the Continent.

The goal of this work is to explain how this epochal development occurred. How did the new postnational common sense about border control emerge and take root in Europe? How was it possible to go against what, until recently, represented the established order throughout the Continent? Why did European governments collectively assent to relinquish part of their sovereign authority on a sensitive issue like border control? Why did they embrace the new common sense? And can similar developments occur outside Europe?

Explaining Schengen: From "Logical Response" to "Normative Shift"

Given their distinctive and constantly evolving features, Europe's borders have, of late, caught the attention of political scientists and other scholars across a variety of disciplines. The literature on the topic is thus burgeoning.[7] Despite the interest, theoretically grounded works specifically focusing on the emergence of Schengen as a new type of governance of borders are rare (Wiener 1999: 442). Accounts by practitioners directly involved in the

6. Telling in this regard is an episode reported by the U.S. Consul in Brussels. In a message posted on the consulate's intranet service, a puzzled staff member candidly asked where the "Schengen-countries" were. He could not in fact locate this entity on a map of Europe (quoted in Van de Rijt 1997a: 47).

7. Relevant works on borders and territoriality in Europe include Parker 2008; Burgess 2006; Bigo and Guild 2005; Walters 2004; Anderson, O' Dowd, and Wilson 2003; Berg and Van Houtum 2003; O'Dowd 2002; Groenendijk et al. 2003; Walters 2002; Meinhof 2002; Zielonka 2001; Christiansen, Petito, and Tonra 2000; Jönsson, Tägil, and Törnqvist 2000; Biggs 1999; Eskelinen, Liikanen, and Oksa 1999; Anderson and Bort 1998; Murray and Holmes 1998; Emerson 1998. For works on borders which make reference to the European case, see Brunet-Jailly 2007; Ansell 2004; Andreas and Snyder 2000; Wilson and Donnan 1998; Anderson 1996; Ruggie 1993.

process represent a valuable source of information on the topic,[8] yet these works mention only en passant the factors that made Schengen possible, and do so without inserting them into a coherent analytical framework.

The neglect of Schengen in the EU studies literature is more surprising. The analysis of the emergence of postnational forms of governance is arguably the defining feature of this academic subfield. Part of the reason for this lacuna is that many EU specialists now look at the European Union as a fully fledged political system, examining its characteristics and functioning, rather than considering it as something unique whose emergence and specificity needs explanation (Hix 1994; Majone 1994). From this perspective, border control is just one of the various domains of the European Union polity. The argument is appealing, but the EU as a polity is still under construction, particularly with regard to its "political" dimension (as opposed to its economic, which is well advanced). The question of why Schengen emerged is thus still significant. A second reason for the topic's neglect stems from the fact that some authors (generally in the international relations [IR] field), although still interested in the origins of the EU and its supranational dimension, have treated Schengen as just a variation of the traditional intergovernmental game characterizing world politics. Moravcsik is a good example of this "business as usual" attitude (Moravcsik 1998). The analysis of the implications of the new regime for borders, and the EU as a whole, that was presented in previous paragraphs should have shown that this "business as usual" argument is both theoretically and empirically untenable.

Neglect does not mean complete oblivion. Schengen's origins have indeed been addressed in the literature. When this has occurred, most commentators have relied on what I call a "logical response" hypothesis. This hypothesis is not always expressed in an explicit and consistent way. It is, however, based on a relatively coherent set of tenets that renders it a distinctive line of argument. Theoretically, most authors relying on this hypothesis use as a frame of reference the insights of what, in EU studies, are known as rationalist and intergovernmental approaches (Steuneberg 2002; Dowding 2002; Rosamond 2000, chap. 6).

In brief, a logical response hypothesis suggests that the emergence of a new regional approach to border control in Europe is the result of a negotiated compromise among key European governments who, acting rationally according to their self-interest and political leverage, were trying to address common problems characterizing the border control domain in the region

8. See, for example, Hrebleay 1998 and the contributions in Meijers et al. 1991; Pauly 1994, 1996; Den Boer 1997a, 1997b, 1998, 2000; O'Keefe 1991.

during the1980s and 1990s (from growing migratory pressure and inter-national crime and terrorism to the obstacles to transnational economic activities across the region). These problems in turn stemmed from either "external" or "internal" contextual factors (Europe's geopolitical position vis-à-vis its neighbors and the creation of a regionwide Common Market, respectively).

Although only peripheral to his work on the European Community, Moravcsik (1998) offers one of the most cogent expressions of this ap-proach. In his "economistic" perspective, Schengen emerged because France and Germany, worried about each other's growing protectionist stance, pressed for a bilateral arrangement to simplify and eventually abolish border controls (ibid., 359–360). The French and German leaders then agreed to include in this arrangement the members of the Benelux Cus-toms Union (Belgium, the Netherlands, and Luxembourg) because of eco-nomic concerns. The idea was "to create a 'Super EEC' (European Economic Community) promoting trade liberalization" (ibid., 359). The negotia-tion phase that followed then was a typical instance of intergovernmental bargaining. This bargaining was part of a strategic game in which France and Germany used the Schengen initiative as "a threat of a two-tier Europe," a threat mainly directed toward the United Kingdom (ibid., 360). According to Moravcsik, economic constraints related to the emerging Common Market shaped European countries' interests and thus contributed to the emergence of Schengen. His model, however, does not preclude the possibility that other noneconomic, more strictly "political" considerations, such as national security, played a role.

Other authors adopting the logical response hypothesis relax some of Moravcsik's intergovernmental assumptions and offer a "bureaucratic" explanation of the emergence of Schengen. This is the case with Monar's "incrementalist" approach (2001) and Guiraudon's "garbage can" model (2003). From their perspectives, the policymaking process leading to the creation of Schengen was more complex and messy than the sole focus on bargaining at a high political level would suggest. Schengen's policymaking was characterized by "various interests, institutions, ideas, problems and solutions which appeared in the process in no preordained sequence, [and yet], the order in which each element appear[ed had] a bearing on the even-tual outcome" (Guiraudon 2003: 266). The actors involved (who include not only high-level decision makers, but also other national, trans-, and su-pranational groups) actively attempted to seize upon the new opportunities offered by the regionalization of the border control domain to pursue their self-interest.[9] In their activities, however, they followed a bounded rationality logic ("do only what suffices to solve a given problem"). Schengen was not, therefore, necessarily an "optimal" outcome.

Over all, the logical response hypothesis seems plausible. It captures some of the core features that characterize the emergence of Schengen, both in terms of process and outcome. The account's appeal also derives from the fact that it reflects the views of most practitioners involved with the day-to-day functioning of the regime. And yet the hypothesis is not fully convincing. The first problematic element concerns the role of contextual factors in explaining the emergence of the new approach to border control in Europe. In most logical response accounts, the relation between these factors and the final outcome (the emergence of the Schengen regime), when explicitly stated, tends to be couched in mechanistic terms. Such is the case with arguments relating Schengen to the emerging European Common Market. The link between economic and political integration is not necessary and automatic. One issue is timing. Explaining the advent of the Common Market as being the cause for the emergence of Schengen is dubious, since Schengen was initiated before the Single European Act[10] was conceived (although the same causes could be at play). Moreover, some of the countries that participated in the Common Market (notably the United Kingdom) did not support the idea of greater integration in migration and border control issues (Lahav and Guiraudon 2000: 60). It should also be noted that Schengen was elaborated not only outside the EC framework but also in competition with it. As an alternative to the Community process, Schengen, despite the cautionary remarks of its proponents, had the potential to weaken or even disrupt the EC as the primary mechanism of European integration.

If, in a logical reaction hypothesis, contextual factors do not provide a clear indication of why Schengen emerged, the same could be said for European states' interests. When the initiative was launched, these interests (which are generally presented as self-evident) did not demonstrate overwhelming support for Schengen. Before negotiations began, the stance of

9. According to Guiraudon, "Law and order officials in charge of migration control seeking to gain autonomy in intergovernmental settings linked their action to the single market and transnational crime. Bureaucrats sitting in interior ministries sought to regain the discretion taken away by courts and the leeway lost to inter-ministerial arbitrage" (Guiraudon 2003: 267).

10. The Single European Act (SEA) was a treaty signed by EC member states in 1986. This groundbreaking document revived the European project after years of stalemate and launched the idea of a "Europe without frontiers" to be achieved by 1992.

most countries toward borders was largely nationalist (particularly France's), or at least mixed (Germany, for example, was particularly active on the Schengen file, but it mistrusted its neighbors and their capacity to render the regime effective[11]). There was also great variety in national approaches to border control across the region (Pastore 2002b). Moreover, no influential national or transnational interest group, or the European population at large, was openly in favor of a regionalization of this policy domain. A rationalist account would leave open the possibility of a change in interests in the period preceding the emergence of Schengen. This, however, did not occur. Given these circumstances, the argument about interests could be turned on its head: how was Schengen even possible given the number of forces opposing it? An alternative option is to consider a trade-off between these interests during the negotiations over Schengen. But this argument is problematic. Schengen entailed a conscious decision by national policy makers to dilute their own country's national sovereignty, a move that went against what rationalists themselves consider a fundamental national interest, that of autonomy in the international system. This development is even more puzzling here, since the issue at stake is national security, a very sensitive issue both in practical and political terms.

The logical response hypothesis represents the mainstream way of thinking about the emergence of Schengen, but it is not the only approach present in the literature. The most influential alternative is represented by what I call the "normative shift hypothesis." Works adopting this line of argumentation draw from sociological theory for inspiration and are consistent with the analytical approach known in EU studies as "sociological institutionalism" or "constructivism" (Jørgensen 1997; Christiansen, Jørgensen and Wiener 2001).

According to normative shift hypothesis, the emergence of Schengen is linked to a change in the ideational context in which key actors dealing with border control in the region are inserted. As a result of this transformation, decision makers across Europe have acquired a new set of "postnational" understandings about the functioning of border control, which in turn have affected their practices and identities in this policy domain. It is in this milieu that Schengen, as a new approach to border control, became possible.

11. According to Wallace and Wallace 2000: 496, the reasons for German activism stemmed from various sources: "A particular sensitive history and geographical position, a citizenship law based on ethnic descent rather than birth within the national territory, liberal asylum law drafted in the aftermath of the Third Reich as the Cold War divided Europe, a large *gastarbeiter* population attracted by its strong economy, and a structural ambivalence about sovereignty and nationhood."

A normative shift account does not deny that material factors such as developments in Europe's geopolitics and economic integration may have played a role in the emergence of Schengen. Unlike rationalist approaches, however, it stresses that the importance of these elements is determined by the way actors dealing with border control have collectively (re)elaborated them. Central in this regard is the role of the normative background in which these actors are inserted. Wiener (1999), for example, in her analysis of the "puzzle" constituted by the British "no" to Schengen (which, *mutatis mutandis*, can be employed to study why other countries did join the regime) argues that Euro-skepticism was not the crucial factor in this decision. Instead, the author emphasizes the "situatedness" of relevant policy makers involved in the policymaking process at the international level. These actors' identities and practices are in fact constituted by "differently established understandings of constitutional norms" (Wiener 1999: 456). The norms informing policy makers can be at odds with each other. This is especially the case in the international arena, where competing national and supranational claims vie for influence on policy makers' identities and behavior.

Whether or not a country decides to join the Schengen regime is determined by battles fought at the national level (Wiener 1999: 454). The acceptance or rejection of the new approach to border control depends on whether its underlying assumptions are compatible with long-established domestic norms and the identities they define. Schengen is problematic in this regard because it impacts the core components that define the sovereign status of nation-states in global politics, such as borders, security, and citizenship (ibid., 448).

In the British case, the option of joining Schengen suggested an identity that did not resonate with the majority of the policy addressees. In particular, some of the more "securitarian" aspects of Schengen clashed with entrenched national principles and practices about justice in fields such as civil rights and citizenship. As a result, the British government couldn't (and still can't) "simply move in and go ahead and change its policies regarding the EU" (Wiener 1999: 447–448).

Since the argument's main focus is on relatively stable domestic constitutional norms, Wiener does not address how a controversial foreign policy decision, such as that of joining the Schengen regime, might originate from a normative change occurring at the international (or, as in the present case, regional) level, and that circumvents the potential problems that incompatible domestic norms create for decision makers. This issue is addressed by Bigo (1994; 2003). Drawing on ideas elaborated by the sociologists Pierre

Bourdieu and Michel Foucault, the French scholar presents the border control domain in Europe as embedded in an emerging "security field" (*"champ de sécurité"*; Bigo 1994). The field represents a social space located at the intersection of the international and domestic political spheres. It is composed of security actors who, through their interactions over time, constitute the field's "forces." The main argument Bigo employs to explain the emergence of this field is a variation of the theme of securitization (Waever 1995; Huysmans 1995; 2000). Hence, the focus is on political strategies involving the increasing salience of border control and the emphasis on the symbolic value of frontiers (here the common European frontier) as protection against danger (Bigo 1998: 149). This dynamic does not follow a "hypothetical political or economic integration" (ibid.); instead, it finds its origins in the activities of practitioners with a specialization in the security field across Europe (police officials, border guards, security consultants). These security entrepreneurs play upon the collective fears and insecurities of European citizens regarding movements of "foreign" populations. Their actions are partly driven by self-interest and aimed at gaining more power and visibility. The security field, however, is not defined by a master plan; rather, it is shaped by the unintended consequences of these actors' practices. By producing and reproducing fear, these practitioners thus create the conditions for the establishment of a new "Europeanized" field of security.

A normative shift hypothesis seems to address some of the problems affecting the logical response account. It is more attentive to the specificity of the border control domain, particularly to the symbolic and "common-sensical" aspects defining it, and is better equipped to analyze the factors influencing their evolution over time. Yet, while promising, this hypothesis, at least in the way it has been applied in the European case, still has shortcomings.

Authors working with this hypothesis need to prove the existence of a clearly defined normative environment functioning as a socializing arena and point of reference around which new ideas are anchored. In this regard, however, Schengen is a hard case, more so than for other policy areas in Europe. The context in which these developments occurred was substantially "thin," both institutionally and in terms of content. Schengen emerged outside the EC/EU, the primary source of integrationist norms on the Continent, and, arguably, the most suitable location for the diffusion of these norms among European countries (thanks, for example, to "norm teachers" such as the European Commission). When the new governance of borders emerged, the institutional context defining the border domain in Europe was overwhelmingly state-centric, both at the domestic and regional level.[12] Therefore there was no "ideal" environment where more prointegration norms could flourish (and actors could be socialized). Rather than its original source, this normative context seems more a consequence of the process leading to the emergence of Schengen.

A normative shift hypothesis thus needs to specify more carefully how a new regional normative background was formed in the first place and how actors were socialized in the process. The way authors relying on this hypothesis have addressed this issue is not completely satisfactory. Bigo relies on security practitioners' activities as the driving force behind the establishment of Schengen. These actors, however, were dragged into the initiative (at least at first), rather than actively supporting it. The process leading to the creation of Schengen was mainly decided at high political levels by key national decision makers. It should be noted that among practitioners there were divisions, many of them opposed (as some still are), to Schengen and its underlying philosophy.[13] Even if we grant that security practitioners played a role in this process, it is not clear how they convinced decision makers to adopt their views, and how they acquired these assumptions in the first place. Bigo also does not explain why Schengen was chosen (and not, for example, a "communitarian" option within the EU). Moreover, although securitization of the border control domain played a part, it was not the initial thrust behind Schengen, since this process started when Schengen was already under discussion.

As this brief overview has shown, even the normative shift hypothesis cannot satisfactorily explain the emergence of Schengen. Despite its shortcomings, however, this line of inquiry represents a valid starting point to examine the puzzle I address in this work. I will therefore now turn to elaborate an argument that builds on its premises. It is my contention that this approach can offer a compelling account of the emergence of the new system of border governance in Europe. The content and details of this analytical framework are developed in chapter 2. In the next section I introduce its main tenets.

12. The same could be said for other areas outside the Continent, which European states could have mimicked.

13. Representative of this critical attitude is the statement made by commissioner of the Bavarian Police in charge of Bavaria's frontiers with the Austrian *Land* of Vorarlberg, Switzerland, and Liechtenstein at the time the Schengen regime became operational: "No alternatives exist to border controls." Quoted in Fortress Europe Circular Letter (hereafter FECL) 32 (March 1995).

Cultures of Border Control and Their Evolution: An Analytical Framework

How did the Schengen regime emerge and become part of the new common sense in Europe? The gist of my argument is that this development should be conceptualized in terms of the evolution of the culture of border control in which members of Europe's border control community are embedded. I argue that the concept of "culture of border control," understood as a set of background assumptions and related practices shared by a policy community in a given domain (here border control), captures the idea of common sense as presented by Margaret Thatcher in her "Bruges Speech." Common sense is, in fact, the status achieved by a mature culture when its underlying assumptions and practices become taken for granted among policy community members and part of their everyday routines. Thatcher was therefore referring to a particular culture of border control when presenting her case for a nationalist approach to the management of borders. I define this culture as "Westphalian" (from the seventeenth-century treaty, which symbolizes the beginning of the modern state system). The Schengen regime did not "fit" into this culture; rather, it was inserted into an alternative, postnational set of assumptions and related practices, which I call the "Schengen culture of border control."[14] Seen in this light, the recent emergence of a new border control regime in Europe can be understood in the context of the evolution from one culture of border control ("Westphalia") to another ("Schengen").

14. By labeling the Schengen project as "postnational," I join the ranks of other social scientists who have used the term to portray recent social, political, and spatial developments affecting Europe and the rest of the world in domains such as citizenship (Soysal 1994), law and governance (Zürn and Joerges 2005), democracy (Curtin 1997), and territory (Appadurai 1996). While sharing the postnationalist literature's key insight ("today we are witnessing new and unprecedented transformations affecting states and their ability to operate domestically and on the world stage"), in this work I do not follow some of its most radical implications, especially the claim that globalization has leveled a fatal blow to the state and made it irrelevant in contemporary world politics. As will be apparent in the following pages, the case of border control in Europe shows that states (or, more precisely, national governments) still matter, although not in the same way they did in the past. The Schengen border control regime's rupture with traditional approaches to territorial governance is reflected in the new transgovernmental modes through which European governments operate, in the mix of inter- and supranational institutional contexts where they carry out their functions and in their relations with supranational and other nonstate political actors. In this sense, Schengen indeed represents a substantial "postnational" reformulation of traditional "strictly national" notions of sovereignty and territoriality in Europe. "Postnational," however, does not necessarily means "poststatist." Claims of the demise of the modern state as a political project are therefore premature. (This theme is elaborated further in the conclusion, where I weigh in on the debate over the future of the European project.)

The use of the term "evolution" to describe this process is not accidental. Borrowing the analogy from biology, I characterize cultural change as being the result of a *variation* in culture and of a process of cultural *selection* leading up to a governance system's final *retention*.[15] The added value of an evolutionary approach to studying cultural change is substantial. First, it averts unilinear explanations that treat the emergence of a new culture as an uncontested (and thus "inevitable") progression (Spruyt 1994). Schengen was not the only option debated at the time. Other potential alternatives were formulated (e.g., the proposals put forth in the context of the European Community/European Union). An evolutionary approach can explain why Schengen was eventually selected over others. Second, this approach is especially attentive to the historical dimension of change, in contrast to the penchant for presentism in many mainstream theories in political science and international relations. The implication of this line of argument is that cultural change does not occur overnight. Culture tends to "settle" over time and acquire a certain degree of inertia. Challenging and eventually "unsettling" a dominant culture therefore becomes a particularly demanding task. Third, this approach leaves space for contingency, which is integral to all political processes. The trajectory a culture takes in fact depends on contextual historical and social circumstances. However, the type of cultural evolution defended here is not completely random. Cultural evolution can be "reasonable," since it is the result of the activities of a community of practitioners collectively pursuing alternative approaches to border control.[16] Moreover, unlike most evolutionary approaches that are applied to ideational phenomena (culture being a typical example), change is not explained in functionalist terms (new ideas are selected because they fit with a given normative environment). What drives the selection process is instead the performance of a culture "in action" (Swidler 1986).

This reasonable and practice-oriented version of cultural evolution can be defined as *pragmaticist*, since it draws inspiration from the work of the American philosopher Charles Sanders Peirce. Peirce defined *pragmaticism* as his own version of the philosophical tradition known as pragmatism (Peirce 1998). Pragmatism has its origins in the early twentieth-century

---

15. On the application of evolutionary theory to the study of cultural change, see Dawkins 1976. On evolutionary approaches in the social sciences, see Modelski and Poznanski 1996. For its application to political science and IR, see Florini 1996.

16. This point is important. By stressing the role of rationality and agency, together with that of process and structure, in the study of change it is possible to avoid one the main pitfalls characterizing sociological works in political science and IR, namely, the overemphasis on structural dynamics.

United States. Instead of being a unified and coherent philosophical system, it is an "attitude," a methodological approach to philosophical inquiry.[17] This strand of thought has had a recent revival that has affected not only philosophy but also other disciplines, including—albeit marginally—international relations (Bernstein 1992; Dickstein 1998; Bauer and Brighi 2008). Peirce is considered the proponent of an analytical and communitarian interpretation of pragmatism—as opposed to other "classical" versions of this tradition represented by William James's *voluntarism* and John Dewey's *instrumentalism* (Goudge 1950; Hookway 1985; Houser 2005). Although generally used as a meta-theoretical standpoint to debate the epistemological foundations of a particular discipline or applied to methodological or normative issues, Peirce's insights (here I refer particularly to his formulation of the logic of inquiry) provide the groundwork for an original and promising analytical framework to address political and sociological questions, including cultural evolution (Wiley 2006). This is particularly the case for the study of the European Union, arguably the pragmati(ci)st political enterprise par excellence (Albert and Kopp-Malek 2002).

Why Retelling the Story of Schengen Matters: Border Control, Europe, and Beyond

Retelling the story of Schengen offers an important opportunity to assess the origins of one of the most far-reaching events in recent European politics. This effort has more than just historical value. Understanding how Schengen emerged can shed light on the dynamics that characterize a rapidly changing political domain and an issue, that of borders, that has acquired a growing political salience in Europe in recent years. Hence, although the main focus of this work is on the events that have led to the creation of the Schengen regime, this work will also sketch some of the main events, actors, and dynamics constituting the story of border control in Europe today and speculate about its possible future trajectories.

17. According to Richard Bernstein (1992: 326–29), there are six common themes that define the pragmatic ethos: the focus on practical consequences (terms related to epistemic and moral values need to be assessed practically); fallibilism (every cognitive, moral, and aesthetic claim is always open to questioning); the emphasis on the social nature of human life (minds and selves emerge socially in critical and creative dialogue with the rest of the community); antifoundationalism (there is no privileged Archimedean point upon which epistemic claims can be solidly based); contingency (the world is not predetermined and its development inevitable, be it by God or man); and pluralism (multiple perspectives on a particular problem help solve it better than a single view).

The story will be outlined using a cultural evolutionary narrative as the main frame of reference. It will not just offer a description of the developments in the border control domain but also provide suggestions on how to *account for* them. This is especially the case for some of the puzzling features that currently characterize this policy domain. For instance, why do Schengen-like intergovernmental policymaking models remain popular despite the fact that Schengen is now incorporated into the European Union, which should be the sole forum for new policy initiatives in this domain? Why is the Schengen regime expanding even though it lacks democratic legitimacy (it is still an élite-centered and top-down initiative imposed on a relatively detached and acquiescent population) and that its new members have very limited influence on its working? Finally, Schengen, even though it was originally conceived as a trade-off between the goals of freedom of movement and security, has become over the years a security-centered and security-driven initiative, and it followed this trajectory well before the recent terrorist attacks on American and European soil. What are the political and normative implications of this trend?

Besides discussing the internal dynamics of Europe's border control regime, this work will also consider some of the added value of applying a cultural evolutionary account beyond this policy domain. One of the subjects addressed is the debate over the future of Europe as political project. Taking as cue the current transformations affecting its borders, is the Continent becoming a superstate, or is it assuming the features of a neomedieval empire? Related to the debate about the European project is the issue of Europe's relations with its "near abroad." To what extent does the evolution of this relationship—both in terms of depth and geographical scope—influence the quest for Europe's identity and sense of purpose? What are the leading assumptions behind the EU's postenlargement foreign policy, such as the recently launched European Neighbourhood Policy initiative?

The application of a cultural evolutionary framework is not limited to Europe. Other cases of potential postnational approaches to border governance around the world will be examined, with special attention given to North America. For instance, does the creation of a North American homeland security field in the aftermath of 9/11 entail a radical break with past territorial practices in the region? Do these transformations indicate that a new culture of border control is emerging across the Atlantic? And if that is the case, are there any parallels with the European experience in terms of the new culture's features and evolutionary trajectory?

Plan of the Book

This work is structured as follows: Chapter 2 outlines the theoretical framework guiding the argument. After reviewing the culturalist literature in political science and international relations and making the case for its usefulness in the analysis of political processes, the argument turns to the concept of culture adopted in this work, with an outline of the main tenets of the three cultures of border control that define the European case ("Westphalia," "Schengen," and "Brussels"). The second part of the chapter addresses the concept of "cultural evolution" by presenting the main mechanisms—*variation* and *selection*—accounting for the emergence of Schengen as a new dominant culture of border control in Europe. The last part of the chapter discusses some methodological issues that this work raises, particularly the operationalization of the concepts of culture and cultural evolution.

Relying on this conceptual apparatus, chapter 3 presents the key assumptions and related practices characterizing the Westphalian culture of border control in Europe. The focus is on the developments in the post–World War II period. In that era, the nationalist approach to border control reached its maturity, but it also faced a growing number of challenges to its dominant position. These developments created a fertile ground for the emergence of potential alternatives to Westphalia. Chapter 4 examines the features of these alternative cultures ("Schengen and "Brussels"), presents the main events that set the stage for their emergence, and considers the reasons why they were pursued.

The following three chapters are dedicated to the process that led to the selection of Schengen and the "weeding out" of the Brussels model in the 1990s. Chapter 5 focuses on Schengen, and in particular on the developments in four areas that characterized the policymaking process over the issue of border control in this period: internal political dynamics, institutional issues, external relations, and the organization of the border control community. The structure of chapter 5 is mirrored in chap. 6, which deals with the (failed) selection of the Brussels culture of border control. Chapter 7 assesses the selection process within both initiatives, explaining why Schengen was successful and Brussels was not. This will function as the premise for the analysis of the incorporation of the Schengen regime into the EU in the second part of the chapter. Chapter 8 examines the consolidation of Schengen culture by looking at the main events that followed Schengen's communitarization and at selected policy initiatives elaborated in this period. Chapter 9 explores the potential of a cultural evolutionary model beyond Europe, focusing on the North American case. Chapter 10 concludes by reflecting on current dynamics and possible future scenarios defining European borders and, more generally, Europe as a political project, taking as a cue the analytical framework elaborated in this work.

TWO

Accounting for Schengen: Cultures of Border Control and Their Evolution

The evolution of frontiers is perhaps an art rather than a science, so plastic and malleable are its forms and manifestations.

—Lord Curzon of Kedleston (1907)

If we were beginning the European Community all over again, we should begin with culture.

— Jean Monnet

Defining Cultures of Border Control

"Culture of border control" is this book's key concept. One may wonder, why *culture?* And what is the added value of using this term to study border control? These are pertinent questions. After all, "culture" is one of the most used (and, in some cases, abused) terms in the social sciences, including political science (Somers 1995: 116–120). Indeed, "culturalist" arguments to examine political phenomena have been the object of scathing criticism. The major objections directed against classic culturalist approaches (e.g., Gabriel Almond and Sidney Verba's work on civic culture in the 1960s) refer to their "wooliness" (the fact that culture is used in a very loose fashion, covering a wide range of phenomena and domains); their determinism (following Talcott Parsons's lead, individuals are considered "cultural dupes," having little autonomy from the context in which they are inserted); and their functionalism (culture is presented as a factor of order and stability in a given society and thus carries with it an inherently conservative bias). Once the behavioralist revolution that swept across the social sciences finally reached political science and its subfields (including international relations), the fate of culture as an analytical category for studying politics was sealed. The concept inexorably lost its appeal and was relegated to the margins of the discipline (Pateman 1980).

After a long period of purgatory, culture has recently "returned" to the mainstream (Jackman and Miller 1996; Kratochwil and Lapid 1995). Dramatic geopolitical transformations (i.e., the end of the Cold War) and changes within political science as a field of study (i.e., the reaction against the positivist diktats on what proper political *science* should be) have rekindled the interest in culture as an analytical tool to examine domestic and international political phenomena.[1] Works adopting a culturalist approach are more eclectic and conceptually sophisticated today than earlier efforts. In the international realm, cultural analysis has been applied to previously unexplored domains, such as security studies (see, for example, Katzenstein 1996; Weldes et al. 1999), and to a variety of levels of analysis, from the national (e.g., Barnett 1999; Johnston 1996) up to the global (Meyer et al. 1997, Bukovansky 2002 1999; Wendt 1999).

The revival of culture is part of a broader movement within political science and IR that has challenged the materialist and individualist bias characterizing the mainstream of the discipline. Authors adopting culture in their analytical framework have therefore put particular emphasis on the ideational and collective elements constituting the concept. Wendt's definition of culture as "socially shared knowledge" is a typical example of this stance (Wendt 1999: 142). To counter the criticism that it is merely an epiphenomenon of other (read material) factors, these authors have also stressed a culture's autonomous impact (be it constitutive, causal, or both) on actors' identities and social outcomes.

In their quest to distance themselves from mainstream approaches, however, most of these authors have sidelined an important dimension included in culture's conceptual field, a dimension that is crucial for its successful application to the border control domain. According to the etymon of the word (the Latin verb *colere*, "to cultivate") culture refers to a "living" entity that is spatially situated and that needs to be constantly nourished in order to survive. This biological imagery indicates that the concept encompasses not only a set of collective ideas shared by a group of actors, but also a more concrete social dimension constituted by this group's activities. The conceptual field covered by the term "culture" is thus richer than the narrow "intellectualistic" interpretation that is often offered in the literature.

---

1. For overviews of the literature, see Hudson 1997; Jacquin-Berdal, Oros and Verweij 1998; Ross 1997; Wedeen 2002.

To be fair, most authors adopting a culturalist approach do make reference to the close relation between cognitive and social structures (their co-constitution and mutual causality), and the fact that in order to have an impact the former have to be instantiated in the latter. These treatments generally do not, however, give equal weight to the two elements of the equation, making the cognitive structures do most of the explanatory work. To fully exploit the potential offered by the concept of culture, it is necessary to counter this imbalance. This can be accomplished by "bringing practices back" into the study of political processes (Neumann 2002: 629; Adler and Pouliot forthcoming; see also Laffey and Weldes 1997). In general terms, practices can be conceptualized as arrays of organized activities in a given domain (Schatzki 2001: 7). These activities assume different forms. They can be verbal (e.g., clichés, scripts, discourses) and nonverbal (mainly gestural; e.g., postures, routines, rituals; Jepperson and Swidler 1994). A fundamental feature of practices is that they instantiate or "congeal" the ideas shared by a group of individuals in their everyday life, rendering a culture "visible" in spatial and historical terms. Inserting them into the analysis of culture adds the concrete dimension that is missing in current culturalist approaches. In turn, this shift of analytical focus would also align political science and IR with other disciplines such as anthropology and sociology, where this "practical turn" has been under way for some time (Schatzki, Knorr-Cetina, and von Savigny 2001).

Practices should therefore be at the core of any definition of culture. In this work, then, I consider a "culture of border control" as a relatively stable constellation of background assumptions *and corresponding practices* shared by a border control policy community in a given period and geographical location. "Background assumptions" are intersubjective cognitive structures that members of the border control community (on this concept see more below) rely on to interpret the reality in which they are inserted and to act upon it accordingly. They are *assumptions* because they suggest what actors should do and who they represent (viz., their social identity) in given contexts and circumstances.[2] They indicate the border control domain's relevant entities and their meaning, specify the range and weighting of the empirical problems to be addressed, identify the "appropriate" members of the community and what counts as a legitimate aspiration, and define the options

---

2. These structures take the form of dispositions activated by a cue in the environment. Their impact is not deterministic, since actors might not follow them. By rendering certain choices palatable and others difficult or socially unacceptable, they establish the conditions of possibility for an outcome to occur. They can therefore be considered as having a "quasi-causal" effect on social reality, although not in a mechanistic way (Yee 1996).

available to members of the community. These assumptions are interrelated and thus constitute a "system." The coherence of this system may vary from case to case and change over time. It can also overlap with or be nested in other, more encompassing systems. The assumptions constituting this system are in the "background" (Searle 1995: 127) because members of the community, while drawing from them, may not be aware of their existence or be able to verbally articulate their main tenets. This is the consequence of the fact that, over time, community members internalize these assumptions until the latter become taken for granted.[3]

Background assumptions render reality intelligible, yet they acquire relevance only when they are instantiated by members of the community in their everyday practices. Culture is in fact a "toolkit" (Swidler 1986) that members of the community employ to address a particular situation or problem they encounter. As we have seen, practices constitute an identifiable and relatively stable pattern of social activities over time; they are what members of a community *do* in their interactions (negotiating, drafting agreements, implementing policies, etc.). In this sense, practices represent a culture's "living" dimension, defining its features and boundaries as well as the identity and purpose of those participating in it.

While background assumptions define the relevant practices characterizing the border control domain, through these very practices background assumptions are reproduced and sustained over time. Background assumptions and practices are thus two sides of the same coin (here the "coin" is culture). Thanks to their interaction, a culture can prosper and secure its continuity. Their interplay also defines a culture's "strength," namely, the capacity to define and organize social reality. This strength depends on the pervasiveness of a culture's assumptions and practices (the degree of diffusion within a community and their level of coherence) and their internalization (the degree of taken-for-grantedness). A culture is therefore dominant (or "mature") when it is the most pervasive and internalized among the community. In other words, it has achieved the status of "common sense."[4]

Thanks to the interaction of assumptions and practices, a culture of border control can prosper and secure its continuity. The production and reproduction of a culture, however, would not be possible without the existence

---

3. On the concept of "internalization," see Müller 1993.

4. Even when dominant, a culture can still be contested. This contestation, however, is minimal, and challengers can be contained. It should also be kept in mind that a culture defining a particular domain such as border control can coexist, overlap, and be nested in other cultures belonging to other domains (e.g., trade, social policy, security, etc.), and these conditions do not necessarily imply a culture's loss of status as an autonomous entity.

of a group of "real" individuals who support its assumptions and enact them in concrete circumstances. In the case of the border control domain, I define this group as a "border control community." The reference to "community" is not casual. Its members share similar background assumptions and participate in common practices in the border control domain; they also know each other thanks to frequent interaction (which might be either personal or mediated through communication).[5] The degree of awareness of the existence of a common identity varies, depending on the strength of the culture in which the community is inserted and the stage of its evolution (emerging cultures tend to be looser than more mature ones; on this point, see below). Moreover, membership in a community is not necessarily exclusive. As cultures overlap or are nested, so are the communities that represent them. Members of the border control community can thus belong to several communities at the same time, and "move" from one to the other according to the circumstances.

Cultures of Border Control in Europe: A Typology

The content and structure of a particular culture of border control, and of the policy community sustaining it, vary according to the particular geographical and historical circumstances. Extrapolating from some of the trends characterizing the treatment of border control in the region in the last fifty years, I have reconstructed three typologies of cultures of border control that I deem representative of the European case. I refer to them as "Westphalia," "Schengen," and "Brussels." The use of these geographical terms is meant to be evocative of the features of each culture. Westphalia and Schengen are historical locations where key agreements having implications for borders were signed (the 1648 Treaty of Westphalia and the 1985 Schengen Agreement, respectively). Brussels is the official "capital" of Europe, and as such represents the very essence of the project of European integration, which, inter alia, entails a particular conception of borders.

Each of these cultures is defined by a set of background assumptions about borders and relevant practices held by a border control community. The background assumptions considered here refer to the characteristics that borders should possess (e.g., linear or discontinuous), to the proper approach to manage them (e.g., national, "pooled," or collective), and to the identity of the relevant border control community (national, intergovernmental,

5. This way of conceptualizing a border control community is consistent with Adler's idea, which he borrows from the field of knowledge management in business administration, of a "community of practice" (Adler 2005; Lave and Wenger 1991; Wenger 1998).

Table 2.1 Cultures of border control in Europe: key tenets

Time frame	Westphalia 1940s–1980s	Schengen 1990s–2010+	Brussels[1]
Borders	Linear, "barrier," functionally integrated, "natural," clear distinction internal/external dimension, nation's outer limit	Semi-linear, "filter," partially unbundled, shared, blurring of internal/external distinction, region's outer limits	Discontinuous, "bridge," fully unbundled, common, continuity between internal/external dimension, EU's outer limits
Border control	National, governmental, absolute, security/military function	International, governmental, "pooled," security/policing function	Supranational, collective, economic/social function
Type of practices	Intergovernmental, bi-/unilateral, symmetric, formal	Transgovernmental, bi-/multilateral, asymmetric, flexible	Supranational, multilateral, symmetric, legalistic
Border control community:			
Identity	National	Regional (intergovernmental)	European (supranational)
Composition	Officials from national governments (ministries of interior, defence)	Officials from EU Council, European Commission, national governments (ministries of interior)	Officials from EU Commission, EU Parliament, EU Court of Justice, EU Council, national governments and parliaments
Relevant texts	Int'l, law (UN Charter, Montevideo Convention); Helsinki Agreement, national constitutions	Schengen *acquis*	Single European Act, Palma Report, External Border Convention, Maastricht Treaty

[1]It should be noted that "Brussels" has not yet fully materialized as a full-fledged culture of border control. So far, it has represented a potential alternative to either Westphalia or Schengen. I return to the issue of "potential cultures" in the section about cultural change.

or supranational). Border control practices consist of what members of the community commonly do when dealing with issues of borders (e.g., debating and drafting political and legal documents, negotiating among themselves and with others, uttering statements, taking political postures, implementing and evaluating policies, etc.).[6] Each of these practices is struc-

6. As this list suggests, the practices highlighted here do not refer to the everyday administration of European frontiers by security practitioners (e.g., border guards), but to the policy making process over borders involving policy makers and their interaction.

tured differently according to the institutional setting in which they take place (e.g., intergovernmental), the number of actors involved (e.g., bilateral), the kind of relations among these actors (e.g., symmetric), and the degree of institutionalization of the policymaking process (e.g., formal).

The three border control communities sustaining these assumptions and practices are regional and consist of policy makers and practitioners active in intergovernmental and EU forums. Among them, we find ministers representing national governments and their delegates, high-level government officials from national capitals or permanent representatives posted abroad, EU officials from the Secretariat of the European Council, and the Commission.

The key assumptions and types of practices constituting the Westphalian, Schengen and Brussels cultures of border control, together with the composition of each border control community and the relevant texts in which the cultures' assumptions are inscribed, are summarized in table 2.1.

Cultures of Border Control and Their Evolution

Being continuously produced and reproduced, a culture of border control is always evolving, even if its core features remain the same. Under certain circumstances, however, a culture may undergo fundamental transformations that lead to its demise and substitution with an alternative culture. In the political field, this process is typically not "revolutionary" in the sense Kuhn (1962) uses the term (i.e., sudden and erratic). The transition from one culture of border control to another should instead be understood as an instance of *cultural evolution*.

Despite some questionable applications in the past (i.e., social Darwinism), evolutionary accounts to explain social phenomena still enjoy considerable popularity among social scientists (Nelson 2004; Sanderson 1990). This is also the case in political science. As Modelski and Poznanski (1996: 316) suggest, authors who employ an evolutionary approach share one methodological trait: "[T]hey reject the model of theorizing represented by classical physics, or mechanics, that is generally implied by conventional paradigms, in neoclassical economics in particular. Instead they endorse methodologies that characterize biology or, more generally, natural history." The shift from mechanical to biological paradigms entails a change from a static to a dynamic type of analysis. It also involves the rejection of determinism and uniformity in favor of an emphasis on probabilities and diversity.

Within the paradigm, different (and sometimes competing) evolutionary models coexist. One important line of demarcation in the literature is between those who believe that there are "real" ontological correspondences between the evolution of the physical/biological and social world and those—the majority—who rely on evolution as a useful analogy to study social phenomena. Authors who support the latter view recognize the differences between the two realms (especially the role of intentionality), and thus believe that it is necessary to reformulate the theory to reflect the specificity of the social world.[7] There are also different views on how the evolutionary mechanism actually works. Darwin's formulation of the theory (the idea that variation is "random" and selection is "natural") is very influential, but not the sole approach social scientists have adopted. A popular alternative is represented by "Lamarckian" versions of evolutionary theory. Unlike Darwin's, this approach stresses the role of human purpose in both variation and selection.[8] There are also diverging views on whether the analytical focus should be put on change in individuals ("ontogeny," in biological terminology) or in a population over time ("phylogeny").

The richness and complexity of the evolutionary paradigm explains why authors belonging to different theoretical traditions within political science and IR have employed some version of evolutionary theory in their analytical framework.[9] While some of these authors mention the role of cultural elements in the evolutionary process (this is particularly the case with those who belong to the constructivist camp; see, for example, Florini 1996), the concept of culture is not central in their analysis. "Cultural evolution" has instead attracted scholarly attention in other disciplines in both the social and natural sciences.[10]

7. These authors prefer to talk about "innovation" rather than "variation" to capture the purposeful nature of human activity, and "reproduction" rather than "retention" to account for the fact that, while a selected character is preserved, it might not necessarily be multiplied.

8. On the debate between Darwinian and Lamarckian evolutionism in the social sciences, see Sanderson 1990; Dittrich 2002; and Hodgson 2001.

9. Examples of rationalist applications of evolutionary models are Spruyt 1994; Poznanski 1993; Modelski 1990; Farkas 1998. For sociological applications, see Adler 1991; Florini 1996; Bernstein 2001; Haas 1990. Modelski and Poznanski (1996) note that evolutionary elements are present in other mainstream approaches in political science and IR. In its emphasis on competition and self-help, for example, neorealism shows a close affinity for social Darwinism. And liberalism, in its search for sources of harmony in world organization, stands close to those strands of evolutionary thought consider cooperation to be a basic organizing principle or survival strategy.

10. In his overview of the current literature on cultural evolution, Nelson (2004) refers to a set of rich bodies of research and writing by social scientists—mostly economists and sociologists— who have been developing evolutionary theories of various aspects of human culture, including science, technology, business organization, and practice.

There are compelling reasons that render a cultural evolutionary approach appealing. At a basic level, the concept of culture seems particularly suited to render more acceptable the transition of evolutionary ideas from the natural to the social sciences. As we have seen, the term "culture" itself embodies an important biological dimension. It is therefore plausible to think about a culture as "evolving" over time. In theoretical terms, the use of culture in an evolutionary framework highlights the fact that, in a social context, change is not just the result of the sum of the new traits acquired by individuals, but instead is a collective phenomenon involving an entire community. Applying the concept of culture in evolutionary accounts also opens up the possibility to include in the analysis the practical dimension of change. As we have seen, practices are an integral part of culture's conceptual field, and in this capacity they can play an important role in explaining the mechanism of evolutionary change. From this perspective, the transition from one culture to another can be conceptualized as the outcome of the dialectical interplay between cognitive structures *and* social activities over time. This move overcomes one of the main problems affecting both rationalist and sociologically oriented approaches that adopt an evolutionary framework of analysis, namely, the tendency to rely on a functionalist argument to account for the mechanism of selection. This argument refers to the "fitness" of innovation to the *existing environment*—be it material or ideational. However, as I already observed in the review of the current literature on Schengen, when the idea of the new approach to border control was launched, there was no clear "environment" in Europe that the emerging regime could "fit to."

For these reasons, an analytical framework based on the concept of cultural evolution represents a promising alternative to either materialistic or ideational perspectives now dominating the literature. As there is a variety of models consistent with the evolutionary paradigm, so a cultural evolutionary approach can take different forms. The one defended here can be defined as "pragmaticist," since it draws inspiration from the work of the American philosopher Charles Sanders Peirce and of other authors who have elaborated on his insights (here the references are mainly to Larry Laudan 1977; 1981; 1984).

Peirce did not explicitly develop an evolutionary framework to study change, and his main term of reference was the "hard" sciences. I argue, however, that his thought is consistent with a cultural evolutionary framework and is applicable to the political domain. Peirce's ideas (and more generally those of pragmatism) were directly influenced by the evolutionary paradigm and in particular by Darwin's theories.[11] This is evident in Peirce's analysis of the logic of scientific inquiry. According to this logic, new collective knowledge can be established when a community of inquirers, challenging existing assumptions dominating a given field, formulates new hypotheses to address unsolved problems and then tests them empirically before reaching consensus over their validity.

The key mechanism in this process is *abduction*. Abduction is "the process of forming explanatory hypotheses."[12] The abductive formulation of new hypotheses is based on the observation of certain facts from which we suppose a general principle that, were it true, would account for the facts being what they are (Anderson 1986; Chauviré 2005). Abduction is therefore a cognitive process that clarifies information that has previously been "surprising." Although human purpose and intelligence play an important role both in the generation of hypotheses and in the acceptance of new empirical evidence, that does not mean that the process is not evolutionary. An innovative practice might fail, and hence it is independent of the outcome of the experimental variation (Campbell 1974; Nelson 2004: 16). The same could be said for the social dimension of change. Peirce stresses how inquiry is a collective enterprise. It is within a community of inquirers that new hypotheses are formulated, experiments are assessed, and validity claims are legitimized (Struan 2006).[13] One of the upshots of this consensualist approach to the evolution of science is that the framing of problems and their solutions are a historically grounded social activity whose structure and dynamics may vary according to the circumstances and the particular community of inquirers involved.

11. Evolutionary theories were particularly fashionable in Europe and North America at the turn of the nineteenth century, the time when Peirce and the early pragmatists formed their ideas. In his work, Peirce incorporated some of the key evolutionary tenets, such as the emphasis on dynamism, creativity, and contingency. On the evolutionary dimension of Peirce's thought, see Hausman 1993.

12. *Collected Papers of Charles Peirce*, 5: 171. References to the *Collected Papers of Charles Peirce* (referred to as *CP* below) will follow the standard procedure of listing the relevant volume and paragraph number.

13. In this sense Peirce's ideas are consistent with Habermas's "logic of arguing" (Risse 2000). This logic accounts for the process through which a community reaches consensus on a particular subject matter. Members of this community may change their identity and interests if they are persuaded during a process of argumentation that previously held norms are not morally justifiable and cannot be sustained in light of the better argument provided by others (Risse 2000: 10). As we will see shortly, pragmaticism's communitarian approach differs from Habermas's because it justifies the achievement of consensus within a community not on transcendental, but on practical grounds.

Peirce's ideas are also consistent with the practice-oriented definition of culture I introduced in this work. Hypotheses must be tested empirically before they can be accepted (Peirce refers to this process as the "fixation of belief"). Experimentation thus plays a crucial role in scientific inquiry. Unlike what positivists argue, the experiment does not just passively confirm a hypothesis. It offers a "lived experience" of the reality the hypothesis entails, which in turn involves a creative interaction between new knowledge and the surrounding social and material environment. Practice also acquires a normative connotation in Peirce's analysis of scientific inquiry. From a pragmaticist perspective, the aim of scientific inquiry is not to unveil (or even get closer to) the "truth" that lies behind the world around us, but to acquire new knowledge that can be used to solve relevant problems. For Peirce, scientific inquiry is not an abstract endeavor, but a practical one. It is justified if it "works" for the community.[14]

Conceptualized in these terms (rational and open-ended, intellectual and practical, socially and historically situated, collective but with an important role for individual actors), the logic of inquiry in the scientific field resembles that which is followed by policy makers when they address a contentious "problem" in the political domain. There are therefore elements in a pragmaticist approach that warrant this conceptual "grafting" and that make it fruitful for the study of political phenomena.[15]

The next two sections elaborate the tenets of this pragmaticist version of cultural evolution and its application to the case of border control in Europe. The argument is structured around the two main mechanisms defining an evolutionary explanation of change. It begins with an analysis of "cultural variation" and then turns to "cultural selection."

Cultural Variation

The premise for the emergence of a new type of governance system is a variation of the culture of border control within which a border control community is inserted. This process involves the emergence at a given historical juncture of alternative cultures challenging the dominant one. It is my contention that, in the European case, this is the role that, in the 1980s,

---

14. There is an interesting parallel here with the work of scholars of technology in the disciplines of economics and sociology of knowledge who assert that technological advance should be understood as an "evolutionary process" driven by the usefulness of new discoveries. For an overview of the literature, see Nelson and Winter 2002.

15. On the political aspects of Peirce's thought, see Ward 2001; Talisse 2004.

"Schengen" and "Brussels" played vis-à-vis the then-dominant "Westphal-ian" culture of border control.

A key element characterizing these two cultures is that in their early stages, unlike the case of a dominant culture, they are not (yet) instantiated into actual practice. They are "potential," each representing a kind of "project" or set of hypotheses about ways in which a particular policy domain could be (re)organized. Potential new cultures can coexist (or even overlap—both synchronically and diachronically) with an established culture and with each other. These projects acquire relevance when they become the object of debate within a policy community. Actors that are external to the community (e.g., pressure groups, experts) may play a role in informing this debate. Yet, at least some members of the community must be the initial "carriers" of these assumptions within the group (which then are passed on to others). Even if taken into consideration, these alternative cultures might not be successful, and therefore "die down" before they are realized. If at a later stage members of the community reconsider them, however, they can "resurrect" and be relevant again.

For the purposes of an evolutionary explanation, the minimum prereq-uisite for the successful retention of a particular governance system is that some sort of cultural variation takes place. To render my framework more compelling, I suggest some general conditions under which this process may be set in motion. Alternative sets of assumptions about borders be-come serious challengers when a dominant culture is increasingly unable to adapt to new circumstances and address in an effective manner the prob-lems (both old and new) characterizing its domain of application (e.g., how to maintain a high level of protection of borders while at the same time opening them for business transactions?). The effects of the weakening of a culture's effectiveness are growing discomfort among the members of the community.[16] This cognitive and emotional condition—which Pierce called "irritation of doubt"—renders members of the community more aware of the culture in which they are embedded. The assumptions and practices that were previously taken for granted are now foregrounded. This "irritation" encourages members of the community to question a culture's relevance and effectiveness. It also motivates them to search for new approaches to address the unsolved problems. When an existing culture becomes so "un-settled" (Swidler 1986: 278), the conditions for change become ripe.

---

16. The concept of "discomfort" is evaluated in terms of the degree of dissonance (a feeling of consistency or inconsistency between two or more cognitions). On the concept of "disso-nance" in cognitive psychology, see Festinger 1957; Cooper and Fazio 1984.

Cultural Selection

Cultural variation creates the groundwork for the emergence of alternative systems of border governance. An evolutionary framework should then explain how a particular system is eventually retained and others are discarded. I argue that in this process there are two (separate but intertwined) selection mechanisms at play. The first one, "pursuit," accounts for why a new approach to border control is initially pursued despite the fact that it clashes with the culture in which, up to that point, a relevant policy community is embedded. (Seen from the community's standpoint, such a move seems "irrational" or inappropriate.[17]) The second one, "anchoring," indicates how members of a community can reach consensus over a new culture (i.e., collectively adopt its underlying assumptions and practices). Such consensus is in fact the necessary condition for the acceptance of an alternative system of border governance.

Selection Mechanism 1: "Pursuit"

In his analysis of the logic of scientific practice, the pragmatist philosopher of science Larry Laudan argues that the adoption by a community of practitioners of a new approach to solve a pressing and yet unsolved problem whose premises lie outside the parameters of an established culture ("research tradition" in his terminology) involves a sort of worldview shift within that community (Laudan 1977). This process may unfold gradually over time, although not necessarily following a linear path. Contingent factors may also influence it. This shift, however, can still be the result of a "reasonable" decision. What Laudan has in mind is not the kind of (instrumental) rationality favored by political scientists. The decision to consider a new approach to address a pressing issue is based on the rate of "problem-solving effectiveness" demonstrated by the culture entailing such an approach (Laudan 1977: 106–108). It is, in fact, by referring to *a culture's overall capacity to solve relevant problems* that a community of practitioners justifies its reliance on a particular approach, and not, as rationalist accounts would suggest, just to the features of the approach taken in isolation.

Yet, since at an early stage a culture's effectiveness cannot be fully evaluated (its practical implications being unknown), a community will pursue the new approach if it considers this approach and the culture entailing it as "fecund"; that is, if they are deemed to have a high *potential* to solve relevant

---

17. On the role of "inappropriate acts" in cultural change see Finnemore and Sikkink 1998: 897–898.

problems (Laudan 1977: 109–114).[18] Laudan defines this pragmatic (instrumental and forward-looking) logic of action as "rationality of pursuit" (ibid., 112). Following this line of reasoning, it is the act (collectively performed by the members of the community) of projecting the new approach and the assumptions of the culture entailing it according to such rationality that "drags" the transition toward a new culture. Rationality of pursuit functions in fact as both a point of reference around which expectations can converge and as a sort of "cognitive bridge," logically supporting a decision that would be otherwise illogical.[19]

Selection Mechanism 2: "Anchoring"

While explaining why a community would pursue alternative approaches to border control and their related cultures, Laudan's argument cannot say how a particular culture (and not another) is eventually "anchored"; that is, how a community comes to accept and internalize its underlying assumptions and practices. (A community's initial choice to pursue a new culture is in fact based on a *belief* in its effectiveness. At this stage, its underlying assumptions are therefore accepted only "in principle.") To understand how a particular approach to border control is eventually selected, we must complement Laudan's pursuit argument with an account of the mechanism that rendered a culture's anchoring possible.

Following Peirce, this can be accomplished by adding a *practical* dimension to the *cognitive* argument I have outlined so far. In this perspective, members of a policy community are eventually persuaded to accept an alternative culture that they have pursued if this culture, when applied to concrete situations, proves actually to be effective (and more so than others) in addressing the problems members of the community encounter in their everyday policymaking activity. In other words, a successful selection will depend not only on a culture's features (its innovative character, coherence, and plausibility—all elements that accounted for its initial pursuit) but, more importantly, on how a culture performs "in action" (Swidler 1986).

18. The criteria that the community will employ in this assessment are related to a potential culture's features. A culture's innovative character (its ability to reformulate problems in new ways and offer original solutions) is key. Other criteria that can be considered are its plausibility (its objectives are attainable) and cogency (it is internally coherent).

19. This conceptualization is consistent with Schutz's argument about cognitive "leaps" from one province of reality (or style of lived experience) to another (Schutz 1971). More pertinent for the present work, the idea of a "controlled projection" also seems to echo what the French politician Robert Schuman had in mind when, in the 1950s, he presented the European Community project as a "leap into the dark."

One of the implications of this argument is that the activities carried out by a community after a culture's initial pursuit can be considered as "experiments" of that culture before it is accepted or rejected. The term *experiment* points to the fact that these activities are not purely random, but structured around the key assumptions of the pursued culture. As is the case when a culture is dominant, practices are repeated over time. They lack, however, the routinized and automatic modus operandi that characterizes practices in a mature culture, since they are not (yet) fully internalized. These experiments are nonetheless crucial in an evolutionary framework because they allow members of the community to "practice" the new culture[20] and provide the supporting evidence that a community relies on to assess a culture's performance. It is thanks to the *results* of these experiments that members of the community are put in the position to either embrace or discard an emerging culture that they have previously practiced. Thus, if a culture's performance is "good enough" (Simon 1996) and comparatively superior to others' in addressing relevant problems, members of the community should be convinced to lift their reservations about the pursued culture and adopt its underlying assumptions. Conversely, a negative performance will have the opposite result. In this sense, a culture's performance plays the same role of pragmatic validation that the experiment has in Peirce's framework.[21]

Performance is thus crucial in a cultural selection process. How a culture actually performs, however, cannot be determined in advance, but will depend on how it is articulated in concrete situations. Here the term "articulation"

20. These structured and repeated activities give the members of the community an opportunity to get acquainted with the pursued culture and to properly master it (to "get good at it") in the same way that it occurs in sport with training or in theater with rehearsals. The importance of such practice in cultural selection lies in the fact that those reproducing a culture might fail to assess its value because they are not able to properly perform it.

21. This process of validation might be unconscious, and members of the community might not be able to explain why a culture actually worked (and similarly, they might not realize they are internalizing the culture's assumptions through practice). Yet they can demonstrate through their actions that they have embraced a culture that worked. Conceptualized in these terms, the deployment of practices during cultural selection represents a kind of "complex" learning process (Nye 1987: 378–382). By participating in a culture's practices, community members do not just adjust their behavior as response to external stimuli (as in the "trial and error" scenario favored by behavioralists); they instead acquire a new set of assumptions and practices that they can deploy to deal with the reality surrounding them. In other words, they are "socialized" in the new culture. Unlike the traditional interpretation of socialization as involving the learning of a set of social norms and practices *that already exists*, be it in a larger or different community, the type of process examined here entails the exploration of new assumptions and practices that are not yet part of the common sense, and this enterprise is a community's internal affair. This process is thus reminiscent of the experimental logic of discovery followed by scientists.

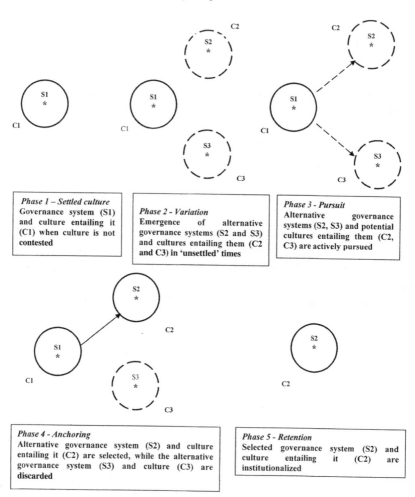

Figure 2.1 Cultural evolution and its phases

should be understood in its double meaning of "to put into words" and "to yoke together physically." Since culture has both a discursive and a social dimension, its enactment involves the arrangement and combination of both utterances and gestures.[22] In this process of articulation, members of the community play a crucial role. Whether acting in self-interest or not, they are instrumental in structuring the debate around a culture's as-

22. On the concept of articulation and its application to studying social change, see Slack 1993.

sumptions, applying the main tenets of a culture, reproducing it over time through their activities, and changing their identities and behavior in the process. A culture's configuration and future trajectory are not determined by these actors' conscious efforts, however (though the overall results might overlap with their interests). Their impact depends to a large extent on the unintended consequences of their actions and is therefore mainly indirect. Consistently with a sociological interpretation of power (Giddens 1976: 102–113), the type of dynamics that ultimately shape the selection of a new culture are in fact diffuse and discursive in nature, rather than stemming from instrumentally driven actions of individuals, as rationalist authors would suggest.

The fact that a culture's performance depends on how it is articulated in concrete circumstances implies that cultural selection is a complex and potentially open-ended process. This process may be slow and incremental, so that positive performance only over time manages to convince a community to accept a new culture. Along the way there can be setbacks to this progression. A culture that has been pursued can fail to persuade a community and "die down" (though, as I have suggested, it can be resumed at a later date if circumstances become favorable again). Once a culture is finally selected and institutionalized (cf. phase 5 in fig. 2.1.), questions about its appropriateness tend to lose momentum. At this stage, a culture is in fact on its way to become "settled" and therefore less likely to be challenged.

Accounting for Schengen: Methodological Issues

Other authors have attempted to account for the recent evolution of border control policy in Europe. The narrative deployed here, however, presents the main events that shaped this policy field from a different perspective, reassessing their meaning and implications and highlighting elements that were previously glossed over. The "retelling" of the story of Schengen thus purports to be original. Yet in terms of its structure and presentation, this endeavor adopts more conventional methods of inquiry. It is based on an *analytical* narrative (Bates et al. 1998; Czarniawska 2004; McLean 2003), which aims to develop a coherent and reasonable account of the main events and processes defining the recent history of Europe's border control policy.

This methodological commitment is reflected in the research design underlying the present work. Although it is applied mainly to one case (Europe's border control domain), the proposed analytical framework is structured in a way that allows the production of multiple "internal" observations that can be used to support the argument. Two subcases are taken into consideration. The first ("Schengen") refers to the intergovernmental initiative that led to the creation of the Schengen regime, while the second ("Brussels") addresses the parallel project developed in the context of the European Union. In an evolutionary account, the Brussels initiative functions as a counterfactual scenario. Despite the fact that each initiative envisions alternative approaches to border control, there are, in fact, similarities in the two initiatives in terms of goals, structure, and time frame. This circumstance offers the possibility of controlling for other factors that could have explained the variation in outcome in the selection process (i.e., Schengen's success and Brussels's failure). To make the argument more compelling, within each of the two subcases, I have examined and then compared four relevant topics: internal political dynamics, institutional changes, external relations, and the border control community's organization. Each of these topics represents instances of a culture's performance in concrete circumstances.[23] The addition of a dedicated chapter on the evolution of North American borders then provides an opportunity to assess the analytical framework's applicability beyond Europe.

Examining empirically a "culture of border control" and its evolution is a challenging task. Cultures in fact "do not stand still for their portraits" (Neumann 2002: 628). They have fuzzy and overlapping boundaries, and they constantly change. It is still possible, however, to successfully operationalize this concept. My starting point is the recognition that culture has a *phenomenic* dimension; that is, it is embodied in actors' lived experience. As we have seen in the previous sections, such experience is expressed through verbal and nonverbal channels that take the form of utterances (i.e., oral or written statements) and behavior (gestures, postures). These elements constitute the empirical "traces" that a culture leaves behind, and it is thanks to them that a culture can be grasped and reconstructed in analytical form. If the traces are nonverbal, they can be identified, either directly through ob-

---

23. The cultural evolutionary argument that I am proposing is also falsifiable. This would be the case if "Brussels" had been selected instead of "Schengen," despite the fact that the former's performance was less impressive than the latter's. In the case of border control in Europe, this was indeed a possible outcome. Brussels, despite its shortcomings, had its appeal, above all because it was based on a well-established and legitimate approach to policymaking at the European level. To generalize this point, a cultural evolutionary account would be falsified if at the end of the evolutionary process under investigation a poorly performing culture is selected over other, better-performing cultures.

servation (including *participatory* observation)[24] or indirectly through actors' recollection of events (as reported in interviews, memoirs, testimonies). If they are verbal, they can be extrapolated from relevant texts. These texts (which might be either written or not, and found in primary or secondary sources) include formal and informal documents (proposals, decisions, memorandums, legislative acts, etc.) and speech acts (generally available in the form of transcriptions/minutes or periphrases) that actors produce.[25]

Once these empirical traces are identified and coded,[26] they can then be "translated" in textual form as a set of propositions (e.g., "Borders are a matter of national security"; "National governments should be in charge of borders," etc.). If these propositions contain recurrent themes, and these themes are interconnected in a meaningful way, they can be read as part of a "narrative." In this context, a narrative is understood as the representation of a series of events or facts related to each other according to an overarching story or "plot."[27]

From this perspective, each culture of border control should be represented by a distinct narrative. As methodological devices, narratives help to capture the multidimensional and dynamic nature of culture as defined in this work. A narrative can have a spatial and temporal dimension (it reproduces events occurring in a given domain over time). Its structure/plot can also assume different configurations (depending on the key tenets, the main characters, etc.) and "modes" (the one employed here is analytic, as opposed to, say, dramatic or epic). In the case of the border control domain, the typical narrative's main tenets should include a description of what borders are, how they should be controlled, and the type of relations

24. This technique, commonly used by ethnographers and ethnomethodologists, involves the full immersion of the observer in a culture, allowing her/him to acquire a deeper phenomenological understanding of its underlying tenets. In summer 2004, I spent three months as an intern at the General Secretariat of the Council of the European Union in Brussels. The job involved attending meetings and briefings of the various groups dealing with border control and interacting with EU officials and representatives of national delegations.

25. The relevant policy groups considered in the present work are the Schengen Executive Committee (1989–1999), the Ad Hoc Working (1989–1993), the Coordinators' Group on Freedom of Movement of Persons (1989–1993), the EU Justice and Home Affairs Council (1993–2007), and the groups set up within the EU after the entry of the Schengen *acquis* in the community institutional framework (the Strategic Committee on Immigration, Frontiers and Asylum and the Frontiers Working Group).

26. The technique adopted in the present work for this task is borrowed from Fairclough 1992.

27. On the concept of narrative and its applications in the humanities and social sciences see Toolan 1997; Ricoeur 1984.

among the main actors. These tenets are extrapolated from the border control practices of a relevant community (negotiations, debates, declarations, etc.).[28] In table 2.1, the key elements of three narratives characterizing the European case ("Westphalia," "Schengen," and "Brussels") are outlined. Each one has a distinctive "plot." The overarching plot for Westphalia is "nationalist," while for Schengen it is "transgovernmental" and for Brussels, "supranational."

Consistent with the methodology applied to study culture in "normal times" (i.e., when it is well established and uncontested), a narrativist approach is employed to operationalize how a culture evolves. In the next section, cultural variation is examined, followed by cultural selection and retention.

Operationalizing Cultural Variation

The procedure to determine the existence of a potential culture is similar to that employed to study a "really existing" culture. Hence, I reconstruct its main tenets in narrative form by looking at how the culture is embodied in relevant practices. The context and type of sources from which the narrative is drawn differ, however, from those of a dominant culture. I look not at those cultural traces present in the border control domain as a whole, but at those within the ad hoc institutional forums created to define and develop new alternatives to current approaches to border control (more precisely, the Schengen Executive Committee in the case of the Schengen initiative, and Ad Hoc Group on Immigration in the case of the Brussels initiative). The material examined in order to define an emerging culture's tenets are the proposals and projects that have been elaborated in the context of these initiatives and the debates that these projects have sparked among members of the community. I translate these elements into texts, and then, as I did for the dominant culture, I examine their structure and content to see whether

28. In this work the main focus is on the activities of the Schengen and Brussels border control communities from the 1980s to today. It is arduous to define these communities' precise size because of their fluctuating nature. A rough estimate would put the number of individuals involved in these two forums at any given time at 600–800. This calculation is based on the fact that both forums were characterized by three levels of decision making: ministerial, coordinators, and working groups. When meetings in each level of decision making convened, they were generally composed of national delegates (two–three individuals per delegation, initially five delegations in Schengen, twelve delegations in Brussels), plus one representative each for the European Commission, the Schengen Secretariat and the General Secretariat of the Council of the EU.

they can be reproduced in a coherent narrative. This narrative will represent a potential new culture.

Operationalizing Cultural Selection and Retention

To operationalize the argument about the rationale for pursuing a new approach to border control, I need to show that each narrative representing the alternative cultures includes references made by members of the community about the types of problems and solutions that these approaches could offer, and to their superior effectiveness (when compared to existing ones). Reference should also be made to the innovative character of the ideas presented in these initiatives (how community members reformulate problems in new ways and offer original solutions) and to their plausibility.

Next, I must examine a community's final acceptance of a new culture's assumptions (that is, a culture's "anchoring"). The operationalization of this process can be accomplished by tracing how the narrative of a potential culture has become the overarching narrative of the border control field (and, in turn, how others did not). A narrative is "overarching" when its main tenets are the most common in a domain, the most coherent and structured, and when a majority of members within the community adopt its tenets in their practices and it is not seriously challenged by other narratives.[29] The relevant textual material used to reconstruct how a narrative in the border control domain in Europe becomes overarching is extrapolated from the negotiation phase (when members of the border control community attempt to define and implement the new initiatives). The main technique used to capture this dynamic process is process tracing.

Applying this methodological approach to each of the initiatives, I look at how the main tenets of a narrative representing a potential culture are articulated during negotiations, and how eventually this narrative overcomes (or not) that of the contending narratives. This interaction with other narratives should look like a series of argumentative exchanges, with one narrative eventually "winning." More specifically, the following dynamics should be observed: when the Schengen initiative is launched, the narrative representing the emerging culture of border control will not be fully consistent and will be challenged by other contestants. Over time, this

---

29. Change is never complete or all-encompassing (remnants of past culture can still survive over the years). To say that a culture has become dominant is, as Ruggie put it, "a matter of balance: of judging ascendancy and decline, reliance and spurious signification" (Ruggie 1993: 166–167; Ruggie was referring to dominant historical forms).

narrative will become more consistent and encompassing (a growing number of community members reproduce it, and among them there could be individuals or groups acting as "cultural entrepreneurs"). It will also defeat challengers, and alternative narratives converge toward it. (In turn, these elements will not be present in the evolution of the culture that was eventually discarded, namely, Brussels.)

In order to establish that members of the border control community were persuaded to accept the assumptions underlying one culture (here Schengen) because of its performance, it should be shown that during negotiations a narrative becomes more powerful if members of the community actually address the particular situation by relying on its main tenets. To render this mechanism more explicit, we should also find evidence of this link in the narrative itself. In other words, members of the community should justify their position on a specific issue (or, more tellingly, a change in this position) by making reference to the approach's performance in addressing that problem.

Finally, to prove that acceptance of a new approach is the result of new culture and not of other reasons (that is, to demonstrate that this outcome is not epiphenomenal of other mechanisms—e.g., material interest, imposition by powerful actors), particular attention should be paid to circumstances in which choosing a certain course of action was not in a community member's material interest, or on instances when the community took a decision consistent with a narrative despite a powerful actor's opposition.

The last stage of the cultural process is *retention*. Retention refers to the mechanism allowing a newly selected culture to persist over time. In the border control domain, this can occur through the signing and ratification of formal documents encapsulating the rules that identify the approach to the management of borders in a given area. In the case of the new "intensive transgovernmental" system that has recently emerged in Europe, the key text is the 1997 Amsterdam Treaty, which incorporated the Schengen *acquis* into the EU framework.[30] The signing of this document signified Schengen's inclusion in a legally binding institutional setting and thus its institutionalization.

The quest for methodological rigor means that the goal of this work is to tell not just any story, but a *good* one. At the same time, this story does not pretend to be the last word on the subject of Schengen and its evolution. Consistent with the pragmatist approach advanced in the previous pages, what is offered is an argument that can plausibly account for the questions

---

30. In EU legal jargon, *acquis* refers to the body of law accumulated so far.

raised by the emergence of a postnational approach to border control in Europe. This argument can be improved or even set aside if a better one is formulated. Incidentally, this method is not dissimilar from the one used by European policy makers in their pursuit and eventual selection of a new approach to border control. In this sense, the model adopted in this work is indeed pragmatist *all the way down.*

THREE

Westphalian Culture of Border Control: From Maturity to Contestation

Frontiers are indeed the razor's edge on which hang suspended the modern issues of war or peace, of life or death of nations. . . . Just as the protection of the home is the most vital care of the private citizen, so the integrity of her borders is the condition of existence of the State.

—Lord Curzon of Kedleston (1908: 7)

[T]he war of 1939–1945 conferred on political frontiers an efficiency equalling or surpassing that of natural phenomena. . . . Whether or not corresponding with natural frontiers, the linear frontiers of Europe have become terrible realities.

—Dion (1947: 6, quoted in Anderson 2002: 16)

Europe, Borders, and the Origins of Westphalia

Territoriality—the control of a defined surface of the globe—and sovereignty—the kind of political authority that is supreme and indivisible—are two of the key principles defining the modern geopolitical vision (Agnew 1994). Borders are an essential feature of this conceptualization of political space. All political systems need some minimum definition of where the boundaries of authority lie, and a mechanism for their maintenance and reproduction.[1] Boundary demarcation, however, acquires a particularly prominent role in the modern state system. In order to distinguish themselves as discrete territorial units, states must possess stable and clearly identifiable borders. Since their key function is to enclose a portion of the globe that

---

1. On the nexus between borders and order, see Albert et al. 2000.

a centralized authority claims as its own and to protect it from external threats, borders must be continuous and fortified lines drawn around the territory. In this sense, states are "bordered power-containers" (Giddens 1976; see also Taylor 1994). Borders also play the "external" function of regulating the interaction among states. The existence of mutually recognized territorial borders is, in fact, a prerequisite for the orderly operation of the international system.

This conception of borders and territoriality, what Murphy (1996) calls the "sovereign territorial ideal," has become so ingrained in everyday life and politics around the world that it seems like the natural way of doing things. Borders have followed the fate that, according to Foucault, characterizes all modern geography: they are treated as "the dead, the fixed, the undialectic, the immobile" (Foucault 1980: 70). This "well-founded illusion" (Bourdieu 1998), however, should not distract our attention from the fact that the sovereign territorial ideal has specific historical and geographical roots, namely, seventeenth-century Europe (Anderson 1996; Zacher 1992). In the medieval era, territorial structures in Europe were complex and overlapping, and no particular hierarchy of governance was dominant. Highly variable senses of territory and space were associated with these structures. The signing of the Treaty of Westphalia in 1648 symbolically represents the beginning of a new phase in which the medieval political space in Europe was reorganized. Gradually, "internal" borders (city walls, provinces, etc.) became less significant. At the same time, the state border took the form of "marked and sometimes fortified line in the landscape" (Langer quoted in Walters 2002). Nation and territory, currency and market, were the end products of this political homogenizing process (Foucher 1998: 238; Walters 2002: 571).

Since its emergence, the historical trajectory of what in this work is defined as the "Westphalian culture of border control" has been inextricably linked with the vicissitudes of the modern state system. This trajectory has not been smooth and linear. In its early stages, the Westphalian culture coexisted with and struggled against contending territorial models. After the seventeenth century, the Church continued to exercise its influence. The same could be said for a variety of other political-territorial arrangements, which, unlike Westphalia, lacked exclusive sovereignty (i.e., the Hanseatic League, the Swiss Confederation, the Holy Roman Empire). Moreover, the Westphalian model was not always applied consistently. Most of the time, states could not or did not want to control borders. As a result, borders were never "hard" (Krasner 1999; Ohmae 1990). Indeed, until the late nineteenth century, administrative barriers to migration between nations in Europe were quite minimal (Castle and Miller 1998: 57–62).[2]

It was only in the twentieth century that the full consolidation of the Westphalian culture of border control occurred. After World War I, European states reinforced the grip over their territories and introduced more systematic checks over their frontiers. Concerns about both national security and the Great Depression played important roles in this development. Protectionism involved the restriction not only of imports but also of potential external competitors in the domestic job market. The foreigner became a "threat." At the same time, a large displacement of population occurred across the Continent. Refugees became a "crisis" and an international "problem" (Sassen 1999: 77–79). Stricter border controls were both a reaction to, and a condition of, the emergence of these events (Walters 2002: 572).

The trends observable in the interwar period continued after World War II. During this period, the Westphalian culture of border control reached its full maturation. The forty years after 1945 represented the phase in which the practical importance of state borders reached its zenith (O'Dowd 2002: 16). The Westphalian model became more pervasive, defining most aspects of the border control domain. It also became more firmly embedded in the imagination and everyday practices of policy makers and the population. However, with the achievement of full maturity, this culture also began to show signs of decline. It had difficulty coping with problems affecting the border control domain, and a growing number of challenges to its authority emerged. Europe was not the only location where these developments took place. Similar trends were occurring in other parts of the world. Europe, however, as had been the case in the past, functioned as the epicenter of and precursor to these transformations. The remainder of this chapter is dedicated to the phase of the Westphalian culture's life cycle that involved the transition from full maturation to contestation. This analysis will function as a launching pad for the study of the emergence of Schengen as an alternative culture of border control, the topic of chapter 4.

Before proceeding further, a methodological clarification is necessary. Much has been written about the evolution of territoriality in Europe in the postwar era. The purpose of this chapter is not to duplicate that literature; rather, it is to use the existing material to complement the analysis of primary

---

2. This was not just the case with Europe. In the United States, a principal destination for migrants, no federal records were kept of immigrants until the 1820s. Immigration into the United States was not regulated until the 1880s (Castle and Miller 1998: 55).

sources and to shed light on the elements that have a direct bearing on the issue of border control. The main justification for this choice is that these developments are preliminary to the discussion of the transition to the Schengen culture of border control, the main focus of this work. This rationale also explains why the following pages will cover mainly key trends, without providing a "thick description" of events occurring in this period. The story of the Westphalian culture's consolidation and contestation in Europe in the decades that followed World War II will therefore be painted only in broad strokes.

European Borders in the Postwar Era: Westphalia Reaches Maturity

World War II had a profound impact on European politics and society, and some of its reverberations were felt in the border control domain. The disastrous consequences of the conflict made it clear to European leaders and the population at large that the violation of the territorial integrity of another state as a means of settling disputes was not only too costly, but also immoral. Rather than displacing the sovereign territorial ideal, however, the war actually contributed to its strengthening. The status quo, namely, fixed national borders, was acknowledged as the only possible solution to the problem of order on the Continent. As Dion put it in the chapter epigraph, borders became "a terrible reality."

The conflict not only legitimized the trend toward the nationalization of borders, but also gave national governments the capacity to accomplish it more effectively. Thanks to wartime mobilization and the economic reconstruction that followed the end of hostilities, European states considerably increased their power of coercion and control over society (Mann 1993). This power had an internal dimension (control over policy domains such as education, health, and welfare provision) and an external one (management of movements across borders, protection against external threats). Thus, despite the shift in policy away from the hypermilitarization that characterized the earlier period, border controls in Europe did not lose relevance. In the postwar era, persons and belongings were individually scrutinized at border posts, borders were patrolled by law enforcement agencies, and the military presence in frontier regions was still substantial (Anderson 1996: 17). Furthermore, since judicial review of executive actions was virtually absent, government agencies' search and seizure powers became almost absolute.

These developments occurred at different speeds and intensity across the Continent, depending on the capacities of the states involved and their geopolitical location. The general pattern was, however, common among European countries. This was true for both Western and Eastern Europe, despite the growing tension between the Warsaw Pact and the North Atlantic Treaty Organization (NATO) alliances and the divisions it created across the Continent.[3] Overall, with the centralization of authority and capabilities, European states had acquired the "monopoly over the legitimate means of movement" (Torpey 1998).

The maturation of the Westphalian territorial ideal in Europe was evidenced by the array of practices characterizing the border control field in the postwar era. This was especially true of the regulation of immigration. The stance adopted by European countries vis-à-vis the movement of populations across borders was nationalist in character. Unlike the nineteenth-century liberal era, access to European countries was strictly regulated and based on short-term permanence.[4] Individuals allowed into a country could reside only for work-related purposes and were granted only limited citizenship rights. One of the dominant models of admission in this period was that of guest worker (Leitner 1997). The policy was based on bilateral agreements between countries of immigration and emigration. This agreement contained the quota of immigrants allowed in the host country and some basic provisions for the protection of workers' rights. Countries that adopted this system included Germany, Austria, and Switzerland. Colonial powers such as the United Kingdom and France instead adopted a model of more permanent labor, which was applied to citizens coming from territories overseas. This relatively open policy changed with decolonization. From the 1960s onward, European governments began to restrict the entry of former colonial subjects (Doty 1996). This nationalist approach to immigration was also clear in the relationships among Western European countries. Rather than cooperating in the post–World War II period, countries of immigration (mostly in northern Europe) competed among themselves to secure the best immigrants and to sign the most advantageous labor immigration agreements with sending countries (Pastore 2002).[5]

3. The Iron Curtain, the militarized line separating the two camps across Europe, represented a special case of a border regime. Its features and implications are examined later in the chapter.

4. One of the effects of greater regulation was that the number of cross-border flows in this period decreased considerably and reached the levels of pre–World War I only in the 1970s.

5. Even when traditional countries of immigration decided, in the early 1970s, to shut the door to new legal entries for economic purposes, that crucial decision was taken in an uncoordinated, competitive way. The only convergence existed between Mediterranean labor-exporting countries and Continental labor importers, but even that limited convergence did not last long (on this point, see below).

Another aspect of the border control domain that underwent important transformations in this period was asylum. The 1939–1945 conflict created a massive displacement of people within Europe. The crisis spurred the international community to create an international refugee regime (Skran 1992; Solomon 1991). The regime's formal rules were codified in the 1951 Convention relating to the Status of Refugees. Its main objective was to ensure that individuals in fear of persecution in their country of origin could seek asylum elsewhere. The regime was originally conceived only for European citizens. Its application had specific geographical and temporal limits attached (these restrictions were lifted only in the late 1960s). Although the regime was international in scope, its administration was strictly state-based. The refugee determination process was, in fact, left to national governments. In practice, until at least the 1960s (and in some cases even later), European countries did not establish an institutionalized system for the protection of refugees and asylum seekers. What existed was largely arranged on an ad hoc basis, and its application varied from country to country.

Both in practical and symbolic terms, the most visible evidence of the changes that Europe's border control domain was undergoing in this era was the diffusion of the passport (Torpey 2000). This state-issued and internationally recognized document had the function of establishing the national identity of individuals crossing borders. It was also used for issuing visas, which determined whether an individual could access a particular country. The passport was therefore the principal institutional means through which borders were defined and regulated. Beginning in the mid-twentieth century, this document became part of everyday life across the Continent (Agnew 2002: 18). Its expansion represented an important step toward the nationalization of European political space.

In these ways, the modern territorial ideal had spilled over into most fields related to border control and had permeated the practices of European governments in the postconflict period. This trend was not only "horizontal" (in terms of the area it covered within the border control domain) but also "vertical" (in terms of internalization of its main assumptions). As noted previously, relevant actors (both policy makers and the population at large) had accepted the new reality as legitimate and commonsensical.[6] This model became the only acceptable political-geographic arrangement and the one

6. This is also true of academia, especially in the social sciences. In the postwar period, most scholars treated states as taken-for-granted units of analysis (Wagner 1989; Häkli 2001).

that others should follow (Murphy 1996: 84; see also Dalby 1991; Ruggie 1993).

One way of establishing the degree of Westphalia's internalization in the decades following World War II is by considering the progressive institutionalization of its main principles in formal legal texts (at the international, regional, and national levels) during this period. Legal codification is proof of the existence of common principles shared in a community. It expresses the consensus of the parties involved. In certain circumstances, it does so even when it is not explicitly articulated, as is the case with customary law. It also formally regulates the practices of the actors involved (its impact depending on the binding legal force of the relevant text). With regard to international law, Westphalian principles are present in various documents drafted in this period. The United Nations Charter, signed in 1948, explicitly mentions states' sovereignty and territorial integrity as two key principles of international peace and stability.[7] The 1978 Vienna Convention on Succession of States in Respect of Treaties recognizes the primordial character of national borders. When a state collapses, previous agreements regarding its borders maintain legal validity. Hence, borders are a preliminary condition for the reconstitution of a state (this rule is known as *uti possidetis*). Westphalian principles were also enshrined in postwar national constitutions and legislation across the Continent. Article 89 of the 1958 French Constitution, for example, stresses the fundamental principle of territorial integrity. This principle cannot be overridden by any attempt at constitutional change that either directly or indirectly might threaten it. In the legislation enacted during this period, the central role that national governments play in regulating access to national borders is evident. In the case of Germany, it is explicitly mentioned in the Grundgesetz, the constitution adopted in 1949. Article 73 states that the federation (as opposed to German regional subdivisions, the *Länder*) has the exclusive power to legislate on freedom of movement, passports, immigration and emigration, and extradition. The principle of territoriality and inviolable borders was also encapsulated in the series of multilateral and bilateral treaties that settled border disputes in the aftermath of World War II (e.g., the peace

7. An earlier example of codification of the sovereign territorial ideal was the League of Nations in the interwar period. Article 10 of its charter stated that all members had "to respect and preserve as against external aggression the territorial integrity and existing political independence of all Members of the League." However, these principles were not forcefully upheld, undermining the league's authority and leading to its ultimate demise (Murphy 1996: 99 et seq.).

treaties involving Germany, the Italo-Austrian agreement on Tyrol, and the Italo-Yugoslavian agreement on Trieste). The Westphalian territorial principles were thus formally recognized as fundamental prerequisites for both internal and international peace and stability.

Besides being incorporated in both international and domestic legal texts, a further indication that the Westphalia culture of border control had reached a high degree of internalization across the region is represented by a less visible development characterizing European politics in this period. Once the remaining outstanding disputes over borders were settled, there was less discussion about borders. This issue almost disappeared from the political agenda (with the notable exception of Germany; more on this point below). The fresh and vivid memories of the conflict, and the chaos that border violation had brought about, certainly played a role in this shift. Borders were still a sensitive issue, and policy makers were careful to avoid raising the subject in their bilateral and multilateral discussions. This silence does not entail the erasure of borders from the political map; on the contrary, it signals the acceptance of their inevitability, of something they had to live with. Williams's description of postwar frontiers captures well this state of mind:

> The sadness of abandoned frontiers. No one wanted them in the first place. Though boundaries are as inevitable as our sense of property, only landlords like them. Though they are a natural response to danger, we forget them when danger is passed. Nothing is less relevant to a people than the boundary of a former people crossing its land. Frontiers are history's orphans.[8]

The fact that national borders after World War II had become less politically visible meant not only that they were taken for granted, but also that there was less need for performative acts to "prove" their existence. Crises over borders in this period were indeed less frequent, and when they did occur, they stirred up less animosity than in the past.

The most notable exception to this trend (but, as we will see, an exception that confirms the rule) is represented by the diplomatic initiative between the Western and Eastern blocs known as the Conference on Security and Co-operation in Europe (CSCE). in the early 1970s. The goal of the conference was to find a way to improve relations between the two opposing sides in the Cold War. Territorial integrity was a key topic in the talks

8. Williams, quoted in Maier 2002: 33.

and one of the most controversial of the entire conference (Ferraris 1979: 115). Being brought back to the top of the political agenda did not mean that national borders were put into question. On the contrary, the debate over this subject showed how the sovereign territorial ideal was strongly upheld by all the parties involved. For the Soviets, inviolability of frontiers was the basis of peace and security in Europe.

> We know of examples of peaceful modifications and we also know of what the consequences were. . . . To speak of inviolability and of the possibility of peaceful modifications is like putting together water and fire: in other words, it means opening the door to revanchism.[9]

All Western states instead insisted that the principle should be defined in such a way so as to avoid the interpretation of a definitive freezing of the territorial and political status quo, which would go against the legitimate manifestations of the sovereignty of the individual states and the legitimate exercise of the self-determination of peoples (Ferraris 1979: 104).

Although the debate at Helsinki seems to contradict the move toward the crystallization of Westphalia, the contrary is actually the case. The peaceful modification of frontiers that the West was calling for specifically referred to the German case. The goal was the return to the prewar status quo, when Germany was a unified nation. It is on these nationalist premises that the West justified its position at the conference. It should also be kept in mind that, on the other side of the negotiation table, the West was facing an actor, the Soviet Union, who, despite its official position at the conference, represented the most dangerous threat to the principles of national sovereignty and territorial integrity. What the West did at Helsinki can therefore be read as the attempt by countries across Europe (and across the Atlantic) to uphold what they considered as a firmly established shared ideal.

Evidence of the internalization of the Westphalian conception of borders in the postwar era can also be found in the developments characterizing the constellation of actors involved with the management of border control in Europe. As we have seen, thanks to the consolidation of the state apparatus, national governments had gained a firmer hold over their states' borders. Border control was mostly a domestic matter, and national governments were the sole agencies responsible for the management of frontiers. What is

---

9. Soviet delegate at CSCE, quoted in Ferraris 1979: 115.

interesting in this arrangement is that, despite the existence of different administrative and bureaucratic traditions, the overall institutional organization of the border control field across Europe was remarkably similar. In most European countries, border control was put under the responsibility of the Ministries of Interior and Foreign Affairs.[10] Although some overlap indeed existed, these two branches of the executive had clearly separate roles and mandates. The Interior Ministry was in charge of border-related issues that had a domestic profile (maintenance of law and order, provision of security and surveillance at borders). The Foreign Affairs Ministry was responsible for the external dimension, such as negotiations over border disputes.

The trend toward institutional isomorphism across Europe meant that the constellation of policy makers coming from the various national agencies began to demonstrate converging views on what the appropriate approach to border control should be, and to be engaged in similar practices both domestically and internationally. While they put different emphases on how to control borders (given the different mandate of each branch of the executive, and because of local traditions), both their vision and practices were nationalist in character, involving—among other things—a clear separation between "inside" and "outside." The movement toward a more homogenous regional border control community in postwar Europe was helped by the increase in interaction among its members. This is particularly the case of Foreign Affairs Ministries, thanks to the experience of peace treaties and other bilateral forums in which they were involved. Interaction was much more limited in the case of Interior Ministries. Participation in the regional community was mostly mediated by similar institutional affiliations, but also through shared nationalistic ideologies. In this sense, Ministries of the Interior were joined together with their colleagues as members of a common "imagined community" (Anderson 1983).

Challenging Westphalia: First Signs of Contestation

Although attempts to confront its dominant position were not new, at least until the early twentieth century the sovereign territorial ideal was rarely

10. Other ministries were involved in the management of borders (e.g., the Finance Ministry for issues related to customs; the Defense Ministry for the military dimension of border control). Their role was only complementary to those of the Interior and Foreign Ministries. An exception to this rule was represented by immigration policy. There is no tradition of "immigration ministries" in Europe as there is for Agriculture or Defence. Immigration is a transversal issue where cross-sectoral conflicts often arise. This issue was, therefore, never confined to a single ministry since it had implications for labor, economics, foreign affairs, social affairs, and internal affairs.

directly questioned. Instead, challenges to the existing order often led to territorial readjustments that winners could exploit to advance that very ideal. More generally, the Westphalian culture of border control adapted to new circumstances and came out of potentially threatening situations strengthened. This is the case, for instance, with the rise of nationalism in the nineteenth century. Until that moment, the state as institution was the fundamental term of reference for the sovereign territorial ideal. Its power and legitimacy were determined by the extension of the territory it included and by the capacity to control it. Who inhabited this space was less relevant than its geographical features. This state of affairs changed with nationalism. A key element of nationalist thinking is the representation of the nation as a group of people who "owns" a particular territory. Political territories are thus the reflections of the nation (Murphy 1996: 97). From a nationalist perspective, it was apparent that the nineteenth-century map of Europe was "unnatural." This situation justified European governments in changing the existing territorial status quo. Indeed, in the second half of the nineteenth century, most wars were fought over territory (e.g., Austria against Prussia and Germany against France).[11]

By threatening the territorial integrity of states across the region, nationalism represented a serious challenge to the Westphalian culture of border control. Westphalia, however, proved to be resilient. In the second part of the nineteenth-century, European states began to adopt nationalist assumptions in their practices. This is the period in which borders and territory became "sacrosanct." Nationalism tightened the link between nations and territory. It also gave new legitimacy to states that approximated the nation-state ideal. As a result, the Westphalian culture not only overcame a potential threat to its dominant position but also became even more powerful.

In the second part of the twentieth century, however, a number of different pressures and arrangements began "to strip away the façade of inviolability of the government within the territorial boundary of the state" (Guild 2001: 3). Two of the most serious challenges to Westphalia were the erection of the Iron Curtain, the fortified barrier dividing Europe in two separate blocs, and the establishment of the European Economic Communities (EEC). The events were quite different in their features and raisons d'être, yet both had a significant impact on how the issue of borders in Europe was treated during this period, and both laid the foundations for the

---

11. The territorial route to aggrandizement manifested itself most strikingly in the colonial enterprise. Until then, colonies were detached from the mainland. Now the goal was to acquire direct control of these territories.

transformations that more recently have characterized the border control domain.[12]

The Iron Curtain as a Cold War Frontier

The new post–World War II world order was centered on the conflictual relation between two superpowers (the United States and the Soviet Union) and their satellite states. The main battleground of what came to be known as the Cold War was Europe, and the Iron Curtain, its most visible symbol. The curtain was a heavily fortified barrier running uninterrupted from Stettino in the North Sea to Trieste in the Mediterranean. It was used as a means to prevent people from crossing from one side to the other (though this was truer for movements from east to west). These controls were particularly effective. The borders it included were in fact the most closed in European peacetime history. In terms of its function as a protective shield against external threats, the Iron Curtain was therefore a traditional kind of border. Yet, if seen through the light of a sovereign territorial ideal, it clearly represented an anomaly. The character of this barrier was not "national." It overlapped with the borders of various countries across the Continent, and in one case (viz., Germany), it actually divided what previously was a unified state. Taken as a whole, the Iron Curtain functioned as a tool of *collective* defense. It was controlled by the two superpowers, indirectly, through political pressure on the country physically containing it, and directly, through a significant military presence on the ground. It was also more than just a territorial line of demarcation. It was a "mental" frontier dividing two ideological camps. From a Western perspective, it was "a line between good and bad, truth and error, justice and oppression, democracy and dictatorship"

12. Although they are my main focus here, the Iron Curtain and the European Community were not the sole challengers to the Westphalian sovereignty principle. One institution that has attempted to overcome the "nationalist" approach to borders in the postwar era has been the Council of Europe. Through its practices, this regional organization has stressed the role of borders as bridges and encouraged cross-border cooperation and the establishment of common legal instruments. However, its actual impact on the border control domain remained limited. Challenges to Westphalia also came from new developments in military technology (particularly the expansion of nuclear capabilities), which altered the strategic meaning of territorial control. The military independence of many states was reduced and their borders became indefensible (Foucher 1989). The nuclear threat certainly played a role in reshaping the meaning of borders in Europe. Their political and symbolic value, however, remained crucial. Herz's claim in the early 1960s about the demise of the territorial state due to the advancement of military technology was thus premature—as the author himself later recognized (1957; 1968).

(Anderson 2002: 17).[13] The curtain was also a vivid reminder of the existence of a powerful enemy, the "other," whose very presence helped cement the idea of a common regional fate. This sentiment was shared by most Western Europeans during the Cold War era. As Margaret Thatcher put it:

> The frontier of freedom here is our frontier, it is America's frontier as well as Germany's frontier, and we are never going to be picked off one by one, and we are going to have a sure enough defence to deter anyone who wanted to cross that wall and come on to Western, free, European territory.[14]

The Iron Curtain was therefore an imposing figure in Europe's political landscape. Yet, it did not seriously threaten the foundations of Westphalian culture. In Western Europe (less so than in the East), the Continent's division was considered an aberration, a temporary phenomenon that sooner or later had to be redressed. This explains the calls for territorial modifications (i.e., from Germany) that would have returned Europe to normality. "Normality," of course, meant strict adherence to the principles of sovereignty and territorial inviolability. But there is also a sense in which the very existence of this fortified barrier actually reinforced the Westphalian model. The relative order and stability (both military and symbolic) that the curtain brought about rendered the idea of national borders dividing Western European countries less problematic, thus paving the way for their "sedimentation" in the minds of governments and citizens across the Continent. This development was supported by the fact that the frontier dividing East and West remained most of the times "cold." The two blocs did not directly interfere in each other's sphere of influence, and that in practice meant respect for national sovereignty—as we have seen in the case of the Helsinki Conference. The stabilizing effect of the Iron Curtain was also felt domestically in Western European countries, where both governments and the population concentrated their attention on growth and welfare (and, more generally, economic issues) and resorted to a more "peaceful" kind of nationalism. National borders did not disappear as a result. They did, however, become less visible in political debates across the region.

---

13. The same could be said of the Berlin Wall, the most visible and controversial part of the Iron Curtain. The wall was a "symbolic axe forced into the body of Europe," "a sign of conflict of power, but it is also a physical expression of the conflict itself, recognizing the limits of dialogue and the limits of reasons" (Tunander 1997: 1).

14. Margaret Thatcher, TV interview for ITN on the occasion of a visit to Berlin, Sept. 25, 1987, COI transcript, Thatcher Archive.

The Birth of the European Community: Doing Away with National Borders?

A potentially serious challenge to the sovereign territorial ideal was represented by the creation of the European Communities (later the European Economic Community and the European Union). As we have seen, World War II can be considered the product of serious violations of both the systemic notion of sovereignty and the sovereign territorial ideal. This explains the renewed emphasis in the postwar era on the respect of these notions as a premise for stability in the Continent. The conflict, however, also showed the dangers of a territorially based system. This system, by putting emphasis on the clear separation among its constitutive units, hindered proper cross-border flows and, more generally, cooperation. The creation of the European Communities can be read as an attempt to overcome the divisions that had so powerfully contributed to the near annihilation of the Continent.

The Community project was officially launched in 1951, with the establishment of a new international organization, the European Coal and Steel Community (ECSC). The key element of the initiative was that the power to take decisions about the coal and steel industry in the member countries (originally Belgium, West Germany, Luxembourg, France, Italy, and the Netherlands) was placed in the hands of an independent, supranational body called the "High Authority." In the following years, the ECSC founders decided to go further and integrate other sectors of their economies. In 1957 they signed the Treaties of Rome, creating the European Atomic Energy Community (EURATOM) and the European Economic Communities (EEC).[15] The latter is the most relevant here, since it dealt more directly with the issues of borders. The main objective of the European Economic Communities was to lift the existing economic and political barriers for the free flow of trade, goods, capital, and people. For this purpose, the EEC Treaty envisioned a single market devoid of internal frontiers and a new supranational model of governance that would supervise and promote this process. As O'Dowd and Wilson note, "the rationality of economic principles was precisely the means employed by the founders of the EU (then "EEC") to desacralize the historically volatile pattern of European national borders" (1996: 9). Economic integration was therefore the instrument that could bring long-lasting peace to the Continent.

The European Community project was not, however, meant to be just an economic custom union. The creation of a pyramid of rights and ob-

---

15. In 1967, the institutions of the three European communities were merged. A single commission and council of ministers, as well as the European Parliament, were also established.

ligations among individual citizens, the member states, and the EC had the potential to fundamentally change the meaning of borders within the European space. Because of the allocation of rights to individuals exercisable if necessary against states and guaranteed by the European Community, intramember state borders would have lost meaning for a substantial number of persons (Guild 2001: 3). This is the case for all kinds of borders (administrative, legal, etc.). The EC project also dealt with the issue of movement of people (for an overview, see Handoll 1995). Part 3, title III of the EEC Treaty sets out the specific rights granted to individuals within the Community in order to effect the abolition of obstacles to their movement. The two key passages are article 48, which guarantees the free movement of workers across the single market, and article 48(3), which allows those seeking work to establish themselves in any member state for the purpose of searching for employment. The directives and regulations taken at the Community level to apply these rights were aimed at member states' nationals involved in economic activity in another member state (workers, the self-employed, and service providers and recipients). With the objective of abolishing internal barriers within the Continent, the European Communities had to devise new arrangements to define what counted as "internal" and "external," and to regulate flows out of and into the Community area. In this regard, the EC Treaty provided a legal basis for the communities to reach international agreements on the freedom of movement with third countries.

Despite its potential, the EC project did not manage to displace the Westphalian model of border control. In the three decades that followed the creation of the European Communities, economic barriers across the Continent were indeed reduced. Yet the objective of achieving free movement across borders remained an inspiration rather than a reality. Progress in easing controls concerning the movement of people across borders was, in fact, minimal. A transitional period was put in place for freedom of movement provisions to take effect. This period ended in 1968, but no major breakthrough occurred afterward.[16] Because of the sensitivity of the issue,

16. Relevant legislation in this period include "Directive No. 68/360 of October 15, 1968," and "Council regulation 1612/68 of October 15, 1968, regarding the freedom of movement for workers within the Community"; "Commission regulation No. 1215/70 of June, 29, 1970 on the right of workers to reside on a member state's territory." In 1974, the Council of the European Union created a working party on passport union and the introduction of a common passport, and envisaged the gradual harmonization of the law affecting aliens. In December of the same year the Commission drafted an action program setting out the basis of action for equality of treatment of workers, granting of political and civil rights, controlling illegal immigration, and coordination of migration policies. The council, however, did not further pursue this program (Handoll 1995: 353 et seq.).

borders were generally left out of community debates (O'Dowd 2003: 17). EC provisions dealing with borders that were approved during this period did not substantially expand the right of freedom of movement. The fact that legislation in this policy area was applicable only to member states' nationals[17] meant that some kind of internal controls at European countries' borders still had to be implemented. As a result, this policy area remained firmly in the hands of governments.

Similar trends characterized the Community's external relations. Although the EC had the legal capacity to conclude agreements with third countries, the fear of overstepping member states' power in matters of freedom of movement meant that in the first three decades of its history the Community did not develop a formal foreign policy on the subject of border control and immigration. In this period, the relationship with third countries was restricted to commercial activities. Over time, with the expansion of the Community's competence, trading agreements concluded with nonmember countries were supplemented with cooperation provisions in the area of development, including the issue of freedom of movement (Niessen 1999: 488). This was true of the first Association and Co-operation Agreements.[18] The freedom of movement aspect of these agreements, however, was limited in scope, since it addressed only the category of workers.

Similar meager results characterized the EC activities with regard to the issue of asylum. As we have seen, the asylum policy in post–World War II Europe was mainly falling within the domain of intergovernmental cooperation. The only relevant action taken within the EC context was a 1964 declaration in which the representatives of the member states' governments meeting in council stated that refugees residing in a member state should be treated as favorably as possible if they wished to enter another member state to work.[19] It did not go further than that.

---

17. In the EC Treaty, the reference is to persons, not EC citizens (art. 3c on freedom of movement; art. 7 on discrimination; art. 48 on workers mobility). But secondary legislation (e.g., regulations) is more ambiguous, referring to "citizens of member states."

18. The most important association agreement was with Turkey (EC/Turkey Association Agreement, signed in September 1963; an additional protocol was added in November 1970). This bilateral agreement envisaged the progressive freedom of movement of workers between the two partners. It offered Turkish workers residing in the EC member state protection against discrimination as regards working conditions, remuneration, and social security. The agreements with Algeria, Morocco, and Tunisia (signed in 1976) contained similar provisions on cooperation in the field of labor.

19. "Declaration of 25 March 1964 by representatives of the governments of the Member States of the EEC, meeting within the Council, concerning refugees," *Official Journal of the European Union* (hereafter *Official Journal*) 78 (May 22, 1964): 1225.

The Gathering Storm: Challenges to Westphalia in the 1970s and 1980s

The major threats to Westphalia emerging in the three decades after the end of World War II were therefore kept under control. Meanwhile, these developments created cracks in the Westphalian edifice, exposing its weaknesses and difficulties in coping with new problems (e.g., the unsolved problem of balancing hard borders with economic integration). Despite being contained, their emergence contributed to the buildup of anomalies within Westphalia, sowing the seeds for future changes.

What made a full-fledged contestation possible was the convergence of a set of developments that, in the late 1970s and early 1980s, seriously put to the test the hitherto dominant nationalistic culture of border control in Europe. During this period, the challenges to the sovereign territorial ideal, and its corollary national approach to border control, became more numerous and serious. Some of the events were global (growth of economic and other types of flows), others more specifically Western European (economic stagnation and unemployment, crisis of the European project, security concerns over terrorism). The following section examines their impact (which varied according to the issue) on the border control domain in Europe.

Immigration Enters Europe's Political Agenda

In the 1970s, European economies underwent a period of stagnation and high unemployment. This situation created pressure for the opening up of borders. Just in bare economic terms, border controls proved more and more costly.[20] At the same time, the economic slump demobilized business interests, which traditionally lobby for openness, while mobilizing anti-immigration political entrepreneurs. Calls for restrictions to immigration (particularly from outside Europe) began to be heard. Immigration patterns were going through a period of major transformations. Until the 1970s, the movement of people across Europe was mainly a regional phenomenon. Individuals moved either within the Continent or out of it (with the exceptions of colonial migration). For the first time, a large number of

---

20. Transportation was one of the sectors affected. In this period, strikes at the borders were becoming more frequent. One of the most serious actions took place in the spring of 1984, when European truck drivers blocked internal border crossings throughout Europe. The strike was in protest of industrial actions by custom officers. It aimed to render European policy makers more aware of the gap between the economic realities, the political discourse over Europe and the daily practice of administrations, and to pressure them to take action (Hreblay 1998: 15).

non-Europeans started to arrive and settle in the Continent. At the same time, longtime guest workers decided to send for their families rather than return home. Migration became an issue not just for its size, but because it was linked to the widespread economic recession. The result was the drafting by European governments of protectionist policies to restrict the entry of foreigners. These policies were introduced first in northern Europe, but the trend soon spread to the entire Continent.

Developments in international politics also helped put the issue of migration on European governments' agendas. In the 1980s, the relations between the two Cold War blocs were warming, at least in Europe. The calmer atmosphere did not necessarily translate into more openness among Western European countries regarding border control, however. The "softening" of the Iron Curtain could in fact imply greater undesired cross-border flows of migrants, criminals, and smugglers. Even before the fall of the Berlin Wall, which occurred only at the end of the decade, Western European governments had become preoccupied with a potential "invasion" from the East.

Regional institutions such as the European Community were neither capable nor willing to challenge European governments in their tough stance toward the issue of migration and border control. The European courts were the only exception. In response to this restrictive approach adopted by member states, the European Court of Justice (ECJ), the court of final interpretation of Community law, became more active in this policy domain. When the European economy was booming, issues arising in the courts about free movement of EC citizens were primarily limited to social security coordination matters. Once member states began seeking to expel migrant workers, including nationals of other member states, the legal caseload at the EC level expanded. Recourse to rights contained in Community law limiting the right to expel on grounds of public policy, security, and health was the territory of dispute between the member states and the individual. In a series of judgments from 1974 onward, the European Court of Justice found in favor of the right of the individual to free movement and thus seriously limited the right of member states to prevent the movement or expel the individual on the basis of Community law in the absence of truly exceptional circumstances. The court's attempt to limit member states' powers over issues that had security implications soured the relations between the two institutional actors. The opposition to the court's activism was apparent in the refusal of EC governments to fully respect the spirit of its rulings in policies and legislation in this period. The tension over the issue of freedom of movement between member states and the ECJ, and more generally the EC institutions, continued in the following years.

The "Euro-sclerosis"

As for immigration policy, economic factors were a crucial variable in the developments characterizing the European Communities since the 1970s. The revamping of the European project (particularly the creation of a common market) was believed to be one way to come out of stagnation and relaunch Europe's economy. Market integration thus became the main objective of the European Community, reversing the traditional means-ends relationship that until that moment had characterized the European integration project (O'Dowd 2003: 19). As a result, in the 1980s national borders were conceived not as barriers to political union but as obstacles to the completion of a European market.[21]

During this time, however, the workings of the EC were stalled. A phase of "Euro-sclerosis" was blocking attempts at reform. The contentious issues on the table were various (Saunier describes Europe as being affected by "ten Achilles' heels"; Saunier 2001: 475). Particularly thorny was the disagreement over the appropriate strategies to overcome stagnation and the controversy over the United Kingdom's budgetary contribution. (The British government wanted to increase the rebate on farm subsidies given to the Community). Some European governments were also nervous about the upcoming enlargement of the EC to include the Iberian Peninsula and its possible economic and social consequences. For example, with enlargement, France would no longer be the net beneficiary of Common Agricultural Policy (CAP) rebates.

At this stage, the focus of the debate over the future of the EC remained restricted mostly to economic issues and did not spill over to the border control domain. The then British prime minister, Margaret Thatcher, made this point very clear: "I did not join Europe to have free movement of terrorists, criminals, drugs, plant and animal diseases and rabies, and illegal migrants" (quoted in O'Dowd 2003: 33, n. 5). The renewed interest in the idea of a common market, however, stimulated the discussion about the entire project of European integration and, in particular, institutional issues, such as the expansion and strengthening of Community competence. This discussion also indirectly informed the border control domain. The creation of the Common Market implied the abolition of border controls (on goods, capital, and services) but also a revision of the existing policies regarding the movement of people, which had to be more open and regulated

---

21. In the 1970s, economic and other types of exchange had grown considerably in the region, again reaching pre–World War II levels.

at the regional level to take into account the new circumstances on the ground. The expansion and strengthening of the EC could also have meant a greater role for its institutions regarding the issue of movement of people. Support for change in the European Community thus grew steadily during the early 1980s.

Security Matters: Terrorism and Cross-border Police Cooperation

Concerns over the effects of rising migration flows highlight another factor that, although indirectly, played an important role in challenging the then dominant culture of border control: security and, more specially, the spike in terrorist activities across the Continent in the 1970s and 1980s. In this period, terrorism affected several Western European countries (the United Kingdom, Italy, Germany, France, and Spain). The origins, organization, goals, and strength of the groups perpetrating acts of violence varied from country to country. They were nonetheless all perceived as a serious threat (either direct or indirect) to state institutions. Moreover, although most of these groups were nationally based, they often had cross-border connections and support bases. The specter of instability created by terrorism spurred a greater involvement of European governments, and in particular security agencies, in the surveillance of national and foreign citizens. It is in this context that a more enhanced cooperation on security matters—something that had always been a jealously kept prerogative of national institutions— began to develop across Europe (Bigo 1996; Walker 1998). The most far-reaching development in this period was the creation in 1976 of the TREVI group (the name is an acronym for "terrorism, radicalism, extremism, and violence"). The group was composed of so-called TREVI Ministers (EC home/interior ministers responsible for policing and security matters), TREVI senior officials (comprising a senior Interior Ministry official from each of the EC states and in charge of preparing the work for the ministers), and a number of working groups and subgroups attended by police officers and internal security agencies. The group's activity involved direct bilateral exchange of confidential information within a common framework. Initially the group's organization and meetings were informal and shrouded in secrecy. Over the years the group was institutionalized and, as we will see, incorporated in the European Union framework.

The implications for border control of this group's activities were not immediately apparent. It was only at the beginning of the 1990s that its remit was extended from terrorism to illegal immigration and border control. In this period, we start witnessing the blurring of internal and external security, which became the key feature of the border -control domain in the following years. In this context, police and security agencies began to act more in common European terms when addressing a particular cross-boundary problem.

The growing salience of immigration issues, economic stagnation, the deadlock of the European Community project, and growing security concerns put borders, which were relatively "invisible" during the previous decades, back at center stage in policy debates across the region. They generated a sense of urgency in addressing problems affecting them. At the same time, they created contradictory pressures on European policy makers. On one hand, they called for more openness of borders (especially with regard to economic issues), and on the other, for more restrictions (mostly visible in the security field). Overall, these trends highlighted the inadequacy of existing national approaches in dealing with the complexity of border control and the need to find alternative solutions. The European Commission encapsulates this sentiment in a progress report on the activities regarding border control in the early 1980s:

> [T]he problems presented by the need to find *alternative and preferably more efficient* means to deal with arms, terrorism and drugs are substantial. Unfortunately Ministers dealing with these problems still seem to be wedded to their present *inefficient frontier controls* rather than actively seeking out *new and better ways* of confronting these issues. [22]

Despite the Commission's somber assessment, the fluid situation characterizing the border control domain in this period offered a political window of opportunity for entrepreneurial actors to seek new approaches to border control beyond the Westphalian model. How these new possibilities were explored is the subject of the next chapter.

---

22. Commission of the European Communities, "Completing the internal market: An area without internal frontiers—The progress report required by article 8b of the Treaty" (COM [88] HSO final, Nov. 17, 1988); emphasis added.

FOUR

The Pursuit of New Cultures of Border Control: Schengen and Brussels

Schengen was Europe's illegitimate child . . . but even illegitimate children are, after all, the fruit of love . . .

—Van de Rijt (1999: 37)

Political frontiers originate from a respectable historical and ethnic evolution, from a long effort of national unification; it would be therefore unthinkable to erase them. In other times, they would be displaced by violent conquest or convenient marriage. Today, it will be sufficient to devalue them.

—Schuman (1963: 23)

Beyond Westphalia: Debating the Future of Europe and Its Borders

The seeds of the new cultures of border control were sown in the first part of the 1980s. This was a time of crisis in European politics. The Continent was experiencing a phase of economic stagnation and an institutional deadlock that had paralyzed the Community for over a decade. It was, nonetheless, a period of political "brewing." Various initiatives and projects were elaborated that aimed at overcoming the impasse.[1] As had occurred in other circumstances, the Franco-German "fire" kept the Community cauldron

---

1. One example was the so-called Genscher-Colombo Plan. The plan (launched in 1981 by the German and Italian foreign ministers) called for greater European integration (including foreign policy). Originally proposed as a treaty, it was progressively watered down to a mainly symbolic "Solemn Declaration on European Union" (Bonvicini 1987). It should also be kept in mind that, in this period, the debate over enlargement to the Iberian Peninsula entered a crucial phase. Spain and Portugal eventually signed accession treaties in June 1985.

boiling and provided the decisive impetus for change (Saunier 2001: 463). Institutional links between Paris and Bonn were ongoing. Various bilateral working groups involving high-level bureaucrats and ministers were active in this period. The relationship between France and Germany was cemented thanks to the activism of the two freshly elected leaders, François Mitterrand and Helmut Kohl. The first sign of the new times was the signing of an informal political agreement, the Latché Agreement, which entailed a reciprocal support at the Community level. From "axis," the relationship was soon upgraded to a "privileged friendship" that, according to Mitterrand, represented "a cornerstone of the European project" (quoted in Saunier 2001: 473, n27).

The two administrations placed their hopes on the relaunch of the EC as a way to overcome the existing political deadlock and used all their political leverage and leadership to persuade their European colleagues of the need for change in the way the Community functioned. In a speech at the European Parliament, Mitterrand called for "a victory of the Community over itself."[2] This victory, Mitterrand suggested, could be achieved through the reform of the EC's decision-making mechanisms and the Internal Market. The strategy used by the two administrations to push this package through—opposed, as it was, by some member states, particularly the United Kingdom—was to move the project forward with only those members who were willing to follow them, thus creating a "two-speed Europe."

The opportunity to put these ideas into practice came in the second half of 1984 when France took over the presidency of the EC. In the run-up to this event, Paris and Bonn worked to fine-tune their common positions and further strengthen their privileged relationship. This involved the signing of a series of agreements. In one of them, the Rambouillet Agreement (May 1984), the two countries formalized their commitment to gradually abolish controls at their common frontiers. The first decisive step in the path toward a postnational approach of border control had been taken.

The first opportunity to discuss this proposal with their European partners arose at the Fontainebleau European Council a month later. The position paper presented at this meeting was ambitious: it called for an intergovernmental conference to study the possibility of a treaty for the creation of a "European Union." It also included the idea of abolishing internal border controls and deepening the Common Market. At the meeting, a compromise was reached on the Common Agriculture Policy (CAP)—which, as we

---

2. "Speech of French president Francois Mitterrand, president of the Council of Ministers, before the European Parliament. Strasbourg, 24 May 1984," Archive of European Integration, University of Pittsburgh. Available at http://aei.pitt.edu/12031/.

saw in chapter 3, was one of the main points of contention at the time. This gave momentum to EC reform, particularly with regard to decision making and the internal market. In the Council's conclusions, European governments called for further internal economic liberalization. Under the section entitled "A People's Europe," they endorsed the idea of abolishing all police and customs formalities for people crossing intra-Community frontiers, and the project of creating a European passport and other symbols of the Community's existence, such as a flag and an anthem.[3]

The Fontainebleau Council's Conclusions outlined a set of objectives and a political mandate to carry them out. The task of EC governments and institutions in the aftermath of the meeting was to clearly define the policy framework that would accomplish these objectives. The European Community was the "natural" institutional setting where these activities would take place. Fontainebleau, however, also gave political impetus to parallel intergovernmental initiatives (outside the European Community), which flourished in the months that followed the Council meeting. Both the Community and intergovernmental initiatives had the same objective: the creation of a Europe without frontiers. However, their content and organization were clearly distinct. Each one was based on a discrete set of assumptions about borders and how they should be managed. In this sense, the launch of the two initiatives set the stage for the emergence of two new cultures of border control.

The story of the border control domain in Europe from the second part of the 1980s until the late 1990s is about the parallel evolution of these two new cultures and their interplay with the then still dominant Westphalian culture of border control. It is also the story of how the proponents of the intergovernmental and Community initiatives justified what were undoubtedly controversial and risky moves (not only did contemplating a post national approach to border control go against the existing nationalist common sense; whether this "leap into the dark" could actually work was far from being certain), and in so doing created the political conditions for the pursuit and eventual selection of a new official culture of border control.

After presenting some background information on the intergovernmental and EC initiatives, the remainder of this chapter examines the leading assumptions underlying the Schengen and Brussels cultures of border control as encapsulated in key proposals advanced in this period and the arguments that supported their pursuit.

---

3. "Conclusions of the Fontainebleau European Council," *Bulletin of the European Communities* 6 (June 1984): 11–12.

The Birth of Schengen

The political momentum created with the Fontainebleau Council bore immediate fruit. In July 1984, the French foreign minister, Roland Dumas, and the German undersecretary to the chancellor, Waldemar Schreckenberger, formalized the commitment toward the gradual abolition of control at their common borders with the signing of a bilateral agreement, the Saarbrücken accord. The agreement envisioned the immediate abolition of control of persons, the easing of control of vehicles, and the transfer of these controls to the external borders; the commitment to harmonize visa policy; the strengthening of police and customs cooperation; and the commitment to harmonize legislation on foreigners, drugs and arms, and passport delivery.

Soon after the signing of the Saarbrücken accord, the Benelux countries (the Netherlands, Belgium, and Luxembourg) began to show interest in the project. The German and Dutch ministers of transport (later joined by their Belgian and Luxembourg counterparts and the Secretariat General of the Benelux Economic Union) were already carrying out consultations and studying measures to expedite movement of goods at their borders. The Neustadt/Aisch conclusions, summarizing the outcome of these discussions, included the decision, taken at a ministerial meeting at the German town of Neustadt an der Aisch on May 1984, to launch a program leading to the reduction of controls and obstacles at common borders. The four ministers reiterated the decision in a technical agreement on December 11. The day after the ministerial meeting, the Benelux Union Ministerial Committee took the initiative to address a memorandum to Bonn and Paris proposing they work together to gradually abolish border controls. The memorandum, along with the Saarbrücken accord, formed the basis of a more comprehensive arrangement whose goal was to abolish border controls among the five participant countries. The principles of this arrangement were laid down in a document signed near the town of Schengen on June 14, 1985.[4]

The Schengen Agreement was more of a working program than a detailed plan of action. For this reason, the five signatories immediately began discussions over an implementation convention that would address the substantive aspects of this document. Unlike the previous agreement, the

---

4. "Agreement between the governments of the States of the Benelux economic union, the Federal Republic of Germany and the French Republic on the gradual abolition of checks at their common borders," referred to as the Schengen agreement [SA]. Available at http://eur-lex .europa.eu/LexUriServ/LexUriServ.do?uri=CELEX:42000A0922(01):EN:NOT.

negotiations over the Schengen Implementation Convention (SIC)[5] proved to be complex and slow. Many political and technical questions were difficult to resolve (Hreblay 1998: 25). The context in which they occurred was also particularly turbulent.[6] After five years of gestation, the five governments eventually reached consensus over a common text (June 19, 1990).

The Schengen Implementation Convention, together with the 1985 agreement, became the cornerstone of a new approach to border control. The two texts did not just codify the main formal rules of the regime; they also contained the underlying assumptions of an emerging culture of border control. It is therefore through a critical reading of these texts, together with an analysis of the main actors involved in their drafting, that we can outline the main features of the Schengen culture of border control.

"Schengen" as Emerging Culture of Border Control

The Schengen conventions redefined the traditional meaning of borders. Two new categories were created: "internal" and "external" borders. The Implementation Convention referred to "internal borders" as "the common land borders of the [Schengen States], their airports for internal flights and their ports for regular ferry connections exclusively from and to other ports within the territories of the [Schengen States] and not calling at any ports outside these territories" (art. 1 SIC). "External borders" were classified as Schengen states' "land and sea borders and their airports and sea ports, provided that they are not internal borders" (ibid.). This "negative" definition of external borders was an attempt to avoid the sensitive issue of who should be legally responsible for their management. The formal distinction between "internal" and "external" was thus presented as neutral. Indeed, in this formulation both internal and external borders still coincided with national borders. Their creation did not entail any boundary redrawing. Yet,

5. "Convention implementing the Schengen Agreement of June 14, 1985 between the Governments of the States of the Benelux Economic Union, the Federal Republic of Germany and the French Republic on the gradual abolition of checks at their common borders." Available at http://eur-lex.europa.eu/LexUriServ/LexUriServ.do?uri=CELEX:42000A0922(02):EN:NOT.

6. The single most important event having a direct impact on the negotiations over Schengen was the reunification of the two Germanys. The Schengen ministers had taken the last necessary decisions to finalize the agreement in November 1989, and the signature was expected for December 1989. West Germany, however, requested more time to address the "East Germany problem" (the recognition of the former member of the Communist bloc as not being a foreign country with regard to West Germany, and the regulation of visas originally granted by Eastern Germany; Hreblay 1998: 43). After the German election on March 18, 1990, these issues were resolved, and the process was set in motion again.

if we go beyond legal formalities, we can see that Schengen outlined a novel way to conceptualize borders. The external border marked the perimeter of a new area comprising the territory of all member states. It was therefore superimposed on national borders and represented a distinct entity with unique features. Internal borders were "subordinate" to their external counterparts (the former was a prerequisite of the latter, but not the other way around). Internal and external borders were also considered a common good. When it is explicitly applied to internal borders, the term "common" seems to refer to the territorial line that two countries share; however, if we look at the equivalent term used for the external border of the Schengen area, it is clear that the term has a collective connotation. The border belongs to all countries in the Schengen area. Indeed, each country needs to take into account the interests of all contracting parties when conducing controls at the external borders (art. 6.1 SIC).

The Schengen conventions redefined not only the meaning of European borders but also their functions. Article 2.1 of the Schengen Agreement stipulates the de facto abolition of controls at internal borders. The function of "filter" played by borders does not disappear, however. The agreement transfers it to the external perimeter of the Schengen area (art. 17).[7] The link between the abolition of internal border controls and their relocation to the external perimeter is deemed necessary. The logic is that of the "security deficit": the abolition of controls inevitably creates a vacuum that needs to be constantly filled.

With the creation of a common external perimeter, controls would not only be transferred but also reinforced. At one level, this is the indirect result of policy harmonization that the establishment of a new regime entails. For example, when deciding on the applicable rules for admission of a person, what applies is the accumulation of rules (i.e., in the absence of common rules, a person must meet the requirements of all states to enter Schengen). At another level, it is a conscious policy choice. In response to the removal of common frontiers, the texts in fact envisaged a hardening of borders through the introduction of new security measures at the external borders (and sometimes even internal borders).[8]

---

7. Nanz characterizes the "Schengen system" as a wheel with a hub and spokes (1996: 64). The hub is article 2.1 (the abolition of internal borders). Around this hub, various compensatory measures are arranged.

8. SIC, for example, entailed (at least on paper) restrictions on the movement of aliens within Europe. These individuals would be allowed to stay legally only for a total of three months, and they would have to report to the local authorities when moving to another country (art. 22 SIC).

The Schengen conventions established who should be in charge of European borders. The institutional framework they developed by and large reflected the intergovernmental approach adopted for the negotiations leading up to the signing of the SIC. The convention mentioned the need to set up an executive committee (art. 132 SIC). Details of the function of this committee and other policymaking structures were defined in a draft document prepared after the signing of the SIC ("Rules of Procedure of the Executive Committee of Schengen").[9] The draft outlined a pyramidal structure with a committee of ministers and secretariats of state, or an executive committee (Comex), at the top. The administrative functioning of this structure was guaranteed by a secretariat and a president (the latter position held by each member state on a rotating basis). Comex, which consisted of ministers responsible for the implementation of the convention, defined the regime's policy objectives, validated the work submitted to it, and set the priorities for ongoing and future works. It could make binding decisions (which had to be unanimous) that became law for the Schengen states.[10] Below the executive committee, and acting under its authority, was the Central Group of Negotiation. Composed of high-ranking officers of the contracting parties, the group would prepare the work of the executive committee. For this purpose it directly activated the groups of specialists (see below) and examined, discussed, and validated their work. The unanimity rule applies to this group as well. Under the central group, and responsible to it, various specialized working groups (WGs) were established (e.g., WG Police and Security, WG Transborder Movement/Circulation). Only representatives of member states were allowed to participate in these structures. Membership to Schengen, however, was open. Other states could join the regime provided that they were EC members and that they accepted the Schengen *acquis* (the regime's existing legislation) in its entirety (art. 140 SIC).

Despite the reference to the objective of achieving European integration in the Schengen conventions (on this point see below), Community institutions

9. For a critical analysis of the content of this draft and more generally of the Schengen Executive Committee's structure and functioning, see Standing Committee of Experts on International Immigration, Refugee and Criminal Law, "Paper regarding the Rules of Procedure of the Executive Committee of Schengen" (CM93–207, Utrecht, 25.8.93).

10. A partial limit to the collective nature of this decision-making mechanism is represented by article 2.2 SIC, which allowed a member state to temporarily reimpose national controls because of public policy or national security concerns. In these circumstances the other Schengen states would have to be consulted beforehand (with the exception of situations where immediate action is required). The competence to reintroduce the checks would remain with the Schengen state concerned; the consent of the other contracting parties would not be required. This rule changed in 1995; Groenendijk 2004: 154; see also chapter 5.

did not explicitly appear in any of the constitutive documents of the regime. The European Commission was included in negotiations leading to the SIC; however, this occurred only late in the process (in 1988), and then it was only granted observer status.[11] The European Parliament (EP) had no role in Schengen, except for being periodically informed by the Schengen presidency on the regime's general policy orientation. The same could be said of the European Court of Justice (ECJ). The ECJ was not competent to judge the lawfulness of the agreement's application by one of the Schengen states or by the SEC itself. The exclusion of the EP and ECJ in Schengen was indicative of a broader issue in the regime: lack of proper democratic and legal supervision (on this point, see Meijers et al. 1991: 5–6). National parliaments could individually verify the functioning of Schengen, but they had very limited access to its activities. Besides the ECJ, no other international court could oversee the regime's legality. Moreover, as the draft rules of procedure of the SEC indicate, the meetings of the executive committee were not public and deliberations of the Executive Committee "fall under secrecy, except for a different decision of the executive Committee" (art. 12.1 of the draft rules).

Schengen as Laboratory: On the Pursuit of a New Culture of Border Control

The ultimate objective of the Schengen initiative was the abolition of border controls across Europe. In pursuing this goal, the original members of Schengen had to demonstrate that they were capable of doing it effectively. At the same time, they had to show that the approach they were proposing was compatible with the European integration project. This approach was clearly at odds with (if not deleterious to) the long-established practice among European states of working together under a common institutional umbrella, and it could have led to the creation of a "patchwork" Europe, with some members "in" and others "out."

The position that the proponents of Schengen took was therefore to stress that their goal was indeed the same as that of the Community. In the preamble of the Saarbrücken agreement, for example, there is a reference

11. The Commission explained that its role at the Schengen meetings was "to help ensure that the Agreements are not contrary to Community rules and, in particular, do not discriminate between nationals of members of the Agreement and nationals of the other member states of the Community." Commission of the European Communities, "Communication of the Commission to the Council on the Abolition of Controls of Persons at Intra-Community Borders" (COM [88] 640 final, 7 Dec. 1988).

to the "continuing and greater (*"sans cesse plus étroite"*) union among the people of the EC states." Similarly, the preamble of the 1990 Schengen Implementation Convention emphasized the complementarity of the project with the "objective of the internal market comprising an area without internal frontiers."

These reassuring statements, however, were not sufficient to dispel the sense of illegitimacy surrounding the Schengen initiative. Its proponents had to find a valid reason for not taking the Community route. In order to get around the problem, they put forward the notion of Schengen as "laboratory of the EC." The laboratory metaphor and the family of related concepts ("testing," "experimenting," "trial," etc.) surfaced in internal and public documents and speeches about the Schengen regime soon after the initiative was launched in the mid-1980s. It was not only used by the proponents of Schengen, but also echoed by other actors who were "external" to the policy circle that had elaborated it. Among them were the EU institutions and, most notably, the European Commission.[12] Commenting on the initiative in its early stages, the Commission defined Schengen as a "parallel and significant exercise" that would function as a "testing ground" or "testbed" for what will happen to the EU.[13] According to the Commission, the Schengen initiative would even "help to speed up the removal of controls throughout the Community."[14] It is on these premises that Jacques Delors, then the Commission's president, could argue that "the solutions arrived at by the Schengen group are an inspiration to Community bodies."[15]

The meaning of the term "laboratory" sheds some light on the question of why the laboratory metaphor was used. A laboratory is a controlled

12. The laboratory metaphor was also reproduced in the academic community (see, e.g., Caloz-Tschopp and Fontolliet 1994; Nanz 1995). Although indirectly, scholars might have played a role in the metaphor's spread, as their references to the idea of Schengen as laboratory were fed back into the political process. On the "Schengen laboratory" metaphor, see Zaiotti 2008. On the role of metaphors in the European politics, see Musolff 2001.

13. Commission of the European Communities, "Commission report concerning the removal of controls on persons at the internal frontiers of the Community" (COM [88] 640, annex); "Written Question No. 413/89 by Mr. Ernest Glinne to the Commission of the European Communities. Assessment of the Schengen agreement," *Official Journal* C 90 (April 9, 1990): 11.

14. COM [88] 640; see also "Replies to Written Question No. 732/89," *Official Journal* 1990: and "Written Question No. 911/89 by Mr. Yves Verwaerde to the Commission of the European Communities. Community policy in Respect of Non-EEC Nationals," *Official Journal* C 117 (May 11, 1990): 13.

15. "Written Question No. 2668/90 by Mrs. Claudia Roth to the Commission. Xenophobia in the Community and the Consequences Thereof for Policy on the Right of Asylum and Emigration/Immigration," *Official Journal* C 144 (June 3, 1991): 10; see also "Commission Report concerning the Removal of Controls" (COM [88] 640).

environment wherein one can experiment with a set of hypotheses that have not yet been verified and accepted. It allows the generation of results that can be evaluated before hypotheses are actually applied in the real world. The working method in a laboratory is that of trial and error, which lets the experimenter correct the previously unforeseen flaws or avoid the negative consequences of the original hypotheses. Applied to the Schengen regime, the laboratory metaphor allows one to visualize how this initiative not only was compatible with European integration but also was a valuable instrument to reach its final goals. The metaphor suggests that Schengen provides a respectable framework to test the potential of a new "postnational" approach to border control. It can produce the results necessary to convince the skeptics of the reasonableness of the enterprise and its usefulness in the achievement of the shared dream of a more integrated Europe.

Charles Elsen (former general director of the Justice and Home Affairs Directorate within the European Council) encapsulated these ideas well when he noted that

> [t]he proponents of Schengen are not working in vain; they are demonstrating a possible and feasible way, creating a laboratory (*"laboratoire d'essai"*) for Europe, and ultimately offering a decisive push to the European construction.[16]

Elsen's reference to the Schengen laboratory as giving a "push" to the European project indicates that the metaphor had a clear pragmatic function. It supported decision makers not only in their effort to formulate a new approach to border control, but also in their quest to experiment with it. Indeed, the language of "testing" was repeatedly employed throughout the period in which the regime was under construction.[17]

For its proponents, the laboratory metaphor helped render the Schengen initiative more palatable to the skeptics. The metaphor's persuasiveness was enhanced by the fact that in the negotiation phase actors external to the regime, especially the European Commission, reproduced it in their discursive practices. The Commission's support of the idea of Schengen as EC's laboratory was certainly controversial. The Commission's main institutional role was to be "the guardian of the Treaties" and of the European project

16. Quoted in Van der Rijt, 1998: 65; author's translation.
17. This is also true of the phase that followed Schengen's launch. The regime went through various "trials" before it became fully operational; on this point see Keraudren 1994; Pauly 1994; and chapter 5 of this book.

as a whole. Here, however, it was embracing an initiative that de facto circumvented these very treaties. The Commission's official position was that this arrangement would be temporary, pending the adoption of the Community measures to achieve the objective of abolishing border controls across Europe.[18] The rationale for this stance was based on a pragmatic assessment of the existing situation. The Commission realized that no matter what its attitude, Schengen would have proceeded anyway; engaging with it was the only feasible way to keep the participants in check and to make sure that the European project remained on track. This attitude meant that the Commission would not interfere with ongoing intergovernmental activities if it was not strictly necessary. When a question was raised concerning which actions should be taken at the Community level and which should be left to intergovernmental cooperation, the Commission considered that "attention should be focused on practical effectiveness rather than on matters of legal doctrine."[19]

Was Schengen really a laboratory for the European project? There are contrasting opinions amongst practitioners and scholars. For some, Schengen was a dangerous development for the EU. Commissioner Martin Bangemann went so far as to argue that Schengen was a potential "graveyard instead of a laboratory for the EC" (quoted in Wiener 1998: 241). The European Parliament was strenuously against it and criticized the Commission for its complacent position. Its main concerns over Schengen were its undemocratic nature and its effect on immigrants and asylum seekers. On various occasions it threatened to initiate legal action against the Commission for its stance on Schengen. Among the few national voices participating in the debate, the Dutch Council of State expressed similar concerns. In its analysis of the legal implications of Schengen, the council argued that Schengen's entry into force "might have an inhibiting effect on the realization of the Community proposal."[20] Other commentators accepted that Schengen was a laboratory, although not necessarily for the EU. Julian

18. Commission of the European Communities, "Communication of the Commission to the Council on the Abolition of Controls of Persons at Intra-Community Borders" (COM [88] 640).

19. Ibid., par. 14a. This position is summarized by Adrian Fortescue, a senior member of the Commission: "We would much prefer to see agreement on concrete measures, adopted by whatever machinery people feel is best, rather than pursue Community legislation for its own sake." "House of Lords Select Committee on European Communities, 22nd Report (1988-89), at Q 1"; Denza 2002: 69; COM (88) 648; "Replies to Written Questions No. 732," *Official Journal* 1990; and 911/89 *Official Journal* 1990, C 117/13.

20. "Opinion of the Dutch Council of State," reproduced in *Statewatch* (Feb. 1992).

Schutte, a member of the Dutch delegation during the negotiation over the Schengen Implementation Convention, contended that the promoters of Schengen envisioned a scenario in which the EC followed in Schengen's footsteps, and not the other way around.[21] This would also explain the late and reluctant inclusion of the reference to the Community element in the Schengen Implementation Convention.[22]

No matter what the reasons for the various actors' stances, the laboratory metaphor nonetheless had the effect of conferring a degree of legitimacy on Schengen. According to Bigo and Guild (2003) the discourse about Schengen as laboratory became so powerful that few dared to move away from it or officially challenge it. It thus acquired the force of "myth." All actors involved converged on the fact that Schengen, despite its questionable origins, was a project they should all embrace. As the president of the Schengen Secretariat colorfully put it in the epigraph to this chapter, Schengen was indeed the fruit of an act of love.

Toward a "Europe without frontiers": The Brussels Initiative

While the construction of the Schengen regime was under way, activities within the EU were also in full swing. Fontainebleau gave a political mandate to the Community institutions to come up with concrete proposals to move the European project forward. The agenda was broader than Schengen's, since it included important institutional matters, plus the objective of creating the Common Market by 1992. The abolition of internal borders was nonetheless a central component of this program. (The catchphrase in this period was, in fact, "Europe without frontiers"). In order to specify how this objective could be achieved, the European Council created an ad hoc committee (known as the "Adonnino Committee") whose mandate was to elaborate the agenda put forward at Fontainebleau.[23] This entailed suggesting measures likely to strengthen the Community's identity and promote a Europe without internal borders (a "People's Europe"). The Adonnino Committee drafted two reports. The first one (which was submitted at the European Council in Brussels in March 1985) dealt with issues such as the

---

21. Julian Schutte, interview with author, July 15, 2004; see also Schutte 1991.

22. It was following a Commission proposal that a reference to the Single European Act (SEA) was inserted at the last moment in the preamble (Bolten 1991: 15).

23. In the same period, member states also set up a second ad hoc committee, known as the Dooge Committee, that would mainly deal with institutional issues. The Committee discussed the feasibility of establishing a common action on—among other things—justice and the fight against terrorism (Keatings and Murphy 1987: 225).

freedom of movement for Community citizens and administrative formalities for border-area traffic. The second report—submitted to the Milan European summit in June 1985—addressed the question of Europe's image and identity, linking it with the issue of borders.

While the Adonnino Committee was at work, the European Commission took up the items of the Fontainebleau agenda that it considered as falling within its mandate. In January 1985 it tabled a "Proposal for a resolution to ease controls."[24] This resolution received a lukewarm reception from the member states, and the council did not pursue it further. A much more successful (and influential) initiative was the publication, in June of the same year, of the White Paper on the completion of the Internal Market.[25] This document set out a program for the removal of internal frontier controls between member states by 1992. It identified a number of key areas "which could have a direct bearing on the highly sensitive question of controls on individuals crossing frontiers" and suggested that action was needed in policy domains such as migration, border control, drugs, and firearms (White Paper, par. 24 and 25).

The ideas and proposals suggested in the Adonnino reports and in the White Paper formed the foundations of the Single European Act (SEA). This act (which was signed in February 1986 and entered into force in July 1987) was the main result of the Intergovernmental Conference called by the Milan summit to speed up the process toward the achievement of the Internal Market. The document envisaged a reform of the EC institutional structure and broadened the scope of the communities. It also formalized the political objective of the achievement of a Europe without borders by 1992. The SEA represented the most important "leap forward" in EC history since the Rome treaties and it marked the official revival of the European project after years of stagnation.[26]

The excitement created with the signing of the SEA did not last long. In the months that followed, the implementation of its ambitious objectives, in particular the part regarding the freedom of movement and a Citizens' Europe, stalled. The Commission called progress in this area "disappointing" and blamed bureaucratic brakes and the multiplicity of institutional

24. "Proposal for a Council Directive on the Easing of Controls and Formalities Applicable to Nationals of the Member States When Crossing Intra-Community Borders," *Official Journal* C 47 (1985): 5.

25. Commission of the European Communities, "Completing the Internal Market: White Paper from the Commission to the European Council" (COM [85] 310 final, 14 June 1985).

26. On the content of the SEA and its significance, see De Zwaan 1986; Ehlermann 1987; Allen 1992.

forums responsible for the file[27] Recognizing the delay in the implementation of the Internal Market program, the Rhodes European Council (December 1988) called on the Council to step up its efforts in all areas where progress was slow, such as in the free movement of persons. For this purpose, it established the Coordinators' Group on the Free Movement of Persons, composed of high-level civil servants from the then twelve interior ministries whose mandate was to expedite the process.[28]

Six months after its creation, the Coordinators' Group drafted the Palma Report.[29] The document outlined the Community program for the practical implementation of the principle of freedom of movement across Europe. After the Madrid European Council (June 1989) adopted it, the Palma Report became the policy framework for the negotiations that took place in the EC context in the following years.

"Brussels" as Emerging Culture of Border Control

As was the case with Schengen, the early policy proposals elaborated in the context of the EC initiative contained a set of assumptions that reformulated the meaning and functions of Europe's borders. The most striking element in these texts is that—unlike the Westphalian tradition, but also Schengen's—borders are conceived in negative terms as barriers that should be abolished (the Commission refers to them as a "nuisance"). Borders impede economic and other types of exchange. Wealth rather than security is the most important objective. The clearest statement of this "liberal" conception is offered in the Single European Act. Article 8a defines the internal market as "an area without internal frontiers in which the free movement of goods, persons, services and capital is ensured in accordance with the

27. See Commission of the European Communities, "Second Report from the Commission to the Council and the European Parliament on the Implementation of the Commission White Paper on Completing the Internal Market" (COM [87] 203, May 11, 1987); and "Completing the Internal Market: An Area without Internal frontiers; The Progress Report Required by Article 8b of the Treaty" (COM [88] 650 final, Nov. 17, 1988).

28. The Coordinators' Group built on the experience of the Ad hoc Working Group on Immigration. This group was created in October 1986 by the United Kingdom (then representing the presidency of the European Council). Its mandate was to prepare a newly established program of regular meetings of the ministers responsible for immigration matters in Europe (WGI [1] SN 3647/86 [IMMIG]). Its institutional structure was ad hoc because it did not belong to the community system and was not inserted in the framework of EC political cooperation.

29. "Free Movement of Persons: A Report to the European Council by the Coordinators' Group." The document was initially kept secret. The British House of Lords Select Committee on the European Communities was the first official source to publish it a year later (House of Lords 1989), 55.

provisions of this Treaty."[30] The notion of "an area without internal frontiers" completes, in terms of results, that of freedom of individuals, as it was introduced in article 3c of the Treaty of Rome. Freedom of movement therefore can only become effective when a space without internal frontiers is realized. In this scenario, "border" is the antonym of "freedom." This freedom is still mainly couched in economic terms. Indeed, as originally conceived in the Treaty of Rome, the free movement provisions—relating to workers, self-employed persons, and service providers—are designed to promote the achievement of economic goals in the context of the Common Market. This approach is echoed in the proposals presented in the 1980s. Yet the new initiative seems to reflect a vision of the Community that is moving toward more than merely economic integration. With the SEA, the link with economic function becomes looser (even EC tourists, for example, could be covered by the service provisions).

The creation of an "area without internal frontiers" does not mean that borders completely disappear. As with the Schengen initiative, there is a clear distinction between "internal" and "external" borders. The former would be gradually abolished, while the latter would remain in place, defining the contours of the new "free" area. Unlike Schengen, there is a more explicit mention of external frontiers as the "Community's borders" (see, for example, the Adonnino Reports). Their role is not just that of redressing the "security deficit" caused by the abolition of internal controls, but also of functioning as symbols of a new collective European identity. This explains the emphasis of the Adonnino Reports on the necessity of removing "anachronisms" such as the sign "Customs" at internal borders and of introducing "visible" items at external borders such as the European flag, and other arrangements such as the European passport and driving license.[31] What the reference to "Community's borders" precisely entails, however, is never fully clear in the original texts of the EC initiative.[32] The term does not seem

30. During the negotiations over the SEA, the Commission had pushed for a more far-reaching definition: "an area in which persons, goods and capital shall move freely under conditions identical to those obtaining within a member state" (McAllister 1997: 179–180). France, the United Kingdom, and (West) Germany rejected this proposal as too sweeping.

31. The European blue flag with gold stars was officially inaugurated in Brussels on May 29, 1986. Member states issued the first European driver's licenses on January 1, 1986.

32. The formal definition of "internal" and "external" borders was offered later, in the Border Convention (examined in the next chapter). Here external frontiers are defined negatively as "(i) a Member State's land frontier *which is not adjacent to a frontier of another Member State*, and maritime frontiers; (ii) airports, *except where internal flights are concerned*; (iii) ports, *except where internal connections within a Member State and regular ferry connections between Member States are concerned.*" Art 91(f); emphasis added.

to have legal implications; rather, it represents a political statement about what the new common area should be.

In the EC initiative the distinction between internal and external borders is reflected in the measures necessary to achieve the area of freedom of movement. These measures are classified in a functional manner. The Palma Report, for example, divided the work plan into "*ad intra*" and "*ad extra*" facets (par. 3). Each set of measures contained a particular conceptualization of what "border control" entailed. With regard to the "internal" facet, the EC initiative stressed that its main goal was the progressive abolition, or at least easing, of controls, not of borders per se. A frontier can exist even if not patrolled. While borders for the purposes of trade or other freedoms should be effectively dismantled, other functional boundaries (e.g., administrative) should remain intact. At the same time, the SEA emphasizes the achievement of all four "freedoms," including that of movement of people. The implication is that all types of borders are linked and thus control over them should be lifted. If economic freedoms are achieved, so must other freedoms.

With regard to the external facet, the EC initiative mentioned the necessity of devising "offsetting measures" to compensate for the abolition of internal controls. These measures should be "common," "tight" and "effective"— all terms used in the Palma Report—and implemented prior to the establishment of an area of free movement. Yet, unlike Schengen, their introduction is secondary to that of the achievement of an area of free movement across the Continent. The link between the flanking measures and the opening of internal borders is not conceived as a "causal link" but as a "logical" one.[33] It also does not necessarily imply a dramatic increase in controls. Security measures must always be related to the objective of achieving freedom of movement and have to be compatible with the fundamental duty of "defending an open society" and therefore should not go "beyond what is strictly necessary for safeguarding security and law and order in the member states."[34] As a result, the security dimension in early EC documents is circumscribed. In the Palma Report, for example, there is only a cursory mention of what should be the "essential measures" at both internal and external borders (on one hand, fight against illegal immigration, drug trafficking, and terrorism; exchange of information, cooperation between law

33. This terminology was often employed by Commission officials to counter the arguments about the "inherent connection" between security and freedom as presented within the Schengen initiative. See, for example, Schengen Executive Committee meeting minutes, SCH/M (92) PV 1.

34. Ad Hoc Working Group on Immigration, WGI (1) SN 3647/86.

enforcement agencies and customs in border areas at internal borders; on the other, combating illegal immigration networks, improving the information system). These measures were directed toward the strengthening of cooperation among member states rather than the establishment of a new "wall" around Europe.

In terms of decision making, the EC texts referred to a mixed competence between member states and the Community over the management of borders. They also referred to intergovernmental cooperation (but within the EC framework). The Single European Act made it clear that in order to achieve the stated objective of completing the internal market, decisions ought to be taken both by the Community institutions and by the member states in accordance with their respective powers. The new powers conferred to the Community in border control issues were only those strictly related to the internal market. Even in this restrictive reading of the SEA, immigration and, more generally, policymaking related to border control, would functionally fall under Community competence. Most European governments, however, were clearly reluctant to delegate their authority over these sensitive issues and opposed the complete abolition of intergovernmental institutional mechanisms. This is evident in two political declarations attached to the SEA, the "Declaration to Art. 13 to 19" and the "Declaration on co-operation over immigration."[35]

In order to render this cooperation more coherent and rational, a hierarchical system similar to that adopted within the Schengen initiative was established. Ministers responsible for border control from the various national capitals would therefore have executive power, while the newly established Coordinators' Group and, below it, various working groups, would support its work.[36]

Despite the limits placed on the European Community's authority in matters of border control and freedom of movement, the EC initiative gave

35. The "Declaration to Art. 13 to 19" states that "nothing in these provisions shall affect the right of Member States to take such measures as they consider necessary for the purpose of controlling immigration from third countries and to combat terrorism, crime, the traffic in drugs and illicit trading in works of art and antiques." The "Declaration on co-operation over immigration" proclaims that "in order to promote the free movement of persons, the Member States shall co-operate, without prejudice to the powers of the Community, in particular as regards the entry, movement and residence of nationals of third countries. They shall also co-operate in the combating of terrorism, crime, the traffic in drugs and illicit trading in works of art and antiques."

36. The SEA did not envisage an official community forum where ministers could meet. As we will see, an ad hoc Council of Ministers dealing with "freedom, security and justice" was established only after the signing of the Treaty of Maastricht in 1992. In the pre-Maastricht era, issues related to freedom of movement were addressed in the Internal Market Council.

more space for supranational actors in the policymaking process than did Schengen. The Commission would play a more active role as policy initiator. The extension of the reach of Community law to issues of free movement of people also gave more scope to the European Court of Justice, although its jurisdiction remained limited. The same could be said of the European Parliament. With the SEA, the EP was officially allowed to participate in the policymaking process, albeit only as an interested party that should be informed of the activities within the Community and that could request information and provide suggestions to the Commission and the council.

Although some intergovernmental elements are still present, in the EC initiative the main institutional framework within which members of the border control community were inserted was the European Community. The EC regulated and gave continuity to their interactions. It also emphasized friendly relations among partners and a spirit of mutual assistance. This element is particularly relevant since member states were now interdependent in matters of border control. In this sense, the EC offered a mechanism to overcome a potentially serious problem stemming from the relinquishment of European governments' competence in the border control field—that of trust (or the lack thereof).

When the Brussels initiative was launched, the main focus was on the relations among existing members over matters of border control. The external dimension was not considered a priority. In the Palma Report there was vague mention of the "solution to the problems raised by member states' agreements with third countries" (particularly asylum), and among "desirable" measures, the conclusion of bilateral or multilateral reentry/readmission agreements. The general rule was that third parties could not actively participate in the policymaking process unless they became EC members. Relations with third parties should, however, involve dialogue and cooperation. In this sense, the approach of the border control community would follow the "normative power" tradition in EC foreign policy affairs (Duchêne 1972; Manners 2002).

"Effective external borders first": On the Pursuit of Brussels

When the EC initiative was launched, all its participants agreed, at least in principle, on the common objective of abolishing internal controls across the Continent. In contrast to Schengen, however, they shared the conviction that this goal should be achieved in the context of the European Community. The United Kingdom was initially reluctant to follow its partners on this issue. London's skeptical views on this subject were known. Yet they were not carved in stone. Even Margaret Thatcher accepted the fact that the creation of a freer common market required a new approach to border control. The British government's reaction to the Adonnino Report, for example, was positive overall:

> We . . . broadly endorsed the first report of the Committee on Citizens' Europe. This contains a number of specific proposals for easier movement across frontiers, higher travellers' allowances, right of residence linked to proof of adequate resources, easier arrangements for road transport and mutual recognition of qualifications—all of them designed to bring advantages to individual citizens.[37]

France and Germany seized on this potential opening and tried to put pressure on the British government to follow their lead. As we have seen, in the run-up to the Fontainebleau summit (and the months that followed), talk of a new approach to the European project intensified. In May 1984, Mitterrand told the European Parliament that Europe at "variable geometry" was "a virtual necessity" (quoted in Saunier 2001: 481).[38] The objective of this innuendo was to threaten the United Kingdom with a "*fuite en avant*" of the most willing members, leaving the others behind. The tactic was risky. Germany and France were fearful of the possible consequences for the EC (delay in EC integration, legal wrangling, and an overall weakening of the European project; Saunier 2001: 483). Yet their proactive stance worked. The United Kingdom took part in the Intergovernmental Conference that produced the Single European Act. With its signing, London formally embraced its objective of abolishing controls at internal frontiers.

Despite the general agreement on the initiative's goal, the idea of lifting controls at Europe's internal borders remained controversial. It was uncharted territory, and thus no one could foresee the exact consequences of this decision. It was also not clear what the path to get there would be. All actors involved (both the Commission and member states) had therefore to persuade themselves of the reasons why the new initiative was worth pursuing.

37. Margaret Thatcher, Commons Debates, April 2, 1985, House of Commons Statement Hansard HC (76/1061–70).

38. The debate over "variable geometry" and more generally "flexibility" as alternative approaches to European integration was not new. In the 1970s, then German chancellor Willy Brandt called for a "graduated integration" ("Abstung der integration") involving a core of willing states (Stubb 2002). In the same period, the claimed that it was "not absolutely necessary that in every case all stages of integration should be reached by all states at the same time" (Tindemans Report [1975], 27, quoted in Stubb 2002: 34). Most of these early projects focused on the economic domain, and they did not materialize.

One advantage with respect to Schengen was that they did not have to make the case about the approach's compatibility with the communitarian spirit. The Brussels initiative was developed within the Community framework and included the Commission as a key player. It was therefore "legitimate." In terms of the content of the initiative, however, the arguments brought forward were different. The Commission relied on an "economic" argument to make the case for the communitarization of the border control domain. Its central tenet was that the abolition of internal frontiers would actually improve border control and render it more effective:

> What we are looking for are more effective controls, and in these days of shortages of manpower resources, above all of more cost-effective controls. The abolition of the internal frontiers offers us the opportunity to do just that.[39]

The Commission accepted that some controls could still be carried out. At the same time, it reiterated its point about the necessity of getting rid of the old way of conceiving of such activities:

> (T)he Commission has never said that frontier zones should be "no go" areas for the enforcement agencies. If evidence or reasonable suspicion exists, of course individual can be stopped or apprehended. *But what must go is the routine, mindless interference with the great mass of ordinary innocent travelers going about their legitimate business.*"[40]

The Commission argued that the new project required political determination at the top and a change in outlook by the actors involved, particularly ministers.[41] But it also made clear that since the abolition of internal frontiers was inextricably linked to the achievement of the Common Market, Community institutions—and particularly the Commission—should be actively involved in its planning. In the work program included in the White Paper, the Commission proposed prospective measures on drug legislation, asylum and refugee status, visas, extradition, and status of non-EC nationals. The 1985 Guidelines regarding the interpretation of the White Paper

39. Commission of the European Communities, "Commission report concerning the removal of controls" (COM [88] 640), par. 7.

40. Ibid., par. 7; emphasis added.

41. Commission of the European Communities, "Second Report from the Commission to the Council and the European Parliament on the implementation of the Commission White Paper on completing the internal market" (COM [87] 203 final, May 11, 1987).

specified that Community action in relation to third-country nationals was to be seen in terms of consultation, experimentation, and information.[42] On the basis of these guidelines, the Commission decided to set up a "communication and consultation procedure on migration policies towards third country nationals."[43]

EC governments agreed on the need for effective border controls. Most of them, however, were uncomfortable (if not outright opposed) to the Commission's activism.[44] Member states were also wary about the implications of the move to abolish internal border controls. These concerns stemmed primarily from the differences over the subject matter under discussion. Although it was often couched in legal terms, member states recognized the political dimension of the debate over article 8a (i.e., the abolition of internal border controls) and their different opinions over its interpretation.[45] These differences were glossed over in Council reports. Indeed, EU councils' conclusions were worded in a way that made the differences not too stark. Reference was generally made to the "full implementation of free movement of persons" or to a similar formula, which each member state could read according to its interpretation.

To avoid the impasse, the focus was shifted from internal borders to the external borders as the preliminary condition to implement the new regime. Given that these measures had to be put into place *before* the abolition of internal control could occur—so the argument went—why not begin with them and come back to the issue of the meaning of free movement later (Nanz 1996: 69)? This reasoning was based on the assumption that the free movement of persons, however defined, depended on the existence of a set of compensatory measures at external borders. All participants in the Brussels initiative agreed on this point. In discussing the *"ad extra"* facet of the measures, the Palma Report argues that the creation of an area without

42. Commission of the European Communities, "Guidelines for a Community policy on migration" (COM [85] 48 final, 7 March 1985).

43. "85/381/EEC: Commission Decision of 8 July 1985 setting up a prior communication and consultation procedure on migration policies in relation to non-member countries," *Official Journal* L 217 (1985): 25.

44. In the Migration Policy Case (joined cases 281–285 and 287/87 *Germany, France, Nederland, Denmark and UK v Commission* [1987] ECR 3245), some member states tried to annul the Decision on Migration policy on grounds of lack of competence. Although the European Court of Justice rejected the claim, the Commission took seriously the member states' challenge, and thus became more cautious in the following years (COM [88] 640).

45. For example, the participants at the June 1988 Munich Council meeting not only put on record their disagreement over article 8a but also questioned whether the decision to abolish intracommunity border control has been taken or not. Similar views were echoed in the Palma Report (see par. 3)

internal frontiers necessitates tighter controls at external frontiers. These controls would have to be highly effective because of the interdependence among partners ("Controls carried out at those frontiers are in fact valid for all the member states") and the necessity of building trust among member states (they "must be able to rely on them"). The emphasis on tighter external controls was also justified by pointing to the fact that these measures were practical in nature and that they would have been taken in any case:

> The [Palma] report in general, and the recommendations for measures to be taken, represent *practical steps upon which all could agree and do not prejudice the legal and political questions* . . . In many instances the measures proposed . . . are ones which are *desirable in their own right*, though equally their implementation assumes greater urgency and importance in the light of objectives of free movement.[46]

These references were meant to render more politically acceptable the implications of the adoption of a common approach to border control. So formulated, the argument about the need for a collective effort to achieve effective controls at external frontiers became the official justification to move the initiative forward. This *"fuite en avant"* allowed participants to overcome—at least temporarily—the politically contentious issue of defining what the abolition of internal borders actually meant and thus to persuade the most skeptical partners—namely, the United Kingdom—to remain on board (Nanz 1996: 59 n7).

On the Relations between the Schengen and Brussels Initiatives

The Schengen and Brussels initiatives developed in parallel. Although both shared the same goal of abolishing Europe's internal frontiers, in their early stages they did not directly clash with each other. As it will become apparent in the next chapter, their "survival" depended on how well they performed, not in trying to suppress their competitor. Those involved in the two initiatives were certainly aware of each other's activities. Some national representatives and members of the Commission were even present in both forums. Yet explicit acknowledgment of the competing initiative was rare.[47]

---

46. "Free Movement of Persons." Emphasis added.

47. References to the Saarbrücken and Schengen agreements were made in Commission documents; Schengen was not, however, mentioned by member states in the EC context. The term first appeared in official documents only at the December 1994 Essen Council.

When it did occur, it was generally expressed in polite terms, demonstrating mutual respect. The Commission was the most candid about the relation between the two initiatives, generally praising their complementarity and compatibility.[48] Representatives within each forum claimed that their approach was worth pursuing because of its effectiveness in achieving the goal of free movement across the Continent. The term of reference against which they made these claims, however, was not the other initiative, but the then dominant "national" approach to border control.

It should be clear from the discussion above that tactical reasons probably explain the basis for these attitudes (Schengen members were afraid of hurting the European project, Brussels members of being left behind). It was not a secret, however, that behind closed doors officials involved in the Brussels initiative would admit to tolerating Schengen only because they considered it a temporary arrangement that would eventually be superseded or incorporated by the Community framework (Schengen worked as "the place where the EU's dirty clothes were cleaned," as one Commission official put it). In turn, some Schengen members deemed that it would be their approach to absorb the Community's, not the other way around.

No matter what the rationale for their attitude toward each other was, both initiatives avoided open conflict and were able to move ahead. Indirect competition is what they would face at the next stage of their trajectory, that of cultural selection. This is the topic of the next chapter.

48. See, for example, Commission of the European Communities, "Communication of the Commission to the Council on the Abolition of Controls of Persons at Intra-Community Borders" (COM [88] 640, 7 Dec. 1988).

FIVE

Selecting a New Culture of Border Control: Schengen

If we want that Europe—even if it is for the moment only a part of Europe—to be understood, be popular, be legitimate, we cannot work with ambiguities and misunderstandings. We must deal with problems as they arise, and we are committed to doing that . . . France is attached to Schengen, but to a Schengen that works ("qui marche"). . . .

—Michel Barnier, French minister of European affairs—press conference, June 29, 1995

Convincing our partners that Italy is capable of patrolling its borders and that we are not, and we won't be tomorrow, the weak link, has required a long and patient work of persuasion, based on immediate visible and tangible proofs, rather than on future commitments.

—Lamberto Dini, Italian foreign minister, *Corriere della Sera*, October 26, 1997

Testing Schengen and Brussels

The flurry of intergovernmental and Community activities that characterized the late 1980s laid the foundations for a major reformulation of Europe's border control domain. In the following decade, the projects pursued in the previous years began to take a more defined and concrete shape. In the context of the Schengen initiative, after the signing of the Implementation Convention in the fall of 1990, the discussion switched to the practical arrangements necessary for the full application of the new regime. In the European Community's framework, after the release of the Palma Report in 1989, the debate centered on how to further institutionalize the border control domain, making it a full-fledged part of the Community framework.

These objectives raised complex technical and political questions. Resolving them was the main challenge of the negotiating forums set up for this purpose in the Schengen and EC context.[1] From a cultural evolutionary perspective, the negotiations and other policymaking activities that took place in these institutional forums represented formalized and iterated social interactions in which members of the border control community practically enacted the background assumptions constituting the emerging Schengen and Brussels cultures of border control. In this way, these activities functioned as a sort of testing ground for the emerging cultures before they could be formally embraced or discarded.[2] Besides providing the "evidence" in the cultural selection process, these experiments also allowed the border control community to rehearse the new cultures of border control. By participating in common practices, policy makers had a chance to acquaint themselves with the cultures they were pursuing. In turn, with the acquisition of a firmer grasp of these cultures' practical effects, they became better positioned to pass judgment on their effectiveness.

This chapter and the next recount the trajectories that the two emerging cultures of border control followed in the 1990s, until Schengen was selected as the new official approach to border control in Europe. The narrative deployed in the following sections traces how in both the intergovernmental and EU forums the practical enactment of the Schengen and Brussels cultures was gradual and dialectical. At the initial stages of negotiations, activities within each forum were often contradictory, and disagreement over the appropriate course of action was common. Over time, practices of the Schengen border control community became more consistent with the main tenets of the pursued culture. In the EU context, by contrast, practices did not cogently build on the main tenets of the pursued culture.

To render the argument more cogent, the evolution of the two cultures of border control is examined by making reference to developments in four topical areas: the border regime's internal political dynamics; the regime's widening and deepening; the regime's external relations, and the evolution of Europe's border control community. Attention will be paid to circum-

---

1. The organization and composition of these forums by and large mirrored those of the previous phase, with ministers responsible for border control, EU officials setting the political guidelines, and senior officials and experts implementing them.

2. Indeed, in this period the border control regimes were not fully operational. As we will see shortly, Schengen's provisions became operational only after 1996, and they did not apply to all Schengen members and all internal borders. In the EU context, there was only some limited implementation of the new approach to border control in selected policy areas.

stances that raised thorny political issues and that were marred by opposition or dissent.

The case of Schengen is addressed first. The item analyzed under the heading "internal political dynamics" is the issue of the necessary conditions for the implementation of the regime. With regard to the debate over the widening of the initiative, the issue taken into consideration is that of enlargement to new members (the two selected cases are Italy and Denmark). The section on the regime's external dimension focuses on Schengen members' practices toward their neighbors in Eastern Europe. Finally, the analysis of the evolution of Schengen's border control community is centered on the tug of war between Ministries of Interior and Foreign Affairs over the control of this initiative.

Schengen's Internal Squabbles: The Debate over the Regime's "Preliminary Conditions"

Schengen was an ambitious and controversial project. It is therefore not surprising that some internal squabbles erupted when the regime's implementation was debated. At different times, and with different intensity, various Schengen members demonstrated concerns, if not open opposition, to certain tenets of the initiative. The most serious bickering occurred over the conditions for the entry into force of the regime. Although it was often couched in technical terms, this issue was eminently political. France's delegation was the most vocal on this subject throughout the negotiation process. If we look at official declarations by French authorities, the various parliamentary reports, and journal articles during this period, Paris seemed in fact to have "more often blew cold than hot" on the project regarding the freedom of movement in Europe (Kerauden 1994: 123). Domestic politics certainly played an important part in shaping this stance. During most of the debate over the regime's entry into force (1993–1997), a center-right government was in power in Paris, and its constituency was markedly nationalist and anti-enmeshment on issues of security and sovereignty. Domestic politics, however, cannot explain why France remained engaged with Schengen throughout this period, and why it was eventually persuaded to lift its reservations and fully join the regime. It is telling that although representatives of the cent-right parties (then in opposition) were openly critical of the treaty during the parliamentary debate over the ratification of the Schengen Agreement (June 1991), they nonetheless overwhelmingly voted in favor of it. It should also be kept in mind that domestic hostility to Schengen was not solely a French characteristic. The Netherlands is a good case in point.

On April 15, 1991, the Dutch government's supreme advisory council, the "Raad van State (RvS), a body that comments on constitutional issues, argued that the Schengen agreement conflicted with international law and in particular the 1951 Refugee Convention, and that the government should therefore not sign it. It was the first time in Dutch history that the RvS gave such a recommendation regarding an international agreement. Despite the RvS's opposition, the government went ahead with its plan.

Given its relevance and seriousness—on many occasions it threatened to block the entire process—the debate over the "preliminary conditions" during the negotiations over Schengen will be the main focus of the following section.

The Debate over the "Preliminary Conditions"

By September 1, 1993, all Schengen members had ratified the Schengen Implementation Convention (SIC). On that date, the agreement officially entered into force. In practice, however, this implied only the establishment of the executive committee (Comex), which had to evaluate whether the preliminary conditions to render the convention operational were met.[3] According to the ministers responsible for Schengen, these conditions were the establishment of external border controls; the issuing of uniform visas; a harmonized system to manage asylum claims; the realization of the Schengen Information System (SIS, a common database system used for the purpose of maintaining and distributing information related to border security and law enforcement); the respect for the provisions of existing drug conventions; the legal protection of personal data; and the creation of a special circulation regime in airports.[4] These requirements were closely related to the quality of border controls and the participants' attitude toward each another. At the Comex meeting held in Madrid on November 6, 1992, all delegations stressed the importance of the effectiveness of controls at the external frontiers, which was guaranteed if these controls "allow to face risks or threats which entail each concrete situation," and the necessity to carry out these controls "in a spirit of mutual trust and taking into account common interests, relying on means considered necessary by each state."[5]

---

3. This requirement is mentioned in SIC article 139 (3).

4. See the declaration issued at the Luxembourg Comex meeting of June 19, 1992.

5. Minutes of Schengen Executive Committee meeting, November 6, 1992 (SCH/M (92) PV 2). In the remainder of the section, the minutes of Comex will be referenced only by their acronym (SCH/M), date, and number. These documents are available at the Justice and Home Affairs Library located at the Secretariat of the European Council's building in Brussels.

Among Schengen members, however, disagreement over the steps that had to be taken in order to meet these conditions soon began to emergence. The diplomatic bickering that ensued represented the first major test of the newly pursued Schengen culture of border control.

The French delegation was the most vocal in expressing its concerns and blamed its partners for lack of political will and laxness at the borders.[6] Frustrated by the lack of progress, in the spring of 1993 Paris announced that it was not ready to go along with its Schengen partners and abolish internal border controls as programmed. Alain Lamassoure, the French minister for European affairs, told the National Assembly Foreign Affairs Commission that there were dangers in "lifting border controls too quickly."[7] Hence France had to maintain its police controls at frontiers as long as the preconditions for the entry into force of the Schengen Agreement were not fulfilled. The other Schengen members were clearly irritated. The Dutch prime minister, Ruud Lubbers, declared that he was "seriously astounded" by the French decision. He added that France would be bound to honor the Schengen Agreement's provisions.[8] Other Schengen members shared this view, though not publicly expressing it.

Despite the French skepticism, in the following months concrete steps toward meeting the criteria were achieved: Schengen members drafted a border manual and common consular instructions, harmonized visa issuance, reached an agreement on asylum processing, and introduced a new circulation regime at airports. In light of these developments, the French delegates reconsidered their position, and, at the Comex meeting in June 1993, accepted to fully participate in the implementation of the regime. The participants, "in order to reinforce the credibility of the Schengen model and to give the long waited positive signal"[9] agreed on a common text, indicating the end of the year as the target by which to apply the convention, but also stressing the need for the "extra efforts" necessary in areas such as drug policy, external border controls, and data sharing. Technical problems with one of the agreement's main pillars, the shared police computer system, SIS, meant that the date had to be postponed yet again. The issue was

6. Troubling for the French delegation was the fact that Germany was unable to ratify the agreement before July 1993, pending the change of its constitutional legislation on asylum; that the Greek and Italian administrations were not in a position to enforce the planned strengthening of controls at the external borders; and that there were incompatible laws on drugs in the Netherlands and other countries (in this period, Spain and Italy decriminalized the possession of some drugs).

7. *Le Monde*, May 3, 1993.

8. Ibid.

9. COMEX meeting minutes, SCH/M (93) PV 1.

solved in the fall of 1994. As a result, the Schengen Executive Committee was able to reach an agreement on a date (March 26, 1995) for the entry into force of the convention.

In the first meeting after entry into force of the SIC (April 1995), all delegations were satisfied with the working of the system. Only few points needed to be fixed. The most pressing problem was the functioning of the SIS, and thus the Committee decided for an initial phase of three months during which the abolition of controls was the responsibility of member states.[10] Following concerns over the right of asylum, drugs, and modalities of border crossing, France requested an extension to this probation period. Other delegations, however, denied this request, claiming that it would go against the spirit of Schengen. In response, France, relying on article 2.2 of the Schengen Implementation Convention,[11] declared that it would maintain controls over land borders with Belgium and Luxembourg as long as it was deemed necessary. France's action spurred an "intense debate" at the following Schengen meetings. The discussion centered on the meaning of article 2.2, particularly on how to define the notions of "public order" and "national security." The goal was to define a more collegial way of approaching this issue and to avoid narrow "national" interpretations of this clause, as France was doing.[12]

In the following months, both in meetings and in public speeches, the French representatives continued to defend their national interpretation of Schengen, justifying their position on the basis of the effectiveness and "Europeanness" of their approach. Exemplary is the response that then French foreign minister Hervé de Charette gave to journalists who were asking how long France would postpone the entry into force of the convention:

> [Schengen] might be at the same time the best and worst thing, *excellent if it works, dangerous if it fails.* For us the question of security holds a great importance, so great that we have to keep in mind that any concession will be made when it *involves the security of France and the French.* . . . Nobody here doubts that I *am a convinced European,* I don't think that being a convinced European must be paid with the price of security of our citizens. If it seems, as it is the

10. COMEX meeting minutes, SCH/COMEX (95) PV 1.

11. SIC article 2.2 allows the resumption of national border control in cases involving "national security" and "public order."

12. See Coordinators Group meeting of spring 1995 (CG 1995 003) and SCH/I (95) 39.

case, that our citizens' security depends also on the border controls, it is understood that we have to keep them.[13]

Without any tangible breakthroughs in sight, however, in the autumn of 1995 France proposed to its Schengen partners a compromise. Paris argued that internal security would be best ensured thanks to a "mobile and rigorous control" in a border area of twenty kilometers on each side of the border, rather than a traditional fixed control. As then French minister of European affairs Michel Barnier put it, "In France, we can see the usefulness of such controls. The Schengen convention does not envisage completely abolishing controls within Schengen, just at frontiers. We now have the concept of mobile controls and mobile frontiers which *could be more effective* than fixed controls."[14]

The idea of "mobile frontiers" (which would be put in place thanks to bilateral agreements between Schengen countries) was the object of a long debate within the Executive Committee.[15] Despite the German support, however, the committee recognized that the French proposition was a source of contention at the level of working groups.[16]

The confrontational dynamic between France and other countries thus continued. In the spring of 1996, the Belgian deputy prime minister and interior minster, Johan Van Delanotte, used a debate to mark the first anniversary of Schengen to attack the French attitude and its unwillingness to lift controls at the Belgian frontier. A month later, Paris announced that, despite the improvement in the bilateral agreements with Belgium and Luxembourg regarding transborder police cooperation, it would maintain its reliance on article 2.2 until a political advancement occurred in the framework of negotiations with the Dutch government over the issue of drug policy.[17] The Dutch position was that France's reliance on this emergency

13. Meeting of French foreign minister Hervé de Charette with the Diplomatic Press Association, Paris, September 21, 1995; emphasis added.

14. Quoted in *Statewatch Bulletin* 5, no. 6 (Nov.–Dec. 1995); emphasis added.

15. COMEX meeting minutes, SCH/COMEX (95) PV4, Oct. 24, 995; "Schengen: 'Mobile frontiers' introduced," *Statewatch Bulletin* 5, no. 6 (Nov.–Dec. 1995).

16. COMEX meeting minutes, SCH/COMEX (95) PV 4.

17. COMEX meeting minutes, SCH/COMEX (96) PV 3. The terrorist attacks that hit Paris in late 1996 made the French government even more nervous about border controls. In December, the French delegation announced the introduction of an antiterrorist plan known as Vigipirate. Its application was on all French territory, including border areas; however, that did not entail the reinstatement of border controls at the frontier with Spain and Germany. COMEX meeting minutes, COMEX Luxembourg, December 19, 1996 SCH/Com-ex [96], PV 5 rév.

clause for such a long period contradicted the very content of the convention and that objectively there was no reason to maintain this position.[18]

As negotiations progressed, France remained isolated, and its stance appeared more and more unsustainable. Paris had to defend itself not only within the closed doors of the Schengen Executive Committee, but also publicly. Tellingly, an embarrassed French foreign minister could not respond to the sarcastic question posed by a journalist on the reasons why France was the only Schengen country requiring derogations from the regime: "Why then do all criminals choose to go to France and not to other countries?"[19]

By mid-1997, the Schengen regime had been operational for more than two years. The experiment had been overall successful. No major security breach had occurred and the system of pooled border management was functioning smoothly. These positive results persuaded other countries to join the regime. In 1995, Sweden, Denmark, Norway, and Iceland became Schengen members (see below). Its enlargement proved that the regime, despite its intergovernmental origins, could indeed function as a laboratory for the EU.

Faced with mounting evidence of the regime's achievements, the French delegation started to soften its "nationalist" position and to slowly move toward that of the other Schengen members. Despite claims to the contrary, in this period France de facto applied Schengen at the Belgian and Luxembourg borders. While the policing of the drug trafficking route to and from the Netherlands continued, no systematic checks were performed along these frontiers. Only in times of sudden crises were border controls reinstated (e.g., the December 1996 bombings in Paris). These actions, however, were generally circumscribed and temporary. Albeit reluctantly, France therefore eventually accepted the Schengen "spirit" when sitting at the Schengen Executive Committee's table and in the everyday practices at the border. It was with this newly achieved consensus that Schengen members could start the debate over the regime's formal incorporation in the European Union.

Enlarging Schengen

In the early phases of the initiative, Schengen members focused mainly on establishing the regime's legal and political foundations. A small and com-

18. COMEX meeting minutes, April 25, 1997, Lisbon SCH/Com-ex (97), PV 1 rév. 2.

19. Joint press conference of Michel Barnier, French minister in charge of European affairs, and Vande Lanotte, Belgian foreign minister and president of the Schengen Executive Committee, June 29, 1995.

pact group was therefore deemed essential for this task. Once the SIC was drafted, however, the existing members felt that the initiative, in order to be fully successful, had to involve other European partners. The expansion of the regime could prove that Schengen was indeed a European project and a precursor of the Europe of the future.

The enlargement option was explicitly foreseen in the Implementation Convention. Article 140 states that all member states of the EC can become part of the agreement. The prerequisite to join is that aspiring members have to accept the *acquis* as it stands at the moment of accession. Formal inclusion in the regime could take place when the 1985 and 1990 conventions entered into force in the candidate country (generally after the conventions are ratified domestically), and all the existing members ratified a protocol of adhesion. The entry into force of the conventions did not mean that the regime could be immediately applied in the new country. Its full implementation required a decision by the Schengen Central Committee, which was based on both a technical and a political assessment of the candidate country's "fitness" to be a full Schengen member. We should therefore distinguish two phases in Schengen's "enlargement" process. The first encompasses the negotiations leading to a country's (or group of countries') formal adhesion to the regime. The second involves a debate among existing members and the candidate country over the practical implementation of the regime. The latter stage was the most complex and controversial. It will therefore be the main object of inquiry in the next sections.

Formally, the negotiation process was the same for all candidates. In practice, there were substantial differences in the approach adopted depending on the country involved. These differences tended to follow a north-south axis. On one hand, this stemmed from the existence of different problems related to movement of people that aspiring members had to face. Southern European countries were more directly affected by external threats than Nordic countries, and they were believed to be less capable of mustering the technical and financial resources (and the political will) necessary to effectively control Schengen's external borders. Existing members were therefore particularly attentive and meticulous when dealing with southern European countries. Nordic countries instead raised complex institutional issues. These issues, however, far from being purely formal, had important political implications, since they entailed a serious challenge to the European project's coherence. To add complexity to the picture, these negotiations (both with Nordic and southern countries) were influenced by the existing relations between the candidate countries and individual

Table 5.1 The expansion of the Schengen regime: key dates

Country	1985 Schengen Agreement	1990 Schengen Implementation Convention	Schengen's entry into force
France	14 June 1985	19 June 1990	26 March 1995
Germany	14 June 1985	19 June 1990	26 March 1995
Benelux	14 June 1985	19 June 1990	26 March 1995
Italy	27 Nov. 1990	27 Nov. 1990	1 July 1997
Denmark	19 Dec. 1996	19 Dec. 1996	19 Dec. 1996
Spain	25 June 1991	25 June 1991	26 March 1995
Portugal	25 June 1991	25 June 1991	26 March 1995
Greece	6 Nov. 1992	6 Nov. 1992	8 Dec. 1997
Austria	28 April 1995	28 April 1995	1 July 1997
Sweden	19 Dec. 1996	19 Dec. 1996	19 Dec. 1996
Norway	19 Dec. 1996	19 Dec. 1996	19 Dec. 1996
Iceland	19 Dec. 1996	19 Dec. 1996	19 Dec. 1996

Schengen members (and, as in the case of Nordic countries, between candidate countries themselves).

As a result, the negotiations over the Schengen regime's expansion did not follow a linear path. These negotiations were mostly multi-bilateral (involving Schengen members and the individual candidate country), but they entailed bilateral and multilateral dynamics as well. Their timing also varied considerably. Some countries began contacting Schengen members early in the process, while others were drawn in much later. For some countries, negotiations were relatively quick, while for others they dragged for years (see table 5.1). The technical and political issues they raised were also different. In the next two sections I consider the cases of Italy and Denmark, two of the most controversial diplomatic exercises stemming from the regime's first waves of enlargement, exercises that contributed to the further "testing" of the emerging Schengen culture of border control.

Italy's Bumpy Road to Schengen

The original group of Schengen members included countries that had the will and capacity to carry out the task of dismantling borders across Europe. In the mid-1980s, Italy lacked both, and this partly explains why it was not among the first participants of the initiative. At the same time, there was a widespread lack of confidence on the part of the five original members concerning the contribution that Rome could offer to the project (Hein 2000). This attitude, as noted in the previous section, also characterized the relation with other southern European countries. What distinguished the

Italian case was that Italy, together with the then five Schengen members, was one of the founders of the European Community. Seen from Rome, not participating in a European project was considered politically embarrassing. The assumption was that Schengen was Europe, and for a self-proclaimed Europeanist country this was not acceptable (Toffano 1989: 542; Fridegotto 1993: 17). The same could be said, *mutatis mutandis*, for the existing members. For them, the inclusion of Italy into Schengen represented a legitimizing move, proof that their project was not only working by attracting new members, but that it was really a European enterprise.

It is in this context that in late 1985, soon after the first Schengen convention was signed, Italian Foreign Ministry officials contacted their French counterparts to inquire about the possibility of participating in the regime. The idea was that of a bilateral agreement (whose content reflected that of the Schengen conventions), whereby France would have functioned as mandatory for all the other Schengen members (a possibility mentioned in art. 28 of the 1985 Schengen Agreement). The dialogue was interrupted in January 1986 over problems in harmonizing visas. Italy wanted to maintain its relations with North Africa and Turkey. France—together with Germany—wanted some action taken immediately. The main fear was that opening the borders with Italy would produce potential mass illegal immigration.

Contacts were resumed the following year. In June 1987, Italy formally requested to be part of the agreement. The application for entry was accepted in principle, with certain conditions attached: the total acceptance of the *acquis* (which in the meantime had grown substantially), and that the entry of Italy would have not slowed down the ongoing proceedings. Other requirements were informally demanded: the introduction of visas for Turkey and North African states; the signing of an admission agreement with other members; and the denouncement of Italy's "geographical reservation" for asylum claimants to Eastern Europe (Fridegotto 1993: 18). With the acceptance of these requests, Italy was included in Schengen as observer. From September 1987, diplomats from the Italian Foreign Affairs Ministry and national experts began to participate in the various Schengen groups.

Negotiations, however, did not take off, and Italy's requests to create a working group to draft the accession agreement were not addressed. The official reason for the delay concerned the delicate phase of the negotiations among the existing members (who, at the time, were finalizing the SIC). It was made clear, however, that there were doubts about the Italian capacity (especially in terms of administrative structures) to join the Schengen system (Fridegotto 1993: 19). Despite the skepticism of the existing members, later that year the Italian embassy sent a letter ("note verbale") to the

Schengen ministers (November 8, 1988) requesting to join Schengen. In the following meeting on December 12, 1988, Comex acknowledged the letter, demonstrating its satisfaction of the Italians' willingness to be a member, as "original founder of the Community," and put in place procedures so that negotiations could quickly lead to adhesion. Yet it asked each delegation to come up with a questionnaire on Italy's structures and practices regarding border control to formulate potential "problems and/or difficulties" its entry might create.[20]

This request further delayed the beginning of negotiations. In May 1990 Italy gave satisfactory technical responses to a memorandum issued by the Schengen group on issues of police and security, movement of persons, transport, customs, and movement of goods. Moreover, the Italian Parliament approved a new law on immigration (the 1990 Martelli Law), which dropped geographical reservations on asylum and "introduced" visas for countries that were the primary sources of immigration in Europe. Official negotiations could therefore start (June 20, 1990). Without further difficulties, Italy was able to sign the accession agreements in the Comex meeting held in Paris on November 27, 1990. The French presidency, in welcoming Italy to Schengen, stressed the fact that this proved the role of Schengen as "laboratory for the 12." The Commission saw in it proof of the role of the "engine" of Schengen, and emphasized its function as "precursor" of the objectives that the Community was trying to achieve.[21]

The signing of the convention did not automatically mean the accession of Italy to the regime (which at that time had not yet entered into force anyway). Italy had to apply the necessary preliminary measures outlined in the convention. As noted in the section on the developments within Schengen, at its first constitutive meeting in October 1993, the Comex announced that the application of the Schengen Implementation Agreement had (once again) been postponed until February 1, 1993. Besides the issues of the control of external borders, the fight against drugs, and the setting up of the Schengen Information System, one of the reasons that was adduced was that Italy (together with Portugal) had not yet deposited its instruments of ratification. Some of the founding members also expressed doubts about the organizational and technical capability of Italy, Portugal, and Greece to effectively implement the agreement's measures in the field of policing and external border control. The executive committee therefore agreed that these three

20. "Conclusions of Ministers and Secretaries of State held in Brussels on December 12, 1988; Note verbale of the Belgian Presidency" (SCH/C [88]).

21. SCH/M (90) PV 3.

countries were not going to implement the agreement on the same date as the existing members.[22]

As previously observed, these preoccupations were not new, and to a certain extent reflected the attitude of Schengen members toward Italy in other political domains. What is interesting to note in this context are the kinds of arguments that were formulated to support these criticisms. In the months that followed the application of the Schengen regime, for example, Germany became particularly vocal about the supposedly lax attitudes of the Italian authorities regarding border control. The then interior minister, Manfred Kanther, told the *Berliner Morgenpost* newspaper that Italy was letting hundreds of illegal immigrants into the EU from the former Yugoslavia, Albania, and Turkey, who then showed up in Germany or France. And he added: "It is not right that on one side Schengen is made to function with great amounts of effort and money and one the other side streams of refugees are allowed into and through the country *against the spirit of Schengen.*"[23] Apart from the irony of the fact that Italy was not yet fully part of the Schengen regime, what the German minister of interior pointed to was the existence of a common understanding of what Schengen was all about, and according to those standards, Italy was breaching this "spirit."

It is about this "spirit" that existing members pressured the new applicants, which at the time included Italy, Austria, Greece, Portugal, and the Scandinavian countries. In the new rounds of negotiations that started in the second part of 1996, however, technical issues were again raised.[24] The Italian delegation openly criticized the impression of political reservation that was given regarding the country's integration into Schengen. The Schengen presidency reiterated that, besides the worries related to the SIS, Italy, Greece, and Austria had to address a series of questions in a questionnaire drafted by Germany and edited by France and Spain. This questionnaire aimed at better knowing and understanding the measures undertaken by these countries to prepare the application of the convention (and thus similar to that adopted in Bonn on December 1994 for the other

22. "The long march towards the implementation of the Schengen agreement," FECL 21 (Dec. 1993–Jan. 1994).

23. Quoted in *Statewatch Bulletin*, "Schengen: the first three months," 5, no. 3 (May–June 1995), emphasis added.

24. In the meetings in the autumn of 1996, the Schengen presidency listed the necessary conditions for the application of the convention to the applicants' countries. It mentioned data protection legislation, external border control having reached a required level, adaptation of airports, and the uploading of SIS.

Schengen members). The Italian delegation agreed to comply with this request, but manifested its disapproval of the approach adopted.[25]

To ease the tension now manifest around the negotiating table, the Luxembourg presidency held a political discussion with Italy, Austria, and Greece on 28 November 1996. There it announced that from a technical point of view it was not possible to apply the convention in any of these countries before May 1997, but it suggested that the date for their inclusion in the Schengen Information System would be October 1997. In the following Comex meeting, the Italian, Greek, and Portuguese delegations begrudgingly agreed to respond to the questionnaire (with the delay it would entail), wondering aloud about the rationale for this exercise.[26]

In the following months the issue of enlargement remained at the top of the Comex agenda. The report of the Frontier Commission—sent by Comex in February 1997 to evaluate the Italian frontiers—highlighted some problems at the Slovenian border; the Albanian crisis also raised concerns.[27] The ratification of adhesion agreements in some member states was also delayed. Despite these obstacles, following a positive report by the Portuguese presidency on the state of the preparatory measures undertaken in Italy (and the other countries), the Comex meeting that took place in Lisbon on June 24, 1997, confirmed the date for the entry of Italy into Schengen (July 1, 1997). The German delegation did not, however, approve the presidency's assessment, and indicated the necessity of further improvement regarding the control of external borders. It also argued that, "keeping in mind the Schengen spirit of solidarity," it was necessary to find a compromise solution that avoided the creation of a Schengen external border between Italy and Austria.[28]

In order to overcome the German doubts, a trilateral meeting between the German, Italian, and Austrian heads of governments was held in Innsbruck, Austria, on July 17. In this meeting, Italian and Austrian representatives gave the necessary political assurance that they would comply with Schengen standards, and committed themselves to improve their mutual

25. GC SCH/C (96) PV November 13–14, 1996.

26. IGC SCH/C (96) PV 15—December 18, 1996.

27. In 1997, thousands of Albanian nationals were landing on the Italian coast. At the height of the crisis (March 25, 1997), Italian interior minister Giorgio Napolitano presented the government's countermeasure to his counterparts in the Mediterranean. Later in the year, Italy led a humanitarian operation (Operation Alba) to stabilize the Balkan country (Perlmutter 1998; Sciortino 1998). According to an executive decree, 16,000 Albanian refugees should have been returned before the end of August 1997; but by mid-August only a third were back in Albania; the deadline was therefore moved to the end of November.

28. COMEX meeting minutes, SCH/COM-EX (97) PV 2.

cooperation on issues related to border control and police cooperation. As a result, the three delegations agreed that the entry into force of the convention could take place on October 26, 1997, for Italy and December 1 for Austria, with the simultaneous abolition of controls in airports.[29]

In September, the Schengen Executive Committee still had on its table the three draft decisions regarding the entry into force of the convention in Italy, Austria, and Greece. The Dutch and German delegations argued that the abolition of controls at airports should occur gradually.[30]

Practical measures at the borders, supported by a good dose of political pressure within the Schengen Executive Committee, persuaded the two skeptical delegations to drop their reservations.[31] In early October, the Schengen ministers took notice of Italy's declaration specifying that all international airports would be completely functional from October 26, 1997. After a long discussion, they reached a consensus on the entry into force of the convention for the candidate countries.[32] The convention indeed entered into force in October 1997 (Greece had to wait until December). Italy finally ended a long and painful period of purgatory.

Denmark and the Scandinavian Dilemma: Schengen beyond the Community?

Despite the widespread Euro-skepticism characterizing Danish politics, there was broad domestic support for the Scandinavian country's entry into Schengen since the regime's very inception. Political calculations played an important part in shaping this attitude. By the early 1990s, all other Continental European countries were either part of Schengen or had formally advanced a request to join. Copenhagen would have found itself isolated.

---

29. Land border control would instead be lifted on July 1, 1998; SCH/C (97) PV 8—July 18, 1997.

30. SCH/C (97) PV 9; "Projets de décisions du Comité exécutif sur la mise en vigueur de la Convention de Schengen en Italie, en Grèce et en Autriche," SCH/COM-EX (97) 27 rév. 2, 28 rév. 2 and 29 rév. 2.

31. In testimony before the Italian commission on Schengen, Mario Monti (then European commissioner responsible for the Internal Market and representative of the EU at Schengen) argued that the problem of the difference of evaluation concerned, in particular, the respect of the conditions relative to effective control and surveillance of the external frontiers. But he added, "While the respect of the other necessary conditions can be verified objectively, in this case the recognition of the prerequisite depends in part from a political assessment, regarding the trust in the effectiveness of the Italian Parliament, means adopted by a member state for the control and surveillance of one's external frontiers." Comitato Parlamentare di controllo sull'accordo di Schengen, Seduta del 15/5/1997.

32. COMEX meeting minutes, SCH/COM-EX (97) PV 3.

From the existing members' perspective, the reasons to support the Danish candidature were eminently political. As was the case with Italy, this development would have reinforced the Schengen initiative and offered it further legitimacy. Moreover, Denmark's powerful neighbor, Germany, was particularly vocal in calling for the Scandinavian country to join the regime.[33]

Overall, there was general consensus over Denmark's entry into Schengen. The Danish case, however, raised complex institutional and political issues, stemming from the country's conflicting commitments with its Scandinavian neighbors (Sweden, Norway, Finland, and Iceland). The following paragraphs consider how these questions were addressed and how—through the diplomatic practices that they spurred—the Schengen culture of border control was once again put to the test.

The idea of involving the Scandinavian countries in the common management of European borders came up not in the context of the Schengen regime but within the EC framework. In 1986 the European Council debated the possibility of an agreement between the Community and the Scandinavian countries on the abolition of controls at common borders. The Council referred to the "ever closer union between the growing number of peoples in Europe" as justification for this move, while making it clear that it should not interfere with the process of easing border checks within the EC.[34]

In the months that followed, however, no concrete action was taken, and the issue remained dormant. As in the case of Italy, Schengen members became seriously interested in the expansion of the regime only after the final drafting of the SIC. The first contacts between the Schengen presidency and Denmark took place in the first part of 1991. The major issue on the table since these early stages was the compatibility of the Schengen regime with the Nordic Passport Union. This agreement, originally signed in 1957, includes Denmark, Sweden, Norway, Finland, and Iceland. Thanks to this agreement, since the 1960s Scandinavian countries' citizens had enjoyed free movement across their common frontiers. Joining Schengen would have meant the creation of new barriers between Denmark and the other Nordic countries; such an outcome was therefore both legally and politically unacceptable for Copenhagen. To complicate matters further, unlike Denmark, none of the Scandinavian countries was then an EU member.

33. It should be noted that as early as June 1986, Denmark had signed an agreement with Germany on the easing of controls at their common frontier. Its provisions, however, were not implemented.

34. Communication of the Secretariat General of the Council to COREPER, 8413/86.

No major breakthrough occurred until 1993, when, unexpectedly, Denmark officially launched its candidature to Schengen.[35] The Schengen Executive Committee responded positively. It drafted a questionnaire and adopted a calendar outlining the steps toward Copenhagen's successful entry into Schengen. The optimism was tamed by the worry about the compensatory measures and their compatibility with those of the Nordic countries (Van der Rijt 1999: 30). Despite these concerns, in May 1994 Denmark requested observer status in Schengen. Meanwhile, an important development had occurred. Sweden and Finland had joined the EU, opening the door for their application as Schengen members.

It is in this context that the second stage of negotiations began. On February 27, 1995, the five Scandinavian countries' prime ministers met in Reykjavik as part of their regular multilateral meetings. The outcome was a declaration stating that the three EU members within this group would be willing to join Schengen on the condition that the free movement of people in the Nordic area was maintained. The problems rested with Norway and Iceland, who were not EU members. The first option at that time was the formal accession of the two countries to Schengen; however, this option was problematic because it was contrary to article 140 of the Schengen convention, which explicitly restricted admission to EU members (Van der Rijt 1999: 32). The alternative was the negotiation of a separate agreement. The Schengen Information System, however, posed serious questions regarding the access, integration, and protection of data. Moreover, Norway and Iceland should have harmonized their visa, asylum, and border policies. The prime ministers eventually agreed on a compromise position whereby Norway and Iceland would remain formally outside the Schengen regime but taking charge of its external border controls.

Existing Schengen members' reaction to the proposal was mixed. In the official meetings that followed the declaration of the Scandinavian prime ministers, some delegations (the most vocal was the Italian) stressed the fact that the adhesion of Denmark was essentially a political question, a testing ground for the EU. Thanks to the Danish case (and the other Nordic countries),

35. At the time of the first contacts in 1991, Denmark had a Conservative-led right-wing government. In January 1993, the government fell and was replaced by a Social Democratic-led centrist government. The previous political reservations against joining Schengen, which until then had found some resonance also inside the Social Democratic Party, gradually disintegrated, leaving only the left and the extreme right in the opposition. Domestic politics thus played a role in defining the timing of the launch of Denmark's candidature, but not the decision per se. The Danish government had already demonstrated its interest in joining Schengen; the change of government simply speeded up the process.

Schengen members could have assessed whether the objective of a "Europe without frontiers" could be implemented within the framework of an enlarged Schengen cooperation.[36] The German position was even more radical, supporting the idea of extending Schengen even to non-EU countries (see the next section on Schengen's external relations). Others were more cautious. The Belgian delegation, for example, noted that the rapprochement with the Nordic Union, though politically important, should have not compromised the current Schengen *acquis* and its eventual incorporation in the EU. Moreover, an accession "*à la carte*" would set a precedent for Switzerland and Eastern European countries. The European Commission was also wary. Its representative at the Schengen meeting stressed the importance of maintaining article 140 in its integrity, which therefore excluded the possibility of the inclusion of Norway and Iceland (CG 1995/00).

Without knowing whether the negotiations would be successful, Finland and then Sweden nonetheless made a formal request for observer status in June 1995 (Van der Rijt 1999: 32). Their accession, however, was explicitly linked to a solution to the question of Norway and Iceland. The Belgian presidency made known that the association of the two countries could not involve voting rights. The possibility of separating "decision shaping" and "decision taking" powers was therefore put on the table: the Norwegian and Icelandic delegations could participate at all meetings and intervene at all levels except for when a vote is tabled, although they could express their opposition, a procedure that would lead to the denunciation of the accord (Van der Rijt 1999: 33).

At this stage of the negotiations an extensive exchange of information on existing legislation and policies took place. Those with doubts were eventually convinced that no major obstacle existed for the candidate countries' accession to or participation in Schengen. As a Nordic Union official commented, "In reality the Nordic countries have had Schengen co-operation for 40 years."[37] In December 1995, after the Danish government answered a comprehensive Schengen questionnaire on the country's immigration, police, and border control policies to the satisfaction of the Schengen group, the Comex granted Denmark and the other four countries observer status starting from May 1996.

Once existing Schengen members reached a political agreement on this issue, the necessary legal instruments (accession agreements for Sweden, Finland, and Denmark and cooperation agreement with Norway and Ice-

---

36. CG 1995/00.
37. *Statewatch* 5, no. 3 (May–June 1995).

land) were drafted. The first meeting of Group Central with the northern countries took place the following May.[38] On December 19, 1996, the Danish government signed the Schengen Implementing Convention. On the same day, the other Scandinavian countries joined the regime. Without much controversy, national parliaments supported their governments' decision and swiftly ratified the agreements.

The Nordic countries' entry into Schengen was a major success, and it bolstered the initiative. The complex institutional architecture of the agreement was, however, to be tested again when the Schengen *acquis* was incorporated into the EU framework. The story of the Nordic countries in Schengen will therefore resume when this development is examined in chapter 7.

Schengen's External Relations in Transition

As was apparent in the analysis of the regime's expansion to Italy and Denmark, Schengen's external dimension was not a priority in the regime's early years. It should be mentioned, however, that at this stage the external borders of the regime included mostly other EC countries. The only "hard" common external border was in the East (specifically, West Germany's border with its eastern counterpart, the German Democratic Republic, and Poland). Until the late 1980s, this frontier was highly fortified and difficult to penetrate. As we have seen, it was an oddity in the Westphalia system since it was not a "national" but a "regional" border and it was permeated by strong ideological undertones. But the Iron Curtain was also in contrast to the spirit of the emerging Schengen culture. Schengen in fact emphasized the "internal security" dimension of borders rather than military and ideological issues. This explains why the Schengen initiative was not directly involved in East-West politics. Throughout the 1980s, therefore, its main focus remained Western Europe.

The interest toward non-EC countries grew as the negotiations over the Schengen Implementation Convention were coming to a conclusion. In this phase, the regime's features and objectives were more clearly delineated, and the need to define the approach to the control of the common external frontiers became more pressing. However, it was ultimately an external event—the fall of the Iron Curtain—that shook up Schengen's foreign policy. As we have seen, this development had a direct effect on Schengen, for it delayed the signing of the implementation convention. More importantly, it created fear among Western European governments of a mass influx of

38. GC SCH/C (96) PV 5—May 7.

migrants from the East. The sharp increase in asylum applications across Western Europe in early 1990s certainly contributed to this state of uneasiness.[39] Border control therefore became an item on the agenda of East-West relations. Given the lack of an appropriate institutional forum to discuss internal security, Schengen members decided to take a more proactive role toward the countries forming their new eastern borders. In parallel to negotiations with potential candidates in Western Europe, Schengen members therefore started a dialogue with their Eastern European neighbors.

The first important foreign policy initiative collectively carried out by Schengen members was the proposal for a readmission agreement with Poland in 1991 (Okolski 1991). A working group for this purpose was set up at the Paris Comex meeting of November 27, 1990. Four months later (March, 29 1991) the two parties signed the accord. This multi-bilateral agreement (formally an agreement between the governments of the Schengen states and the government of Poland) envisaged the repatriation of illegal immigrants to the country whose external border these individuals had crossed first (art. 2[1]). Thanks to this arrangement, on April 8, 1991, the Schengen members introduced a visa exemption for Polish citizens. In commenting on the agreement, Schengen members stressed its political value, inserting it in the broader context of post–Cold War East-West relations. The then German presidency argued that maintaining an open policy regarding visas proved that the regime "was not about the construction of a Fortress Europe."[40] In cultural evolutionary terms, this practical achievement in the regime's external relations represented an early sign of the Schengen culture's potential.

The approach adopted by Schengen governments with regard to cooperation with Eastern European countries over the issue of immigration and border control was considered a success. In fact, it inspired similar intergovernmental initiatives in the months that followed. In October 1991 ministers from thirty-three Western and Eastern European countries met in Berlin to discuss ways of coordinating immigration control and, in particular, combating illegal immigration across Europe. The "Berlin group" met again in Budapest in February 1993 and discussed enlarging the Schengen-Poland readmission agreement to other Eastern European states. The initiative's content and spirit reflected those of Schengen (and the link was explicitly mentioned).

39. For a quantitative analysis of asylum applications in EU member states in the 1980s and 1990s, see Vink and Meijerink 2003.

40. COMEX meeting minutes, SCH/M (91) PV, June 1, 1991.

Another set of initiatives that was launched in this period was that of the Vienna Group. This group was set up in 1978 by interior ministers of Austria, France, Germany, Italy, and Switzerland to combat terrorism across the Continent. The countries involved called a ministerial conference in January 1991 to discuss migration movements from Eastern to Western Europe and invited EC and Eastern European ministers. From that conference emerged the Vienna Group (Immigration), which in turn produced the Working Party on a Solidarity Structure (Burden-sharing), with a brief to examine "collective European cooperation with respect to the movements of people." The working party first met in March 1993, and other meetings followed. As for the Berlin group, the Vienna Group's main assumptions reflected those of Schengen. The main focus was security (and, indeed, it was originally created to combat terrorism). The "solidarity" referred to was not for refugees or migrants but for the prevention of their "disorderly movements" across Europe.[41]

Besides multilateral efforts, in this period Schengen also inspired other bilateral readmission agreements. Some were negotiated individually by each Schengen member. For example, in the early 1990s, most of them either signed or were close to signing agreements with Slovenia, and opened negotiations with Romania, the Czech Republic, and Slovakia. Readmission agreements de facto became a prerequisite to join Schengen. EU candidate countries therefore became very active on this front. Between 1991 and 1993, for example, Austria signed mutual readmission agreements with Hungary, Poland, Romania, Slovenia, and the Czech Republic; similarly, Denmark reached an agreement with Latvia and Lithuania and was in negotiation with Estonia.

Despite the success of the Schengen model, the regime's foreign policy was not formalized. It was still carried out mainly in an ad hoc and decentralized manner. Neither the Schengen Executive Committee nor the presidency had special authority on the subject. The situation changed when the first discussions began over EU enlargement to the East. It was under the Portuguese presidency in the first semester of 1997 that the character of Schengen's external relations was more clearly defined. The Comex

---

41. Multi-bilateral contacts were also developed with countries that, although not EU members, were considered to be low-risk in terms of immigration and other border-related threats. This was especially the case of Switzerland. This country showed interest in Schengen from the beginning of the 1990s. Even if landlocked, it risked becoming "an island in an ocean of free movement" (Van de Rijt 2000: 45). At this time, however, an agreement could not be reached. Switzerland was dealing with the anti-EU sentiment of its population but also with the conviction of elites of the inevitability of the entry into the EU.

decided to set as an objective institutionalizing the presidency's procedure in this domain, so as to avoid duplicating the action of the EU. The central idea was that of subsidiarity. All external relations had to maintain a subsidiary character to that of the structured dialogue within the third pillar of the EU (on the "structured dialogue" with Eastern European countries, see chap. 6). At the same time, Schengen member states had to maintain an attitude toward third countries that could not be interpreted as a rejection of their aspirations. Contacts had to avoid any kind of formal commitment by Schengen member states, such as granting observer status or accession (Van de Rijt 1997: 46–47).

The formalization of Schengen's foreign policy, however, opened up a rift among Schengen members. Some of them (most notably Germany) criticized the cautious and subordinated approach that was adopted under the Portuguese presidency and pushed for a more aggressive and independent stance. In a report published in the fall of 1996 by the German government on the progress made under the Schengen Agreement and the perspectives for its future development, Bonn did not agree with the "majority opinion" within Comex that the association agreements with Norway and Iceland should be seen as exceptions. It argued that whether non-EU states remain "associates" or join the EU as full members after the incorporation of Schengen cooperation into the EU makes no difference, as the EU "ultimately benefits." Furthermore, this document proposed the creation within Schengen of a "participant status" (*Mitwirkungsstatus*) for third countries that planned to join the EU or Schengen in the mid- or long term.[42]

The heated debate over the future of the Schengen regime's foreign policy continued throughout 1997. Exemplary of the tone of the discussion was the Comex meeting that took place in December.[43] On the table was a document drafted by the Coordinators' Group regarding contacts with third countries, with a focus on Eastern Europe and Russia.[44] Many delegations deemed that the text expressed a too defensive attitude. The German delegation declared its willingness to present a bolder proposal. Compromise positions were also suggested. The Norwegian delegation suggested a formulation according to which Schengen external contacts would be placed in the context of the structured dialogue within the European Union, rather than being subordinated to it. Both the German and the Norwegian delega-

---

42. Report of the German government on the Schengen Agreement, "Experiences and Perspectives," 1996; reproduced in *Statewatch* 6, no. 5 (Sept.–Oct. 1996).

43. COMEX meeting minutes, Vienna, December 15, 1997, SCH/Com-ex (97) PV 4.

44. "Contacts avec les pays tiers," SCH/IV (97) 2 rév.

tions argued that their proposal would have strengthened the regime and helped the European project. In the eyes of most delegations, however, the German position was not convincing. The independent approach Bonn was proposing was going too far. It could have seriously damaged the ongoing process of enlargement within the EU rather than supporting it. The Norwegian compromise was not sufficient to overcome these doubts. The majority of Comex members therefore decided to stick to the "subordinate" approach. This approach eventually prevailed and became the official blueprint for Schengen's foreign policy in the early 1990s. Comex did not establish formal relations with EU candidate countries (although the protocol integrating Schengen into the EU foresaw their inclusion in the regime). In the meantime, the Schengen presidency limited itself to exchanging information with candidate countries and to inviting them to Comex meetings. Formal contacts would have begun only once the adhesion process had been officially determined and the status of the Schengen *acquis* defined. As we will see in the next chapter, it was only after the Schengen culture's formal selection, sealed with the regime's incorporation into the EU, that a new and more proactive phase in Western European countries' foreign policy regarding border control would open up.

"Home affairs": The Evolution of Schengen's Border Control Community

As for practices more generally, changes in the configuration of the Schengen border control policy community in the 1990s represented a sign of the culture's strengthening. The most noticeable development in this period was the growth in the regime's membership. From the initial five proponents, at the end of the decade Schengen included fifteen European countries. Besides expanding in size, the Schengen border control community's internal dynamics changed as well. Schengen was mainly an intergovernmental affair and remained so throughout the decade. The main institutional actors were ministers and other officials constituting the various national delegations. While other ministries such as that of transportation were involved in the preparatory stages of the regime,[45] its day-to-day management was handled by officials from Foreign Affairs and Interior/Home Affairs (see table 5.2).

45. As a result of the spring 1984 pan-European truck drivers' strike to protest the long waiting time at borders (cf. chap. 4), European ministers of transportation were spurred to find a "European" solution to the problem, and their activism played a role in the birth of Schengen.

Table 5.2 Representation in Schengen groups by country and ministerial affiliation (1990s)

Country	Executive Committee	Central Group
Belgium	Interior	Interior
Denmark	Justice	Justice
Germany	Interior	Interior
Greece	Foreign Affairs	Foreign Affairs
Spain	Foreign Affairs	Foreign Affairs
France	European Affairs	Prime minister (SGCI) coordinator
Ireland	—	—
Italy	Foreign Affairs	Diplomat (perm't representation)
Luxembourg	Justice	Justice
Netherlands	Foreign Affairs	Justice
Austria	Interior	Interior
Portugal	Interior	Foreign Affairs
Finland	Interior	Interior
Sweden	Justice	Justice
UK	—	—

Source: Adapted from Turk 1998.

National traditions initially dictated who would be participating in the meetings of the Schengen Executive Committee and the Central Group, the regime's decision-making organs. In the 1990s, there was a clear shift in these meetings in favor of officials from the Interior Ministry (Hreblay 1998: 28; Guiraudon 2003: 266). Representatives of this ministry within the various negotiation groups became more numerous, and their political clout grew considerably. This reconfiguration of power did not occur smoothly. Other ministries had a stake in the initiative, such as Foreign Affairs, with regard to visa issues. Hence there was no a priori reason to expect a monopoly of Interior personnel (Guiraudon 2003: 267–268). Battles over the control of this portfolio were therefore common. Representative of this tension is what occurred in France around the time the Schengen regime came into effect. In response to the concerns raised about the dispersion and lack of coordination in French policy regarding border control, the French minister of European affairs, Michel Barnier, told the French Senate that the government would have given the Schengen file to the Interior Ministry at the end of the intergovernmental conference (IGC) that took place in the second half of 1996 (see chap. 7), stressing that the delay was only because of the transition from the regime's negotiation to its everyday management.[46]

46. Intervention of the Minister of European Affairs, Micheal Barnier, to the French Senate; Paris, March 26, 1996.

When the Senate asked again at the end of the IGC about the timing of the reform, the new minister (Moscovici) replied that this issue would be solved when the Schengen *acquis* was fully incorporated into the EU, and that "the links between the ministry of interior, justice and foreign affairs still have to be defined."[47] The French Foreign Ministry was clearly unwilling to cede power to its Interior counterpart.

The political tug of war between ministries at the national level did not spill over into the Schengen working groups. National civil servants involved in the various groups' meetings showed a spirit of cooperation and mutual understanding. Within each initiative people called each other by their names, and colleagues were even friends. Being part of these negotiations fostered a sense of common belonging. What Hayes-Renshaw and Wallace argue about the European Council in general can therefore be extended to Schengen's border control policy community: "Decision makers . . . , in spite of their national roots, become locked into the collective process, especially in areas of well-established and recurrent negotiation. This does not mean that participants have transferred loyalty to the EU system, but it does mean that they acknowledge themselves in certain crucial ways as being part of a collective system of decision making" (1997: 279, quoted in Laffan 2004: 91).

The predominance of Interior Ministries within Schengen meant that this sense of common belonging and purpose was translated into a mostly security-oriented agenda when issues of border control were on the table. As the former British home secretary Jack Straw candidly put it, "whenever two or three Interior Ministers are gathered together, they tend to talk about nothing else than asylum and migration."[48] Indeed, by actively advocating the expansion of "protective" measures to compensate for the abolition of internal borders, Interior Ministries contributed to the further securitization of the Schengen regime.

The securitarian outlook that Schengen acquired over time had consequences not only for the national delegations represented at Schengen, but also for the European Commission. Suspicious of supranational institutions interfering on their turf, Schengen delegates were not enthusiastic about the European Commission's involvement in their intergovernmental affairs. It was not surprising therefore that only after long pressing was the Commission's representative allowed to participate in the Schengen meetings.

47. Senate Session of October 14, 1997.
48. Testimony at UK House of Lords Select Committee on the European Communities, "Prospects for the Tampere Special European Council" (House of Lords 1999).

The Commission's actual contribution to the regime was nonetheless marginal. Its most relevant impact was mostly symbolic. As had been the case in the previous years, what the presence of a Community institution in an intergovernmental setting outside the EU provided was an element of legitimacy to the initiative.

SIX

Selecting a New Culture of Border Control: Brussels

Europe will not be made all at once, or according to a single, general plan. It will be built through concrete achievements, which first create a de facto solidarity.

—Robert Schuman, May 9, 1950

The idea is clear: political Europe will be created by human effort, when the time comes, on the basis of reality.

—Jean Monnet (1978: 431)

Negotiating Brussels: The Border Convention and the Troubles with "Europe without frontiers"

The ongoing testing of the new cultures of border control taking place in Europe throughout the 1990s was not restricted to the intergovernmental practices of the Schengen initiative. Similar evolutionary dynamics were evident in the European Community's (soon to be "Union") context. Indeed, after the signing of the Single European Act (SEA) in 1986, an intense debate ensued over the project of a "Europe without frontiers." Despite the differences of opinion on the subject, European governments and their representatives in the EC, with the support of the European Commission, informally agreed to begin negotiations to achieve the goals set out in the SEA. In the summer of 1989, the then French EC presidency submitted to the Ad Hoc Group on Immigration two draft conventions. The first document addressed the issue of asylum ("Convention determining the State responsible for examining applications for asylum lodged in one of the member states of the European Communities," also known as the "Dublin Convention"). The second dealt with border crossing ("Convention between the Member States of the European Communities on the Crossing of Their External Frontiers" or "Border Convention"). Taken together, the two conventions covered most of the topics included in the Palma Report, the working plan adopted in 1989 to address the lack of progress concerning freedom of movement within the community. Without much debate, all member states accepted these texts as the basis for negotiation, and special working groups were set up to examine the various aspects of the conventions.

While the Dublin Convention was agreed upon in a relatively short time,[1] the debate over the Border Convention turned out to be a tortuous and controversial affair (O'Keefe 1996). The delegations participating in the negotiations had to overcome several legal and technical obstacles (e.g., British and Irish separate and incompatible systems for granting visas; the lack of common rules on data protection; Denza 2002: 72). The most contentious issue was the definition of "borders" for the purpose of the convention and the implications that their abolition would have for member states. As we have seen, the negotiators had decided to postpone any decision regarding the meaning of "free movement" as expressed in article 8a of the EC Treaty until the end of the negotiating process. They soon realized, however, that this would be impossible. The dispute involved substantial matters, such as the distribution of competence between member states and community institutions, which needed to be resolved before a final agreement on the content of the convention could be reached.

In the first rounds of negotiations, two camps emerged, which by and large mirrored divisions at the time of the signing of the SEA. On one hand, a group of "historical" Community members, supported by the Commission, defended a communitarian interpretation of article 8a, which established the goal of "progressively establishing the internal market," defined as an "area without borders." According to this group, because the area was equated to an internal (i.e., domestic) market, the abolition of borders should apply to both EC and non-EC citizens, even if the term "persons" included in the Treaty of Rome (art. 3c) did not clarify this point. Indeed, if it did not apply to both EC and non-EC citizens, controls had to be reinstated to determine the nationality of individuals, and this would clash with the agreed common objective of abolishing internal borders.

1. The convention was finalized after ten months of negotiations; however, it only entered into force in 1997 as a result of the long process of ratification in some of the member countries. On the Dublin Convention, see Marinho 2000; Müller-Graff 1995.

On the other hand, a group of recalcitrant countries led by the United Kingdom (the others were Ireland, Denmark, and Greece) opted for a narrower nationalist interpretation of article 8a. Although in principle they accepted the goal of a Europe without borders,[2] these delegations deemed that the SEA did not create any obligation to abolish controls at internal borders for non-EC nationals. They emphasized the fact that the SEA left open the possibility for member states to control (and possibly limit) the process leading to the creation of an "area without borders."[3] This interpretation was backed up by reference to the two declarations added to the SEA ("Declarations on Art. 13 to 19"; and "Declaration to article 8a"), which explicitly mentioned the centrality of member states in the border control field. These delegations also claimed that the goal of the Common Market could be achieved through simple intergovernmental cooperation, and therefore supranational methods (i.e., through the Community) were not necessary. To support this claim, they repeatedly pointed to the fact that border control had an important security dimension, which only national governments could appropriately address. Geographical arguments were also brought forward to justify the need for national approaches to address the issue (particularly by the United Kingdom, but also by Greece[4]).

Despite these differences, a final text of the Border Convention was agreed upon in June 1991. Given the diverging interpretations of its content, the likelihood of the convention becoming operational in the near future was very low. Nonetheless, what prevented its formal approval was an issue that came up late in the negotiation between Spain and the United

2. The Thatcher government was enthusiastic about the neoliberal emphasis on free markets underlying the Single European Act (the White Paper, the document that laid the foundation of the SEA, had been drafted by Lord Cokfield, a former cabinet minister). Geoffrey Howe, then a minister in the British government, shared this favorable sentiment about the SEA: "Broadly we relished the idea of a Europe that was frontier-free . . . In the end we [came] as close as possible to achieving that prospect" (quoted in Moravcsik 1998: 325). At least in principle, the Irish government supported the idea of abolishing border controls with Continental Europe. However, because of its free travel agreement with the United Kingdom, Dublin maintained a cautious attitude within the EC when debating issues of border control so as to avoid straining the special relationship with London.

3. They referred to the part of article 8a that states that measures in this field should be "in accordance with the provisions of this Treaty," which allows member states to trump Community competence for matters of national security.

4. See, for example, the *Times*, June 14, 1991: "Baker says border controls must stay."

Kingdom over the status of Gibraltar (the disputed British enclave in Spanish territory) for the purposes of the convention.[5]

While the negotiations over the Border Convention stalled, the European Commission became more vocal in its attempt to convince member states to meet the 1992 deadline for the complete abolition of border controls. The Commission started to raise its voice against the European Council, which seemed to drag its feet on this issue. Telling in this regard is the fate of a proposal for a directive to "progressively reduce controls at common borders," which the Commission introduced in January 1985. It was a transitional proposal before all the objectives of the White Paper were met. However, the Internal Market Council, which should have decided its approval, first watered it down, and then, in 1987, transferred the file to the ad hoc working group of Ministers responsible for immigration, further delaying it. No agreement was reached on the wording of the resolution, and the Commission was eventually forced to withdraw the proposal.

The Commission's criticism was directed not only to the Council as a whole, but also to individual delegations. This was especially true of the United Kingdom's. In the spring of 1992, the Commission publicly warned London that the abolition of border controls was "a clear and straightforward objective. It imposes an obligation to produce results and leaves no margin of discretion. All controls must go, whatever their form and whatever their justification."[6] The British government flatly rejected the Commission's argument. The home secretary at the time, Kenneth Clarke, argued that "it is for individual member states to take the measures they consider most appropriate to control immigration from third countries and to combat terrorism, crime and drugs."[7]

Failing to provide concrete evidence of the effectiveness of the new border model, in the following months the Commission turned to a more conciliatory approach. After meeting with the British home secretary in Lisbon (July 1992) and London (September 1992), Martin Bangemann, vice president of the European Commission, suggested a pragmatic solution that

5. Spain accused the United Kingdom of failing to respect Community legislation by not applying several directives in Gibraltar and disregarding its sovereignty claims over it. Conversely, the British (and Gibraltar) authorities considered unacceptable the excessive controls imposed by Spain at its border with Gibraltar, as well as the nonrecognition of identity cards issued by Gibraltar authorities. The negotiations of several Community instruments were blocked for years because of this dispute (see, e.g., the fate of the "Joint Action establishing a European Judicial Network" [*Agence Europe*, no. 7115, Dec. 6, 1997], and the directive on security checks on third-country aircrafts [*Agence Europe*, no. 7354, Dec. 2, 1998 and n. 7404, and Feb. 13, 1999]).

6. *Guardian*, May 8, 1992.

7. Ibid.; see also *Times*, "Major to fight on for border checks," May 15, 1992.

would lead to "no systematic border controls" after January 1, 1993. The idea, widely reported in the press as the "Bangemann wave," entailed that EC nationals entering the United Kingdom would not be subject to thorough checks, but walk through passport control holding up their passports or national identity cards.

The other delegations (particularly those also involved in the Schengen initiative) were lukewarm about the Commission's proposal. Discussing the issue within the Schengen framework (Madrid, November 1992), the ministers in charge of immigration and border control insisted on the "inseparable link" between the abolition of controls at internal borders and the existence of controls at the external frontiers. They added that if the United Kingdom wanted to take a unilateral step, they would not oppose it. Yet, they deemed that a provisional solution "seems not the most appropriate for such a fundamental question."[8]

In any case, the solution proposed by the Commission was not enough to convince the British government. The Commission had assumed that the compromise reached by Clarke and Bangemann would apply to all entries to the United Kingdom by EC nationals. London argued instead that the "Bangemann wave" was applicable only to seaports and not airports—the point through which most people entered the country. Moreover, this measure would not be introduced until the Schengen countries removed their internal controls (expected to cover sea and land entry by the summer and airports by the end of 1993). The British government thus maintained its commitment to keep controls at its borders indefinitely.

Meanwhile, the position of other members of the recalcitrant group began to change. The long-standing difference between, on one hand, the United Kingdom, Ireland, and Denmark and, on the other, the rest of the EC, had often been presented by London as a united front determined to maintain border controls to check for terrorists, drugs, and illegal immigrants. Starting from 1993, however, Denmark started to distance itself from the British position. This was clearly demonstrated at the Copenhagen meeting of ministers in June 1993. On this occasion, the Danish government hinted that when three conditions were met it would remove internal border checks with Germany. These conditions were the ratification of the Dublin and the Border Convention and the establishment of a European Information System ("EIS," a Community-wide computer database covering immigration, policing, and legal matters). In this period, Greece also softened its position, assuming a more "communitarian" attitude.

---

8. Schengen Executive Committee meeting minutes, SCH/M (92) PV 2.

Despite the growing isolation of the British, negotiations over the Border Convention did not advance in the following months. According to an EU official who participated in its activities, the Frontiers Working Group (the group responsible for the Border Convention file), was "dead." Not even the creation of a Community-based justice and home affairs (JHA) policy domain in 1993 (on this point see below) helped to revamp the process. In November 1993, the Commission tabled a proposal regarding the Border Convention.[9] The proposal resumed the text agreed upon on June 1991 and updated it in light of the newly established JHA policy domain; however, the Commission's activism was not enough to overcome the impasse. From 1994 onward, this proposal was under examination by the Frontiers Working Group. There it languished and was never approved. In the meantime, relevant working parties within the EC continued discussions on the convention. Still, it could not overcome the main problem blocking the negotiations, namely, the question of its territorial application to Gibraltar.[10]

The stalling of the Border Convention reflected the failure of the Community to respect the deadline to achieve a "Europe without frontiers." In July 1993, the European Parliament, after repeated threats, decided to initiate legal proceeding against the European Commission for failing to make sure that the twelve EC member states met their commitment on time.[11] In July 1995 the Commission responded to this challenge by introducing three new proposals for directives. These proposals (the so-called Monti Proposals[12]) were never adopted because of a lack of consensus in the Council. They nonetheless eliminated the grounds for the European Parliament's complaint over the Commission's inertia.

The lack of progress regarding freedom of movement within the European Community was recognized by the European Court of Justice. In the 1999 case *Wijsenbeek*, the ECJ held that, at the time when the main events in the proceedings occurred (1997), there were no common rules or harmonized laws for the member states on controls at external borders and immigration, asylum, and visa policy. Thus, even if according to the EC law nationals of the member states had an unconditional right to move

9. Commission of the European Communities, "Proposal for a Decision about the Conclusion of the Border Convention . . . ." (COM [93] 684 final).

10. "Progress report from Presidency to Council," 8097/1/95, June 16, 1995.

11. "Case C-445/93, European Parliament v European Commission," *Official Journal* C 1/24 (1994).

12. Commission of the European Communities, "Proposal for a council directive on the elimination of controls on persons crossing internal frontiers" (COM [95] 347, July 12, 1995); *Official Journal* C 289/16 (1995).

freely within the territory of the member states, the latter retained the right to continue identity checks at the internal frontiers of the Community to determine whether an individual was a national of a member state and thus possessed the right of free movement within the EC.[13] The dream of a Europe without frontiers was clearly still far from becoming reality.

Maastricht and Justice and Home Affairs: Great Expectations and Unfulfilled Promises

The debate over the Single European Act was not restricted—as in the case of the Border Convention—to the practical steps necessary to achieve the objective of a regionwide area of free movement. It also touched upon broader institutional questions, in particular whether the SEA gave the European Community sufficient power to fulfill its new, expanded mandate. These attempts to reshape the EU's "infrastructure" played an important role in the evolution of the emerging Brussels culture of border control, for it is through these efforts that border control's viability as an independent and coherent "European" policy domain could be appraised.

The idea of deepening the reforms envisioned in the Single European Act started to circulate soon after the act's ratification. A proposal to create a monetary union was formally tabled at the Hanover European Council in June 1988. Nonmonetary matters (including freedom of movement and border control) entered the agenda only later. As had occurred for the SEA, the French and German governments took the initiative. High-level consultations began before the March 1990 elections in Germany, the first after the fall of the Berlin Wall. In these talks President Mitterand and Chancellor Kohl flagged the idea of a "Political Union," which would be elaborated alongside the "Monetary Union" initiative. Political union meant a deeper integration of foreign and defense policy and home affairs.

On the basis of this discussion, on April 18 the French and German leaders forwarded a formal request to their EC counterparts for a parallel conference, "taking into account the deep transformations in Europe, the establishment of the Common Market and the realization of the Economic and Monetary Union."[14] The objectives of the proposal were to reinforce the

---

13. *Wijsenbeek,* EC case C-378/97, (1999) ECR I-5221; Guild 2001: 10.

14. "Joint message by François Mitterrand, President of the French Republic, and Helmut Kohl, chancellor of the Federal Republic of Germany, addressed to Charles Haughey, president of the European Council, on the necessity to speed up the construction of Political Europe" (Paris, April 19, 1990), Agence Europe, 20 April 1990, no. 5238. On the origins of the 1992 ICG, see Corbett (1992).

democratic legitimacy of the EU, render more effective its institutions, ensure the unity and coherence of community action, and define and implement common foreign and security policies. The issue of freedom of movement (and more generally "internal security") would form an important part of the emerging political union, although at this stage the topic was not explicitly addressed.

The reaction of the other EC member states to the Franco-German initiative was mixed. At the following council meeting in Dublin (June 1990), British prime minister Thatcher and her Danish and Portuguese colleagues were openly opposed to any attempt to impinge on their national prerogatives. The more "communitarian" delegations (e.g., the Netherlands) were concerned that talking about "Political Union," and not just "Community" might have weakened the entire European project. In its conclusions, the Council argued that in order to achieve "the Union it wishes," it was necessary to take action in various fields (including free movement of persons) "with a view of enhancing the benefits which our peoples derive from belonging to a Community which has as its *raison d'être* the promotion of their rights, their freedoms and their welfare."[15] Despite some reservations, the proposal for the new Intergovernmental Conference (IGC) on Political Union was accepted.

A decisive orientation on the content of the IGC was again suggested by the Franco-German duo shortly after the Dublin Council. On December 6, Kohl and Mitterand sent a letter to their partners outlining their vision of a future political union. Here they proposed an enlargement of the Community competences, which would have led to the inclusion of policy issues hitherto treated in an intergovernmental framework. These issues included immigration, visa and asylum policy, and international crime. Mitterand and Kohl also recommended the creation of a special council of ministers entirely devoted to justice and home affairs.

The Franco-German proposal formed the basis of the negotiation at the IGC on Political Union. The conference began in 1991 and worked parallel to the one on Economic and Monetary Union (EMU). Unlike the case of EMU, the agenda was not defined, and negotiations were open-ended. The key political question for member states was whether to integrate into the Community the various intergovernmental activities that had been undertaken previously outside the Community. Various proposals were submitted

15. "Dublin Council Presidency Conclusions," Dublin, June 25–26, 1990, *European Council Presidency Conclusions (Dublin, 25.–26.06.1990)*, SN 60/1/90 (Brussels: Council of the European Communities, June 1990).

during the IGC. Germany was the country that pushed most forcefully for the communitarization of the immigration and border control policy area. Other countries traditionally in favor of more integration supported this view, although the degree of enthusiasm varied considerably (France, for example, had mixed feelings about the German activism). The Commission was in favor of putting all intergovernmental cooperation under the Community framework. Its views, however, carried little weight in the context of the IGC (Denza 2002: 75; Den Boer 1998: 3–4).[16] On the other side of the spectrum was, once again, the United Kingdom. London supported the idea of creating a stronger and more coherent structure to deal with home affairs issues, but only using intergovernmental methods. It also strongly opposed the abolition of internal borders and further communitarization efforts in this policy domain.

After having heard the views of all the delegations, in January 1991 the Luxembourg presidency drafted a paper containing various options for the future of justice and home affairs issues in the EC, ranging from the maintenance of the status quo to full communitarization. The United Kingdom, Ireland, and Greece favored the idea of putting a brief reference in the treaty to the principle of cooperation and let the Council define the details. The Netherlands, Belgium, Spain, and Italy instead favored full communitarization (Corbett 1992: 284). The Luxembourg presidency, however, decided to push forward an intermediate option (to elaborate a set of provisions defining the field to be covered and the decision-making procedures with a view to achieving full communitarization), a position that was supported by France and Germany.

This compromise option was included in the presidency's "non-paper" of April 1991, which proposed a new institutional arrangement to include the political union in the Community. The proposal envisioned a new pillar system for the EC. The first of the three pillars would represent the already existing European Communities (the European Community, the European Coal and Steel Community, and the European Atomic Energy Community), now strengthened with enlarged competences (including the monetary union).

---

16. Aware of its limited influence, during the ICG the European Commission adopted a stance sensitive to the fundamental issues of national sovereignty inherent in questions of border control (Uçarer 2001). This attitude was evident, for example, in the communication drafted in the autumn of 1991 to stimulate debate on the attitudes and practices of member states over the issue of migration in advance of the ICG on Political Union ("Communication to the Council and the EP on Immigration," SEC [91] 1855 final, Brussels, October 23, 1991). In this document the Commission recognized that the Community and its member states have "shared principles and individual variation" (ibid.). It also advocated dialogue with all the forums where these discussions could take place (both within the EC and outside).

The other two pillars (Foreign Policy and Security, and Justice and Home Affairs) would function instead according to an intergovernmental method, although still under a common umbrella, that of a newly created "European Union."

The ministers discussed this proposal in various meetings between May and June 1991. France, the United Kingdom, Denmark, and Portugal supported the pillar arrangement. A majority of delegations (Belgium, Germany, Italy, Ireland, Spain, the Netherlands) thought that this proposal was too minimalist (Corbett 1992; Pryce 1994: 47). The Commission was also opposed (its then president Delors called it "crippling"). The presidency was not convinced, however, that the "maximalist" majority view would have achieved the necessary consensus. In June it therefore only made some adjustments to take into consideration some of these critiques in a "Draft Treaty on the Union" (Corbett 1992: 279). In this revised text it was emphasized that the pillar structure would have represented a step toward the communitarization of the two noncommunity pillars. Not all members of the procommunitarian camp were fully satisfied with the changes (ibid.: 280). As a compromise, the Luxembourg Council accepted the text as the basis for continuing the negotiations, but added that it should take into account the principles of "the maintenance of the full *acquis communautaire* and developments thereof [and] a single institutional framework."[17]

The Dutch presidency that took over in July 1991 attempted to reopen the issue, presenting a new "Draft Treaty towards European Union" based on a unitary "tree" structure, in which all new policy areas (including justice and home affairs) would be fully integrated into the EC. The draft was circulated in September. For most delegations, however, it was too late to revive the debate. Since only Belgium supported it, the new text was withdrawn later that month. As a result of this debacle, this date was also known as "Black September."

In the following months, there was skepticism that a satisfactory solution to the impasse could be found. In this climate, late in the fall a new text that resurrected the pillar system was presented before a meeting of foreign ministers (November 12–13). The part on justice and home affairs reflected almost in toto Luxembourg's early proposal. The main differences were the inclusion of a visa policy in the first pillar and a *"passerelle"* ("bridge") clause that provided for the possibility of further transfers to the first pillar if the

---

17. Luxembourg European Council, "Conclusions of the Luxembourg European Council," in *European Council (Luxembourg, 28 and 29 June 1991). Presidency Conclusions,* SN 151291 (Brussels: Council of the European Communities, 1991).

Council unanimously agreed (Corbett 1992: 280–281). Given the lack of valid alternatives, this text became the basis for discussion at the Council meeting in Maastricht the following month. Without much discussion, EU leaders officially approved the revamped pillar system, which became the central feature of the Treaty on European Union (Maastricht Treaty).

The relevance of the agreement reached at Maastricht for the issue of border control was that this subject officially entered into the EC (now EU) institutional framework.[18] A new title was added to the treaty (art. K), whose provisions had the objective of "facilitating the free movement of people, while ensuring the safety and security of the member states' peoples" (title K, preamble). Among the areas listed as "matters of common interest" in this new field, the treaty mentioned asylum policy, control of external borders, migration by nationals of nonmember states, judicial cooperation in civil and criminal matters, customs, and police cooperation. The forms of cooperation within the new policy domain could take the form of policy guidelines to be followed by each member state ("Recommendations" and "Declarations") or legally binding legislation by the Council ("Conventions" or "Joint Actions"/"Joint Positions").

In organizational terms, Maastricht significantly reshaped the structure of the border control policy community. The Council, previously excluded from home affairs matters, was given a central role in the new legal framework. A new ad hoc Justice and Home Affairs (JHA) Council of Ministers and a coordinating committee of senior officials ("K.4 Committee," which took over the role previously held by the Coordinators' Group) were set up. Maastricht also led to the creation of new steering and working groups, whose mandate was elaborated in the first meeting of the JHA Council.[19]

Maastricht also brought some important changes for the European Commission (Uçarer 2001: 3). Hitherto the Commission only had observer status in the existing cooperation involving border control and immigration. It could make suggestions to the policies when input was solicited, but it

18. For analyses of Maastricht's pillar structures, and specifically the Third Pillar, see Monar and Morgan 1994; Müller-Graf 1994; Dehousse 1994; see also Curtin 1993.

19. The three new steering groups, together with the working groups (WGs) under their responsibility, were the following: 1) Immigration and Asylum (WGs Migration; Asylum; Visas; External Frontiers; Forged Documents, 2) Security, Law Enforcement, Police, and Customs Co-operation (WGs Terrorism; Police Co-operation; Organised Crime and Drugs; Customs; Ad Hoc Group on Europol), and 3) Judicial Co-operation (WGs Criminal-judicial Co-operation; Civil-judicial Co-operation). The Immigration and Asylum Steering Group was also responsible for two permanent bodies: the clearinghouse house on asylum (Centre for Information, Discussion and Exchange on Asylum [CIREA]), and the clearinghouse on immigration (Centre for Information, Discussion and Exchange on the Crossing of Frontiers and Immigration [CIREFI]).

could not submit policy proposals, nor could it offer unsolicited opinions or feedback. This role was strengthened by article K.3, which gave the Commission a shared right of initiative in a substantial portion of JHA matters. It also allowed the Commission to be represented during the deliberations and engage in policy discussion.

All these institutional changes were consistent with the "communitarian" tenets of the emerging Brussels culture of border control. However, the compromise solution found at Maastricht was very complex, and doubts were immediately raised about the workability of the new system. For some commentators the temple metaphor used to describe the institutional arrangement adopted at Maastricht was misleading, since it implied completion, order, and permanence, all elements that the treaty lacked. Müller-Graf, for example, argues that while the first pillar was of granite, the third had the quality of "legal sandstone" (Müller-Graf 1994). For Curtin, the pillar structure was joined "by means of a loose, tarpaulin-like structure—under the heading of an undefined European Union—suspended artificially and tenuously above both the loose pillars and the Community as such" (Curtin 1993: 23). The confusion was heightened by the fact that well after the signing of the treaty, the content of the EU *acquis* regarding JHA was still unclear. The pressure to define such *acquis* came from the upcoming accession to the EU of Sweden, Finland, and Austria (accession in fact required the acceptance of the existing EU *acquis*). The final version of the *acquis* was presented only the day after the Maastricht Treaty entered into force (November 2, 1993), and it was eventually incorporated into the treaty concerning the accession of the three new EU members.[20]

The legal complexity of the Maastricht arrangement also made it particularly problematic to assess the degree of communitarization that the Justice and Home Affairs domain had actually achieved. While the subject had been moved under the EU institutional umbrella, this policy domain maintained a substantial intergovernmental imprint. The Council (and, through it, its member states) became the fulcrum of the new arrangement. While the stipulations in the treaty elevated the Commission's level of involvement and secured it a meaningful seat at the discussion table, they were not comparable to the privileged position the Commission held in the first pillar, where it had the exclusive right of initiative. Though an improvement from its previous standing in the intergovernmental discussions relating to third pillar affairs, a shared right of initiative was clearly an indication that

20. The treaty of accession was signed on June 24, 1994, and entered into force on January 1, 1995.

the Commission was envisioned as one of sixteen actors in the third pillar to take initiative in JHA matters, and not one of the most powerful (Uçarer 2001: 1).

For some member states, the new arrangement was definitely intergovernmental in nature. In the United Kingdom, for example, the sections of the Maastricht Treaty concerning the second and third pillars were excluded from the provisions to be given the status of "European Community Treaties" and thus were ratified by the executive branch of the government under prerogative powers (European Communities [Amendment] Act of 1993; Denza 2002: 82). The British Parliament accepted without much discussion the government's position. The British government was not alone in supporting this approach. The German Constitutional Court also argued that cooperation in JHA after Maastricht would have remained an intergovernmental issue (see the case *Brunner v European Union Treaty* [1994]).

Despite these controversies, for most European governments the important point was that with the Maastricht Treaty the process of European integration had been set in motion again, and that the situation would have improved with time. The German chancellor Helmut Kohl was one of the European leaders that expressed this sentiment more vocally. In the address given to the Bundestag after the signing of the treaty, the chancellor mentioned that the deal would have eventually born fruit, and that the achievements regarding the JHA field represented an important step toward a closer union.

> I agreed to this outcome convinced that *it was the only way to achieve rapid practical advances* [in the JHA domain]. A decisive consideration for me was the fact that we pushed through a timetable and a set of provisions that open up the possibility of bringing these policies within the Community domain.[21]

Soon, however, this optimism vanished. Problems emerged with the domestic ratification of the new Treaty. France, Ireland, and Denmark held referendums on the subject. France narrowly voted in favor. The Danish population rejected it, and only after a new agreement (which gave Denmark more concessions) was arranged was the document eventually ratified. The treaty thus did not enter into force until November 1, 1993, almost two years after it had been agreed upon at Maastricht. The impact of this bickering on the issue of border control was mainly indirect, however. During

---

21. Helmut Kohl, address to the Bundestag, December 13, 1991; emphasis added.

the entire ratification process there was in fact little discussion about the third pillar.[22]

More worrying than the lack of debate over JHA issues was the fact that the activities within the newly created policy domain did not achieve the concrete results that Chancellor Kohl, among others, had hoped. The initial workload at the EU level (both by the Council and the Commission) was heavy, and so it remained in the following years.[23] This activism was, however, deceiving. Most of the initiatives being discussed were in fact carried over from the pre-Maastricht intergovernmental cooperation, and despite long discussions, little tangible progress on these files was made (Hailbronner 1998: 161–175). At the level of practical cooperation, the most relevant developments were a series of recommendations on effective control practices at the external border for applicant countries (agreed in 1997), the provision of forgery detection equipment (1998), and the launching of the Odysseus program (1998), which provided funding for common training measures, exchanges, and studies in the area of external border crossings and controls. Moreover, the areas in which the Council did focus its attention often involved restrictive policies, such as those setting the conditions of entry for third-country nationals.[24]

The Council was not only dilatory with regard to justice and home affairs, but it also put the brakes on the Commission's involvement in this field. Member states continued to regard the Commission with suspicion and were unwilling to confer it more power. In February 1994, for example, the Commission issued a new communication on immigration and asylum policies. This document reviewed progress made on the 1991 program and set out a new framework for action for the Union. It suggested that the *passerelle* pro-

22. Among the most important factors affecting the debate over the ratification of Maastricht was the fact that Europe in this period was going through a serious and deep economic crisis that caused governments and public opinion to set aside issues of European construction. Second, there were serious monetary tensions that challenged the European Monetary System and the objective of a future economic and monetary union. Third, the EU appeared unable to implement a common foreign and security policy regarding the crisis of Yugoslavia.

23. The first Council meeting held in Brussels in November 1993, for example, had an enormous agenda of 44 items. Estimates from within the Secretariat General of the Council suggest that roughly 40 percent of meetings and workload in 1999 directly or indirectly related to JHA (Monar 1999).

24. Two Council resolutions passed in 1994 made this objective very clear: "Council Resolution of 20 June 1994 *on limitation on admission* of third-country nationals to the territory of the Member States for employment," and "Council Resolution of 30 November 1994 relating to *the limitations on the admission* of third-country nationals to the territory of the Member States for the purpose of pursuing activities as self-employed persons." *Official Journal* C 274 (Sept. 19, 1996): 3–6, 7–9, respectively; emphasis added.

vision be used in regard to asylum. The Council responded to this request by arguing that "the time [was] not yet right to propose such an application so soon after the entry into force of the Treaty on European Union."[25]

An early critical assessment of the failures of the JHA field was offered by the Reflection Group. This group was created by member state representatives and the president of the Commission at the June 1994 Corfu European summit to draw up the agenda for a new intergovernmental conference planned for 1996 (cf. chap. 7). In their report, which was completed in December 1995, the group discussed the existing situation of JHA cooperation (par. 45–48). Although recognizing that JHA cooperation had been in force for a very short time and had been a step forward compared with the previous situation, it "concluded unanimously that the magnitude of the challenges is *not matched by the results* achieved so far in response to them" (par. 46; emphasis added). The high hopes that Maastricht had created had clearly not been fulfilled, leaving the fate of the Brussels culture of border control in a limbo.

The EU, Border Control, and External Relations: Exploring Uncharted Territory

In the years that followed the signing of the Maastricht Treaty, the importance of the external dimension of border control in shaping the Brussels culture's trajectory grew significantly. This subject in fact became a central element in the European Union's political agenda throughout the 1990s. The reasons for this development were both internal (the pressure on European governments and institutions to adopt a more common foreign policy as a result of the move toward the Common Market) and external (the fall of the Berlin Wall and the resulting anxiety over mass migration from the East; Niessen 1999: 486). The 1991 "Work Programme on migration and asylum policy" prepared for the Maastricht European Council explicitly recognized that the complex nature of current migratory movements worldwide required a comprehensive approach.[26] This entailed tackling the root causes of migratory movements by expanding economic, social and financial cooperation between the European Union and migrants' countries of origin.

25. "Council Conclusions of 20 June 1994 concerning the possible application of Article K.9 of the Treaty on European Union to asylum policy," annex 3.1, *Official Journal* C 274 (Sept. 19, 1996): 34; Denza 2002: 203.

26. Council of the European Union, Ad hoc Group on Immigration, "Report from the Ministers responsible for immigration to the European Council meeting in Maastricht on immigration and asylum policy" (SN 4038/91 [WGI 930] Dec. 3, 1991).

The delegations at Maastricht agreed that more activism was needed in external affairs. The final text of the treaty mentions in its first title that the EU should strive to "assert its identity on the international scene." As we saw in the previous section, with Maastricht a new institutional system was created based on two new "pillars" (foreign and defense cooperation, and justice and home affairs). Taken together, the two pillars offered—at least on paper—the opportunity to develop a more coherent EU external policy regarding border control.

In the post-Maastricht period, the EU did indeed become more proactive in this field. In May 1992, the Union concluded an agreement with countries belonging to the European Free Trade Association (EFTA), which then included Austria, Finland, Iceland, Liechtenstein, Norway, Sweden, and Switzerland, to create the European Economic Area (EEA). This agreement (which entered into force on January 1, 1994) expanded the freedom of movement to all countries involved, although it did not envision the abolition of internal borders. In December 1992, the Edinburgh European Council adopted a declaration ("Declaration on the principles governing external aspects of migration policy"), in which EU leaders outlined the linkage between external relations and international migration. This document identified some key "liberal" elements involved in the reduction of migratory movements: the preservation of peace, respect for human rights, the promotion of democracy, and a freer trade policy. It also stressed the need for coordination between foreign policy, economic cooperation, and immigration and asylum policy.

The call for a closer link between migration and EU foreign policy was echoed by the European Commission. In 1994 it published a communication that identified three areas for Union action: migration pressure, controlling migration flows, and strengthening integration policies to benefit legal migrants.[27] Its balanced and comprehensive approach to migration issues was, to a great extent, based on the work program adopted by the Council of Ministers and, in fact, identified policy areas similar to those under discussion in the Council.

The primary method that the EU adopted to put into practice the link between foreign policy and immigration was that of multilateral agreements with third countries. The most important among them were the so-called

---

27. Commission of the European Communities, "Communication from the Commission to the Council and the European Parliament on Immigration and Asylum Policies" (COM [94] 23 final, Feb. 23, 1994).

Europe Agreements with Central and Eastern European countries (CEEC).[28] These agreements were aimed at adjusting the former Communist states to a market economy. When addressing the issue of freedom of movement, the Europe Agreements contained provisions on workers, right of establishment, and supply of services. References to justice and home affairs, however, were only marginal. Questions of border control were completely excluded.

In the early 1990s, the European Union was also considering the establishment of a comprehensive approach to the Mediterranean region. Thus, in 1995, the Euro-Mediterranean Partnership was launched. This partnership was designed to create a vast Euro-Mediterranean free-trade area by 2010. The central instruments of this policy were the Euro-Mediterranean association agreements, which replaced previously existing agreements with Mediterranean countries, and the MEDA program, a financial instrument to support the various aspects of the initiative. Although not a central element in the Euro-Mediterranean Partnership, the association agreements did address the issue of movement of persons. Some of their provisions referred to the freedom of establishment and liberalization of services. In addition, the new agreements set up a dialogue in the social domain between the parties. This dialogue was meant to address—among other issues—problems relating to migration, clandestine immigration, and the conditions of return of persons in an irregular situation.

Besides the "near abroad," EU institutions and their member states also made contacts with their "faraway" neighbors. Partnership agreements were negotiated with countries belonging to the former Soviet Union. These documents, which were signed between 1994 and 1996, replaced the 1989 "Agreement on Trade, and Commercial and Economic Co-operation" between the EC and the USSR. Their main focus was economic cooperation. However, they also made reference to collaboration on the prevention of illicit activities, including illegal immigration.[29]

The new attitude toward the issue of migration and border control also influenced the relations with other regions deemed as reservoirs of would-be

28. This group of countries includes Bulgaria, the Czech Republic, Estonia, Hungary, Latvia, Lithuania, Poland, Romania, Slovakia, and Slovenia. Hungary and Poland signed Europe Agreements in 1993, while Bulgaria, Romania, the Czech Republic, and Slovakia did so in 1994.

29. Co-operation clauses on justice and home affairs matters were included in the agreements with Armenia, Azerbaijan, Belarus, Georgia, Kazakhstan, Kyrgyzstan, Moldova, Russia, Tajikistan, Turkmenistan, Ukraine, and Uzbekistan. In the agreement with Russia there is a separate section on this subject. For an overview of JHA cooperation between the EU and former Soviet states in the 1990s, see Potemkina 2002.

migrants. The EU introduced "third pillar" clauses in its relations with groups of countries with which the Community shared a particular and institutionalized link, such as Latin America's Rio Group, San José Group, the Andean Community, and Mercosur.[30] It also strengthened its relations on this subject with African, Caribbean, and Pacific (ACP) countries. Policy cooperation with ACP countries had started in the mid-1970s. Cooperation included trade and investment policies, financial and technical cooperation, and the protection of human rights. Migration was not considered in the various agreements signed between the two sides over the years (also known as Lomé conventions). This situation changed with the Fourth Lomé Convention, concluded in 1990. Two declarations annexed to this document required that each member state accord to legally employed ACP workers treatment free from discrimination based on nationality with regard to working conditions, pay, and social security benefits linked to employment. Other provisions referred to EU support in the professional training of ACP nationals and the commitment of the parties to discourage illegal immigration.

In parallel to the negotiations and signing of cooperation agreements with its near and far neighbors, EU institutions and member states' governments began to consider the issue of enlargement. At the June 1993 Copenhagen Council, European leaders agreed to allow central and Eastern European countries to apply for EU membership. The topic of justice and home affairs was one of the items on the agenda in the accession negotiations. Cooperation between the European and candidate countries in this field was mentioned for the first time in December 1993 in the letter addressed to the president of the European Council by the British and Italian ministers of foreign affairs. The goal of the Hurd-Andreatta initiative, as well as of the second letter from the two countries' foreign ministers ("Hurd/ Martino letter of July 1994"), was to strengthen and intensify political dialogue with the associated countries under the conditions laid down in the conclusions of the Copenhagen Council.[31] The ministers proposed to develop new linkages between the associated countries and the two inter-

30. "Note from Presidency to K4, External relations in the framework of the third pillar," Brussels, May 13, 1996, 6891/96.

31. At the December 1993 Copenhagen Council, the EU had set a series of conditions for EU membership (the so-called Copenhagen criteria): the candidate country must have achieved "stability of institutions guaranteeing democracy, the rule of law, human rights and respect for and protection of minorities, the existence of a functioning market economy as well as the capacity to cope with competitive pressure and market forces within the Union." "Copenhagen European Council, 21–22 June 1993; Conclusions of the Presidency" (SN 180/1/93 REV 1), 13.

governmental pillars of Maastricht, namely, foreign policy and justice and home affairs (Lavenex 2001: 32).

The rapidly expanding intergovernmental cooperation between individual member states and accession countries led the European Commission in the summer of 1994 to urge JHA ministers to take a decision on the procedures for consultation within a more formal relationship (Lavenex 2001: 33). Following this suggestion, the heads of state and government meeting at the Essen European Council in December 1994 agreed that there should be cooperation with the countries of central and Eastern Europe to "fight all forms of organised crime."[32] This cooperation would be added to the instruments of preaccession. The Council conclusions also referred to bringing justice and home affairs into a "structured dialogue." This dialogue would have entailed discussions between the respective justice and home affairs ministers on measures to be adhered to by countries applying to join the EU, and making available the PHARE program[33] to fund activities under the third pillar.

The practice of including JHA provisions in agreements with third countries signaled a new era of European Union foreign policy. It entailed the willingness to adopt a more comprehensive strategy, which included not only sticks but also carrots in its relations with non-EU partners. This was particularly true for the accession process. Enlargement seemed to open a new chapter in the external policy of the EU on issues of border control and JHA more generally. The prospect of inclusion in the EU represented a more substantial incentive than previous engagements. This new arrangement would have also been the basis of a more symmetrical relation between the two sides.

Despite the high expectations, throughout the 1990s the results in the JHA domain with regard to its external dimension were disappointing. After the Essen Council, EU member states attempted to put into practice the idea of a structured dialogue with central and Eastern European countries. This dialogue was to develop in a series of regular meetings between the EU institutions and the associated countries. From the time of the Essen Council (December 1994) and the summer of 1997, however, EU ministers of justice and home affairs and their CEEC counterparts met only on two occasions. Mounting frustration with the structured relationship led to a change

32. Essen European Council, Conclusions of the Presidency, in *Bulletin of the European Union* (December 1994), no. 12.

33. PHARE is a financial program launched in 1989 in order to help central and Eastern European countries to reconstruct their economies following the collapse of Communism.

in strategy and the introduction of a more focused and practically oriented approach through "accession partnerships." These partnerships outlined a common framework for all applicants (both those who had already begun negotiations and those who had not), and indicated the short- and medium-term priorities for each country in their effort to adopt the EU *acquis,* including the part on JHA (Lavenex 2001: 33).[34]

Also discouraging were the lack of results characterizing the Euro-Mediterranean Partnership. As mentioned previously, migration and border control played a limited role in the initiative. Nonetheless, cooperation in this field did not take off as expected. Among all the commitments with regard to migration, progress was achieved only in the field of readmission (see below). Other questions relating to migration were not translated into action. The implementation of the MED-Migration program was, for example, suspended only a few months after its launch for lack of concrete results.

Distinguishing the EU policy toward its neighbors during this period was a trend toward the downplaying of the "carrot" component that the EU had stressed in earlier strategy plans. The Commission noticed this situation as early as 1994. It regretted that, with regard to intergovernmental cooperation in the JHA field, the emphasis had been on the fight against organized crime, despite the fact that closer cooperation in asylum and immigration matters was urgently needed.[35]

An official confirmation of this change of attitude by EU member states came with the release in October 1995 of the Langdon Report. This document was drafted by a team of experts under the instruction of the Commission to "identify appropriate measures to promote integration through cooperation in the field of Justice and Home Affairs, especially those necessary to prepare the countries concerned for accession to the EU."[36] Its recommendations became the basis for EU policy toward the applicant countries. In setting the priorities for cooperation in the JHA field, the report suggested that the member states and the associated countries should have an "immediate and shared concern to deal with the pressures of unauthorized migration and serious crime that have arisen as an unwelcome concomitant of the

---

34. The European Council concluded accession partnerships with each of the applicant countries (with the exception of Cyprus, Malta, and Turkey) in 1998.

35. Commission of the European Communities, "Follow-up to Commission Communication on 'The Europe Agreements and Beyond: A Strategy to Prepare the Countries of Central and Eastern Europe for Accession'" (COM [94] 361 final, 27 July 1994). On this point, see Lavenex 2001: 3.

36. "Preparation of the associated Central European countries for EU membership: Justice and Home Affairs—the Langdon Report," Working Document of the Commission Departments, CK4 5, confidential, ref: 4660/96, 30.1.96; *Statewatch* 6, no. 2 (March–April 1996).

freedoms of the democratic transition process" (ibid.) The report's drafters thus called for the adoption of measures to combat illegal immigration and to enforce border controls, the creation of institutions and procedures necessary for a functioning asylum system, and a fiercer fight against drug trafficking. In contrast to the earlier political conditionality imposed on foreign policy, instruments like the PHARE program, and general cooperation and association agreements, the issues of asylum and immigration now did not refer to the fundamental freedoms of their own citizens, but touched on the respective countries' own external relations and their policies toward foreigners. The Langdon Report clearly signaled a move away from the approach the EU had envisioned in the 1991 work program, with its more balanced mix of stick and carrots.

The securitarian trend in the EU policy was not restricted to the relations with candidate countries. In 1995 the EU decided to insert a "standard clause" into a number of its association and cooperation agreements. This provision required the signatory country to readmit its own citizens when any EU member state asked, and "without further formalities." It also asked these countries to agree to negotiate a further readmission treaty with any member state as a condition for progress in cooperation.

Besides introducing the standard clause and pressuring third countries to sign new readmission agreements, EU countries were also refining the concept of "safe country of asylum." This idea was originally articulated in the 1990 Dublin Convention. As we have seen, the convention allowed any signatory state to send an applicant for asylum to a third state, once that state had been assigned the responsibility to process an asylum claim. According to this principle, refugees and asylum seekers who traveled to the country of asylum neither through Eastern Europe nor through Morocco (with which the EU had readmission agreements) could still be returned to countries of origin or transit if these countries were deemed to be "safe."[37] After signing the convention, European governments felt the need to refine and harmonize their approach to the issue of safe countries. This was accomplished with two resolutions (known as the "London Resolutions") passed at the end of 1992 by the European ministers for immigration.[38] The wording of the resolutions makes clear the critical stance of the member

37. Since it threatened the right to seek asylum, the introduction of this provision led to legal challenges in some European domestic courts. In Germany and in France, the issue was circumvented with the passing of constitutional amendments that enabled the government to adopt the "safe third country" rule.

38. "Resolution on Manifestly Unfounded applications for asylum" and "Resolution of 30 November 1992 on a harmonised approach to questions concerning host third countries."

states toward the issue of asylum. The original draft's preamble contained even harsher language, referring to "economic migrants" and to the fact that "intercontinental travel [is] seldom necessary for protection reasons." These parts were cut in the official version because of concerns over their "presentational impact" (Guild 2001: 59).

During the discussions over these resolutions, the German interior minister suggested the drafting of a list of safe countries of asylum. Other delegations considered this to be controversial and denied the intention of drawing up a common list. Yet one of the tasks of CIREA (the EU's Centre for Information, Discussion and Exchange on Asylum created with the Maastricht Treaty) was to compile and gather country information designed to assist the receiving EU state in deciding whether the country of origin or transit was safe. No consensus on this matter was achieved, however. A survey commissioned by the European Council in 1997 showed that variation was still broad with reference to the countries considered "safe" (Denza 2002: 198).

One major reason for the limited accomplishment in the EU external policy on border control issues was structural. The complexity of the compromise reached at Maastricht (most notably, the fact that JHA matters were now under the EU institutional umbrella, but not under Community competence) were reflected in the unclear status of the external dimension of JHA and its limited scope (Nissen 2000: 487). Organizational uncertainty was highlighted, if not compounded, by a lack of political will from all the major parties involved. Despite the good intentions expressed in the 1991 work program and at the Edinburgh European Council, the Council of Ministers (meeting as the General Affairs or Development Councils) hardly ever tabled the issue of linking foreign policy and immigration. This lack of activism stemmed from caution in mixing foreign policy and migration, above all if inserted in a common approach.

Lack of political will was strictly related to another problem: the lingering mistrust of European governments toward their neighbors. In discussing the inclusion of migration clauses in agreements with third countries during the first JHA Council, the ministers responsible for this portfolio explicitly mentioned that these agreements would take into account the "past behavior of that country" on immigration matters. Cooperation was also, for the most part, imposed by the EU on its partners. This was true in the negotiations over accession with CEECs, and with Mediterranean countries in the context of the Euro-Mediterranean Partnership, even if both initiatives were supposedly based on reciprocity, and, as in the latter case, they explicitly addressed issues of asymmetry. This imposition took the form of a new type of political conditionality. Onerous requests on the part of the EU not only pushed these countries toward adopting a more restrictive stance in border control issues but also created confusion about the scope of the *acquis* reached in this field and about the measures that the CEECs would have to adopt in order to become member states (Lavenex 2001: 33). This conditionality also showed the opportunism of EU countries, for they gave the impression of using accession to put pressure on CEECs in issues that concerned them most (Grabbe 2000: 519–520). Despite the rhetoric, the reliance on strict conditions and the lack of real dialogue demonstrated that the relations between the EU and the candidate countries remained by and large asymmetrical. The image of cooperation in justice and home affairs as a moving train is appropriate here. Future member states could have eventually jumped on, but once they did, they would not have been able to change its course, let alone stop it. As for the initiative's internal dynamics, the lack of tangible results stemming from the EU border control foreign policy, coupled with a progressive distancing from the liberal tenets that originally defined the project of a "Europe without frontiers," represented a further blow to the culture's evolutionary path toward full institutionalization.

Still a Work in Progress: The Evolution of the EU's Border Control Policy Community

Unlike Schengen, the Brussels border control policy community included all EU members since the very launch of the initiative. Its organization, however, was still in a state of flux. One of the main developments characterizing this community in the 1990s was the more prominent role that the Commission gained in JHA-related issues, especially after the signing of the Maastricht Treaty. The institutionalization of the JHA field in the EU framework also conferred a greater coherence to the hitherto confusing constellation of intergovernmental groups dealing with border matters and gave a more influential role to the Council Secretariat in this domain. These developments seemed to indicate that the supranational credentials of the Brussels border control community were finally becoming more established.

But beyond the surface, problems were nonetheless still present. The institutional structure agreed upon at Maastricht made a "potentially awkward actor" of the European Commission in the third pillar (Uçarer 2001: 1; see also Meyers 1995). Its right of initiative was in fact shared with member states, which thus kept a decisive role in this policy domain. In institutional terms, only the small Task Force for Justice and Home Affairs was created to liaise with the Council, rather than a full-fledged directorate-general, one of the most powerful bureaucratic units in the Commission's organizational structure. As a result, in the phase that followed the ratification of the Maastricht Treaty, the Commission experienced "pronounced bureaucratic inertia" (Papademetriou 1996: 60).

The realization of its limited room to maneuver convinced the Commission to become more pragmatic. With constitutional constraints putting the brakes on its activities, the Commission adopted a strategy of "not pushing its luck" in competence terms, even as this applied to legislation necessary to complete the project of accomplishing free movement of persons (Fortescue 1995: 21). An example of this cautious attitude is represented by the "Communication on Immigration and Asylum policies" that the Commission tabled in 1994.[39] The emphasis on the root causes of immigration aside, this document appears to be merely a summary of existing policies across the Continent, carefully worded to avoid antagonizing member states. The Commission's stance implied that it preferred to appease member states rather than push through its agenda. More problematically, it also entailed a move toward a securitarian discourse. In various circumstances the Commission supported powerful member states and restrictively interpreted certain rules, such as those regarding the right of asylum (Bigo and Guild 2003). Even the internal composition of the new JHA task force reflected the Commission's new approach toward issues of free movement and border control. Most of its staffers did not come from the units that traditionally had defended the rights of third-country nationals (namely, the Employment and Social Affairs and the Internal Market Directorates-General). Personnel in the newly created task force considered them as "old fashioned" and "maximalist" (Guiraudon 2003: 269).

Questions lingered too with regard to the evolution of the intergovernmental groups in Brussels, now all falling under the European Council institutional umbrella. As within Schengen, iterated interactions within a common institutional framework cemented the social relations between the officials involved in these groups and fostered a sense of being a part of a shared European project. The fact that the number of policy makers active in the EU context was greater than in Schengen (thus diluting the cozy atmosphere that characterized that forum, especially in its early stages)

39. Commission of the European Communities, "Communication from the Commission to the Council and the European Parliament on Immigration and Asylum Policies" (COM [94] 23 final, Feb. 23, 1994).

Table 6.1 **Representation in EU-level groups dealing with border control by country and ministerial affiliation (1990s)**

Country	Council of Ministers	K4 Committee
Belgium	Justice + Interior	Justice
Denmark	Justice + Interior	Justice
Germany	Justice + Interior	Justice + Interior
Greece	Justice + Interior	Foreign Affairs
Spain	Justice + Interior	Foreign Affairs
France	Justice + Interior	Prime minister (SGCI) coordinator
Ireland	Justice	Justice
Italy	Justice + Interior	Diplomat (permanent representation)
Luxembourg	Justice	Justice
Netherlands	Justice + Interior	Justice
Austria	Justice + Interior	Interior
Portugal	Justice + Interior	Foreign Affairs
Finland	Justice + Interior	Justice + Interior
Sweden	Justice + Interior	Justice
UK	Interior	Interior

Source: Adapted from Turk 1998.

was compensated by the EU's "thick" institutionalization and the greater involvement of EU officials, which helped create a more structured and supranational context for the activities of the various negotiating groups.

Yet the communitarization of what were previously intergovernmental groups did not lead to a radical change in the way they operated. National delegations remained reluctant to give up power. As in Schengen, interior ministers acquired a more prominent role (see table 6.1) and brought with them a more nationalistic outlook on matters pertaining to border control. In a report commissioned by the French Senate on the international role of the police and Interior Ministry, these actors are described as having a "hexagonal" (viz., France-centered) worldview, and to consider European files as not that attractive (Turk 1998). Moreover, they have "neither the habit nor the spirit" ("n'ont pas l'habitude ni le gout") for negotiation or compromise that characterize international relations (ibid.). This characterization accurately describes the worldview of most Interior Ministry personnel across the Continent.

Despite its communitarian credentials, the European Council and its Secretariat were closer in institutional culture to the member states, and the latter seemed particularly comfortable in dealing with its officials. This can explain why the inclusion of TREVI (the secretive group created in the 1970s to address terrorism and now also covering border-related issues; cf. chap. 3) in the JHA Council that occurred after the Maastricht Treaty did not raise particular concerns.[40]

As for practices within the Union more generally, in the 1990s the EU border control policy community clearly drifted away from the liberal tenets that defined the Brussels culture of border control when it was launched a decade earlier. It moved instead closer to those of its main competitor, namely, Schengen, which at the time was already on its way to becoming the dominant culture of border control in Europe.

40. In the late 1980s, TREVI's remit was extended to include illegal immigration, border control, police cooperation, drugs, and serious crime. The TREVI 1992 Working Group was set up in April 1989 specifically to consider the "policing and security implications of the Single European Market" and to improve cooperation to "compensate for the consequent losses to security and law enforcement" in the members states (Bunyan 1993). Although with its inclusion in the EU TREVI lost some of its most secretive elements, this structure was still organized around intergovernmental rules.

SEVEN

From Selection to Retention: Schengen's Incorporation into the European Union

Enhanced co-operation exists, it exists in the Treaty, for instance with the Monetary and Economic Union. It exists aside the Treaty, as in the case of the Social Protocol; it also exists outside the Treaty, as in the case of Schengen. . . . Should we encourage the development of this enhanced co-operation within the Union, within the unique institutional framework of the Union, or should we take the risk—I stress this—the risk, for the European idea, which is ours—that it develops more and more outside the Union?

—Michel Barnier, French ministers of European affairs, Joint Press Conference with Werner Hoyer, German minister of European affairs, Brussels, October 22, 1996

Schengen will never die.

—Charles Elsen (2000: 11)

On the Dynamics of Cultural Selection in Schengen and Brussels

The 1990s was a decade of feverish activity in Europe's border control domain. Whether in the European Union or in the context of the Schengen initiative, the constellation of policy makers constituting Europe's border control community engaged in prolonged and heated debates about the conditions for the creation of a "Europe without frontiers," proposed new rules and measures aimed at abolishing internal border checks and at reinforcing Europe's external frontiers, supervised the implementation of these proposals, negotiated the entry of new members into the regime, and expanded the relations with third countries beyond Europe. All these activities contributed to the realization of the project of a common area of free movement across the Continent. Through them, members of Europe's border control policy community instantiated the assumptions of the two emerging cultures of border control ("Schengen" and "Brussels"), and the results of these practical enactments paved the way for the ultimate selection of Schengen as the new official approach to border control in Europe.

The process leading to this outcome was not straightforward. Initially, in both Schengen and the EU, practices consistent with the new cultures of border control were challenged by those belonging to the still-dominant nationalist culture of border control. Examples of these "counter-practices" in the internal dynamics within each forum were the repeated French reliance on article 2.2 of the Schengen convention (which allowed member states to reinstate national border controls when issues of national security were at stake) and the British resistance to the communitarization of the border control field. In both cases the justification for these positions was that *collective security* could be achieved through *national* means, and that the establishment of a common external border would not work because it required a level of mutual trust among partners that was difficult, if not impossible, to obtain. Other delegations tried to counter this nationalist stance by demonstrating the virtues of a postnational approach to border control. They did so by reiterating the "logical" link between the creation of a shared European border and the need for a common arrangement for its control, and exposing the inconsistencies of the opposing side's position. If we turn to the two cultures' external dimensions, in both Schengen and Brussels there was a clear tension between a more proactive multilateral approach to dealing with third countries and one that emphasized less ambitious bilateral agreements.

This dialectical process followed different trajectories in each institutional forum. Over the course of negotiations, practices within Schengen became more consistent with the main tenets of the pursued culture. If we consider the regime's internal dynamics, for example, the achievement of freedom of movement was not the main term of reference in policy makers' activities. Instead, the litmus test for the regime's application became the establishment of the "necessary" compensatory measures. The balance between freedom of movement and compensatory measures clearly tilted toward the latter. Even the activities of those who supported a nationalist approach to border control practices converged toward the tenets of the Schengen culture. France's attempt to find a compromise (i.e., the proposal on "mobile frontiers") is clear evidence of this trend.

Similar dynamics characterized Schengen's external relations and the evolution of Schengen's border control policy community. As the Italian case showed, the regime's enlargement was often problematic, and it demonstrated the lack of trust on the part of existing members toward some of the candidate countries. With regard to the relations with third countries, the policies proposed or implemented became progressively more security-oriented and were mostly imposed by Schengen members. This was the case, for example, concerning the readmission agreements signed with Poland. The securitarian orientation of the regime was also strengthened by the growing power and influence that ministries of interior acquired in the policymaking process. The result of these developments was that the assumptions underlying the Schengen culture became dominant, leaving less "discursive space" for alternative accounts.

In the EU context, the pursuit of the new culture of border control was not as coherent as in Schengen. If we consider the initiative's internal dynamics, we can notice that some timid attempts to push forward the issue of freedom of movement were made, especially after the signing of the Maastricht Treaty. The limits of the new institutional arrangement, however, soon came to the surface. Progress in the EU on the issue of free movement was stalled. Practices remained mainly intergovernmental, and securitarian—rather than "liberal"—principles acquired a greater importance. Despite the EU's experience in dealing with external affairs, the issue of border control remained low on the Union's foreign policy agenda, and no major breakthrough occurred in this period. Most interactions remained bilateral and outside the EU institutional framework. Moreover, EU member states (and, to a certain extent, even the European Commission) adopted a suspicious attitude toward their neighbors. Hence the focus was put on restrictive policies, especially with regard to issues such as visas and readmission. As to the relations within the border control community, disagreement over the underlying principles and objectives of the initiative was still rife, while the European Commission acquiesced to the general securitarian orientation that most European governments had taken in this period.

As in the case of Schengen, over the course of the negotiations within the EU there were attempts at mediation between the postnational and nationalist approaches to border control. This is demonstrated by the presentation of compromise proposals to persuade skeptical members within the border control policy community to overcome their reservations about a common approach to border control (e.g., the "Bangemann wave"). Unlike with Schengen, the offer came from supporters of the pursued culture (the European Commission), and it was the "communitarian" argument that accommodated the main recalcitrant party (the United Kingdom). The latter maintained its opposition of the abolition of internal borders. The final result was that practices in this initiative became inconsistent, and no dominant narrative emerged.

Why did the Schengen and Brussels cultures of border control follow different trajectories? Why was Schengen successful, while Brussels failed? To answer these questions it is necessary to look at the two cultures' performance, that is, the practical results they obtained when members of the policy community instantiated their underlying assumptions in the course of the negotiations that took place in Europe throughout the 1990s. On this account, Schengen fared better than Brussels. What defined Schengen's superior performance was that its formula, balancing the apparently contradictory requirements of freedom and security, proved itself to be more effective in addressing the relevant practical and political problems that European policy makers had to face in this period. Positive results (e.g., the regime's entry into effect, the expansion to new members) created political momentum for following rounds of negotiations, and diplomatic successes were in turn translated into new policy initiatives. This did not occur in the EU context. Successes were circumscribed (e.g., the signing of the Dublin Convention; the Maastricht Treaty), and they had a limited impact on the establishment of the regime. As a result, the pursuit of the culture progressively lost momentum and ultimately stalled.

It is thanks to the new cultures' practical results over time that members of Europe's border control policy community were put in a position to formally embrace Schengen as the new approach to border control and to discard the work done in the EU. In the late 1990s, a growing number of government and (more cautiously) EU officials publicly talked about the idea of incorporating the Schengen *acquis* into the EU, arguing that the time for this decision had finally arrived. (It should be recalled that incorporation into the EU was referred to in the Schengen founding documents as the regime's ultimate goal.) The decision to communitarize Schengen, however, was not unproblematic. Although couched in technical terms, this question was eminently political. Some members of the EU border control policy community (especially representatives of the European Commission), while welcoming Schengen into the Union, deemed that they could tame some of the regime's intergovernmental tendencies (which were likely to remain even after the prospective incorporation in the EU), and maintain some control over it. They agreed that Schengen had indeed been successful, yet at the same time argued that it had exhausted its "laboratory" function and therefore should complement the EU *acquis*, not completely replace it. For Schengen supporters the EU should have instead accepted the new regime and its *acquis* in its entirety and maintained Schengen's role as institutional laboratory even within the EU. The battle between these two visions of Schengen and its institutionalization (or, using evolutionary language, its "retention") is the topic of the remainder of this chapter.

Schengen in the EU: The Road to Amsterdam

The idea of transferring certain subjects related to border control to the Community framework was mentioned during the negotiations leading to the Maastricht Treaty. At the time, this proposal did not receive wide support, and so a Third Pillar was created. At Maastricht, however, European leaders indicated their intention to reconvene in the near future to assess the achievements of the new treaty provisions and make the necessary changes. The headline with which the French newspaper *Le Monde* commented on the signing of the treaty was telling: "À suivre . . ." ("To be continued . . .")[1] The need for a revision of the Maastricht arrangement became even more pressing after the decision to accept Sweden, Finland, and Austria as new EU members.

The early political window of opportunity to revamp an initiative that had not yet ripened came in 1995 with the launch of a new intergovernmental conference (IGC). The fate of the Third Pillar, and thus of border control, was not originally the main focus of the conference. Yet by the end, it was the subject area that had been transformed most thoroughly. According to a commentator, these changes were "dramatic" (Monar 1998: 9). The discussion of the IGC primarily dealt with the issue of reform of the Third Pillar's specific objectives and type—legal or political—of instruments used to realize these objectives. At issue were the deficiencies that resulted from its intergovernmental nature and the ineffectiveness of the instruments hitherto adopted (De Zwann 1998: 17; Den Boer and Corrado 1999: 398).

Schengen was not on the agenda when the IGC officially began in March 1996. The proposal to incorporate Schengen into the EU was in fact advanced quite late in the negotiations. Yet even if not on the table, Schengen loomed large over the IGC. Indeed, even before the conference, talks of its incorporation were already under way. This subject was addressed by the Reflection Group, which was set up to outline the agenda for the IGC.[2] The discussion within this forum about the future of Schengen led to the

---

1. *Le Monde*, Feb. 8, 1992, 1.

2. "Report of the Reflection Group" (SN 520/95 [REFLEX 21]), 18 (point 54). The group consisted of personal representatives of the foreign affairs ministers, the president of the Commission, and two representatives of the European Parliament.

outlining of two different scenarios: a "minimum" and a "maximum" option. The "minimum option" envisioned the coexistence between the two systems by means of flexible arrangements if some of the EU member states decided not to accede to the Schengen convention. The "maximum option" entailed the Union accepting Schengen, which would be merged into the rules and structures provided for in the Treaty on European Union.

The majority of national delegates represented in the group were opposed to incorporation altogether (the ones in favor were the Benelux, Austria, Germany, Italy, and Spain; Hix and Niessen 1996). The main argument against its integration was that Schengen concerned an intergovernmental body of law and thus would "taint" the community legal order. Those in favor argued that the idea of Schengen as "laboratory of the EU" had run its course, and thus the regime's incorporation was its "natural destiny." This position was supported by the European Commission and the European Parliament. According to the Commission, all items under the Third Pillar, except criminal law and police cooperation, should have been transferred to the First Pillar (i.e., Community law).[3] A briefing on the intergovernmental conference and the Schengen convention presented by the Working Party Secretariat of the European Parliament's Task Force on the IGC stressed that Schengen was "the precursor of or a sort of testing ground for the creation of a European area without frontiers where people can move freely." It insisted, however, that Schengen "can and must be replaced by Community regulations valid for the whole Union."[4] Given the wide range of positions of the subject, in its final report the Reflection Group made a set of clear recommendations for the Second Pillar (foreign and defense policy), but not for the third.[5]

Before the beginning of the Intergovernmental Conference, the fate of Schengen was still uncertain. Adding complexity to the already fluid scenario, some of the supporters of its integration started having second thoughts. Germany, for example, although it earlier favored a rapid merger of Schengen with the EU, became more cautious as the IGC approached. In March 1996, the State Secretary at the Interior Ministry, Kurt Schelter, stated that incorporating Schengen in the EU was "premature at the moment."[6] Schengen was "an engine for EU development and has proved successful

3. Commission of the European Communities, "Reinforcing Political Union and Preparing for Enlargement. Commission Opinion" (COM [96] 90 final, Feb. 28, 1996).

4. European Parliament, "Briefing on the IGC and the Schengen Convention," Luxembourg (Jan. 30, 1996, PE 165.808).

5. "Report of the Reflection Group," 45–55.

6. "Note of State Secretary Kurt Schelter, Interior Ministry, to the Internal Affairs Committee of the German Parliament," Bonn, April 29, 1996; reproduced in FECL 43 (April–May 1996).

in the respect," therefore Germany feared that a rushed integration could "stall the dynamic Schengen cooperation while not bringing cooperation within the EU any further."[7]

The arguments over the future of Schengen and the potential implications of any decision on the subject for cooperation in the JHA domain became clearer only after the IGC started and the timetable for final decisions got closer. The progress report drafted for the special meeting of the European Council in Florence in June 1996 indicated the options regarding the Third Pillar (partial transfer to the First Pillar; the creation of a new Third Pillar) and addressed the issue of the new structure of the Justice and Home Affairs Council.[8] The report also considered alternative forms of enhanced cooperation, such as an enabling clause opening the door to closer cooperation between member states, and the incorporation of the Schengen regime into the Treaty on European Union.

The explicit reference to Schengen was the premise for the formal introduction of this issue on the negotiation table. In a position paper ("non-paper") issued in July 1996, the Dutch presidency presented this option to its EU partners. The document referred to the fact that "the Schengen Agreement has never been thought of as existing outside the political and institutional framework of the EU. For the majority of the member states, the integration of Schengen into the EU is a priority" (De Zwann 1998: 18).

The first reaction to this proposal was negative overall. The British and Irish delegations were particularly opposed to it, arguing that they did not know the content of the Schengen *acquis* (not being members of the regime). More generally, they had reservations on the very idea of communitarizing Third Pillar items (De Zwann 1998: 18). On this point they were openly supported by Denmark, while other delegations shared some skepticism on the transfer but hid behind the British position. Besides political issues, the main concern was about the technical complexity of this exercise, and in particular how and when Schengen provisions would be transformed in EU texts. As a result of these concerns, the Dutch proposal seemed at the time destined to fail.

To find a compromise, in the fall of 1996, Germany and France came up with a proposal to introduce in the EU a general clause allowing for enhanced cooperation among member states.[9] Key tenets of the proposal were

7. Ibid.

8. "Progress report from the Presidency on the Intergovernmental Conference" (CONF 3860/1/96 REV 1).

9. For a full text of the proposal, see Europe Documents no. 2009, p. 2.

the preservation of a single institutional framework, which implied that any Union member, if willing or capable of participating, would not be excluded, the respect for Community law and for the objectives of the Treaty, and the granting of a supervisory role to the Commission over enhanced cooperation in the First Pillar. The rationale of this proposal was to avoid the "risk" that cooperation outside the EU would continue to grow unabated.[10]

In light of the discussions carried out during the winter months and the various proposals submitted to the IGC until that point, in early February 1997 the Dutch presidency presented a new non-paper to the negotiating table. This proposal was more modest than earlier versions circulated by the Dutch delegation, suggesting that the IGC would only agree on general principles, leaving the details for negotiations after the signing of the Amsterdam Treaty. In substantial terms, it envisioned two options, this time both making it possible for Schengen member states to continue their cooperation without the participation of the United Kingdom and Ireland, but within the institutions of the EU.[11] Under the first option ("enabling clauses" flexibility approach) the Treaty on European Union would contain enabling provisions allowing for "enhanced co-operation" between particular groups of member states in each of the three pillars. Under the second option ("predetermined" flexibility approach), the existing Schengen countries would be authorized through a particular protocol (attached to the Treaty on European Union) to continue to develop within the Union's institutions the Schengen *acquis,* which would be applicable only to them (cf. table 7.1). The non-paper justifies the incorporation of the Schengen *acquis* into the Union since it is "a gradual process which is already under way" (ibid.).

A change in government in London in the run-up to the June 1997 Amsterdam summit eased the tension at the negotiation table. Although not lifting its reservations regarding the abolition of border controls (and thus precluding a full participation in the Schengen regime), the new Labour government took a more flexible stance than its Conservative predecessor. Instead of an "opt in" clause to the Schengen Agreement and its *acquis* taken as a whole, it wanted to "opt out" or, effectively opt in on a case-by-case basis (see more below). Various delegations were openly grumbling about Great

---

10. Michel Barnier, French minister of European affairs, "Joint Press Conference with Werner Hoyer, German Minister of European Affairs," Brussels, Oct. 22, 1996 ; cf. the chapter epigraph.

11. "Schengen and the European Union," non-paper, IGC Secretariat, Brussels, Feb. 4, 1997, Conf/3806/97, limite; annex 1: enabling clauses flexibility approach; annex 2: draft Schengen Protocol.

Table 7.1 Types of flexibility in the European Union

Type of flexibility	Definition
Multispeed	Mode of flexible integration according to which the pursuit of common objectives is driven by a group of member states that are both able and willing to go further, the underlying assumption being that the others will follow later.
Variable geometry	Mode of flexible integration that admits to unattainable differences within the integrative structure by allowing permanent or irreversible separation between hardcore and lesser-developed integrative units (Old Schengen).
"À la carte" mode	Mode of flexible integration whereby respective member states are able to pick and choose, as from a menu, in which policy area they would like to participate, while at the same time holding only to a minimum number of common objectives.
Transitional clauses	Mode of flexible integration characterized by two-way transitional periods that allow either of the member states to adapt to a particular policy area, the underlying assumption being that the adaptation period is temporary.
Enabling causes	Mode of flexible integration that enables the willing and the able members to pursue further integration—subject to certain conditions set out in the treaties—in a number of policy and program areas within and outside the institutional framework of the Union.
Case-by-case flexibility	Mode of flexible integration that allows a member state the possibility of abstaining from voting on a decision and formally declaring that it will not apply the decision in question, while at the same time accepting that the decision commits the Union (UK, Ireland, and Denmark on Title IV and Schengen).
Predetermined flexibility	Mode of flexible integration which covers a specific field, is predefined in all its elements, including its objectives and scope, and is applicable as soon as the treaty enters into force.

Source: Adapted from Stubb 2002: 32–33.

Britain's having-its-cake-and-eating-it-too stance, and insisted that other states should have the right to veto such ad hoc British participation.[12]

An agreement on the integration of Schengen into the EU was eventually reached at the Amsterdam summit. This agreement was part of an overall package on EU policy on movement of persons that included the issue of visas and a reform of the objectives and structure of the Third Pillar. With the signing of the Amsterdam Treaty, the JHA field was redefined as "an area of freedom, security and justice; [an area] in which the free movement

12. *Statewatch Bulletin* 7, no. 3 (May–June 1997).

of persons is assured . . . in conjunction with appropriate measures with respect to external border controls, asylum, immigration and the prevention and combating of crime."[13] Border control, immigration, and asylum were transferred from the Third (intergovernmental) to the First (Community) Pillar. Under German pressure, toward the end of the negotiations the delegates decided to introduce a five-year transitional period before these changes could take effect. In this phase the right of initiative would be shared between the Commission and member states, voting would be based on unanimity, the European Parliament could only offer opinions, and the European Court of Justice would have limited competence in Third Pillar issues.

At Amsterdam, European leaders also agreed to outline the rules for the integration of the Schengen *acquis* in a separate protocol.[14] The central element in the protocol is the definition of a series of derogations and opting outs for some member states that did not fully accept the incorporation of Schengen into the EU (United Kingdom, Ireland, and Denmark), and for nonmember states that were previously affiliated with Schengen (Norway and Iceland). In the new arrangement, the United Kingdom and Ireland would in principle not be bound by the Schengen *acquis* but may at any time request to take part in some or all of the provision of this *acquis*. On such a request, the existing Schengen members would decide unanimously, granting them the power to veto the participation of the United Kingdom or Ireland.

The position of Denmark was even more eccentric than the British and Irish "opt ins." Copenhagen was a Schengen member, but it was opposed to the regime's inclusion in the EU framework. The compromise found at Amsterdam was that Denmark would not, in principle, participate in the adoption of measures in the JHA field now falling under the First Pillar, although it may at any time inform the other member states that it no longer wished to avail itself of such a derogation (art. 7 of the protocol on the position of Denmark). However, as regards the measures built upon the Schengen *acquis*, it would decide within a period of six months from their adoption whether to implement them in its national law or not. In any case, this would only create an obligation under international law (as opposed to Community law) between Denmark and the member states adopting these measures (art. 5).

13. "Treaty of Amsterdam amending the Treaty on European Union, the Treaties establishing the European Communities and related acts," *Official Journal* C 340 (Nov. 10, 1997).

14. "Protocol integrating the Schengen *Acquis* into the Framework of the European Union." For an analysis of the Schengen Protocol, see Den Boer and Corrado 1999; Elsen 2000; Kuijper 2000.

In the case of Norway and Iceland, the main problem was institutional. Norway and Iceland were linked to the Schengen states by a cooperation agreement signed in December 1996, when Denmark, Sweden, and Finland joined the Schengen group (cf. chap. 5). The transposition into a Community context of the content of this agreement—provided for by article 6.1 of the Schengen protocol—was controversial, since it entailed two nonmember states participating in Council meetings, even if only in the capacity of observers. The compromise solution was to set up a cooperation mechanism outside the institutional framework of the European Union, enabling all the parties to be involved in an appropriate fashion. For this purpose, a "mixed committee"—composed of the members of the EU Council, the representatives of Norway and Iceland, and of the Commission, meeting at the level of experts, senior officials, and ministers—was established.[15]

Sorting Out Amsterdam: Schengen's "Ventilation"

Soon after the conclusion of the Amsterdam summit, some government leaders began wondering what they had actually signed up for. The legal consequences of the agreement had not been scrutinized in detail when the final text of the treaty was agreed upon. The task was rendered particularly arduous because of the complexity of the new arrangement. The Amsterdam Treaty resembled an "impenetrable labyrinth" (Denza 2002: 82), which had been "baroquely decorated with facultative arrangements, time-clauses and protocols" (Den Boer and Corrado 1999: 398). From a political perspective, the Amsterdam Treaty seemed to be more straightforward: it represented a "marriage of convenience" between Schengen and the EU, whereby Schengen could gain on legitimacy, while the Third Pillar could gain on operational capacity (Den Boer and Corrado 1999: 399). For the most fervent supporters of the European project, this arrangement represented the end of Schengen's sui generis status and its dissolution in the EU legal and institutional framework. Yet, on closer inspection, it is evident that the Amsterdam Treaty instead reflected the reality that had characterized the border control domain in the previous years, namely, the ascendancy of Schengen as the dominant culture of border control in Europe. Hence, rather than its communitarization, the incorporation of the Schengen regime in the

---

15. "Article 3 of the Agreement concluded by the Council with Norway and Iceland concerning the latter's association with the implementation, application and development of the Schengen *acquis.*" The agreement was signed on May 18, 1999 (*Official Journal*, L 176 [July 10, 1999]: 35).

EU entailed the *Schengenization* of the newly established "Area of Freedom, Security and Justice" in the European Union.

One of the most visible examples of this development is the acceptance of the series of flexible arrangements included in the Schengen protocol attached to the treaty. As we have seen, these arrangements were devised to rationalize the eccentric position of some countries that did not want to fully participate in the Schengen regime or that did not accept it as part of the EU framework. In the agreement achieved at Amsterdam, "flexibility" was not restricted to these ad hoc arrangements. The Amsterdam Treaty for the first time codified into EU law the flexible method of integration that had been the hallmark of Schengen. The term used in relevant provisions in the treaty is "closer co-operation." The innovation introduced with the treaty is that flexibility has to be within the institutional framework of the EU (previously the treaty allowed this cooperation to occur outside). One of the consequences of this arrangement is that it could have led to a two-track community, with a "first class" consisting of states that make full use of enhanced cooperation, thereby accelerating the process toward a federalist and centralized union, and a "second class" made up of "antifederalist" member states and, possibly, future new member states, regarded as not yet able to meet the requirements of "enhanced" cooperation. In this way, Amsterdam seemed to reproduce the scenario that characterized the formative years of the Schengen regime.

The Schengenization of the EU brought about with Amsterdam was also apparent in the reorganization of the Council's structures, which occurred in the months that followed the signing of the treaty.[16] In the new institutional arrangement, the Council maintained a pivotal role in the policy-making process. At the same time, it had to be readjusted to reflect the new organization of the EU.

Some of these changes reflected the communitarization of some items that previously fell under the Third Pillar. The new Strategic Committee on Immigration, Frontiers and Asylum (SCIFA) was thus formed.[17] In other cases, however, the existing mandates of some working parties of the Coun-

16. See "Responsibilities of Council bodies in the field of justice and home affairs" (6166/2/99 REV 2. LIMITE CK4 12, 10 March 1999).

17. A special committee ("Article 36 Committee") was set up to deal with issues that remained in the Third Pillar (police and custom cooperation, judicial cooperation in criminal matters, organized crime). This group took over from the "K4 Committee," the body within the Council that was responsible for solving technical issues before a question passed to the Committee of Permanent Representatives in the European Union (COREPER) and then to the JHA Council of Ministers.

cil had to be enlarged, and where no corresponding working parties of the Council existed, they had to be created *ex novo* in order to ensure the continued application of the provisions of the Schengen *acquis* and their further development.[18] This was the case for the working groups responsible for the exchange of information and data protection (issues related to the Schengen Information System). The new JHA structure also included the former Schengen Standing Committee (now "Schengen Committee"), with the task of monitoring and ensuring the correct implementation of the Schengen *acquis*. The establishment of this working group was particularly problematic, since its powers within the EU institutional framework potentially encroached upon the competences of the Commission, the official "guardian" of the treaties and of their application (Den Boer and Corrado 1999: 413).

Another concrete piece of evidence of how Schengen "took over" the EU is represented by the debate over the modalities of integration of the personnel of the Schengen Secretariat, which was previously associated with the Benelux Secretariat (an intergovernmental body). This question created tension among member states and within the European Council Secretariat, and it even caused a strike (the first one of its kind in the EU).[19] Eventually, the Council decided (by qualified majority), to integrate about sixty officials of the Schengen Secretariat into the Council Secretariat, by way of derogation from EU staff regulations. With them, officials from the Schengen Secretariat carried over the regime's institutional memory into the EU, and thus guaranteed its preservation and reproduction in the following years.[20]

Finally, the Schengenization of the EU with Amsterdam is also evident if we consider how the Schengen *acquis* was incorporated into Community law. As part of the agreement at Amsterdam, the issues of the definition of the *acquis* and the establishment of the legal bases of each of its provisions (also referred to as "ventilation") had been left pending, to be finalized while the treaty ratification process in the various national capitals was still ongoing. As had occurred in the past, these seemingly technical questions became the object of political wrangling. With regard to the definition of the *acquis*, the main concern was the possible "contamination effect" that executive measures taken without any parliamentary control—sometimes

18. On this point, see *Action Plan* 12028/1/98.

19. France, in particular, was strongly against the integration of the Schengen Secretariat without a prior selective competition; in favor were Spain, Belgium, and the Netherlands, with the other member states having intermediate positions. See *Agence Europe*, no. 7202, 17 April 1999.

20. This "transfer" included the regime's official documentation, which was now located in the Council Secretariat's JHA library in the Justus Lipsius building in Brussels.

adopted "informally"—could have on Community legislation (Den Boer and Corrado 1999: 402). Eventually, only five decisions of the Schengen Central Group were included in the Council decision defining the *acquis*.[21] The most controversial issue was the determination of an "appropriate" EC/EU legal basis ("First" or "Third" Pillar) for each provision to be incorporated. The political squabbling over the "ventilation" of the Schengen *acquis* is particularly relevant here, because it represented the last installment of the process leading to the selection of the Schengen culture of border control.

The Schengen *Acquis*

1 The 1985 agreement between the governments of the states of the Benelux Economic Union, the Federal Republic of Germany, and the French Republic on the gradual abolition of checks at their common borders (Schengen Agreement).

2 The 1990 convention implementing the Schengen Agreement of June 14, 1985, between the governments of the states of the Benelux Economic Union, the Federal Republic of Germany, and the French Republic on the gradual abolition of checks at their common borders (Schengen Implementation Convention).

3 Accession protocols and agreements to the 1985 agreement and the 1990 implementing convention with Italy, Spain, Portugal, Greece, Austria, Denmark, Finland, Sweden, Iceland, and Norway.

4 Decisions and declarations adopted by the Schengen Executive Committee.

5 Acts adopted for the implementation of the convention by the organs upon which the executive committee conferred decision-making powers.

To address this issue, a working group ("Schengen I") was set up after the Amsterdam summit.[22] The tensions of the negotiations in the working

---

21. Council Decision 99/435/EC; see table 7.2. Council Decision concerning the definition of the Schengen *acquis* for the purpose of determining, in conformity with the relevant provisions of the Treaty establishing the European Community and the Treaty on European Union, the legal basis for each of the provisions or decisions which constitute the *acquis*"; and "Council Decision determining, in conformity with the relevant provisions of the Treaty establishing the European Community and the Treaty on European Union, the legal basis for each of the provisions which constitute the Schengen *acquis*," both published in *Official Journal* L 176 (July 10, 1999): 1 and 17, respectively.

22. The "Schengen II" working group was in charge of the negotiation and drafting of the association agreements with Norway and Iceland.

group—which met on a fortnightly basis—were considerable.[23] Stubborn negotiation tactics were used by large delegations, notably France and Spain, which gave frequent rise to rivalries and stalemates. Spain, for example, because of the contentious political issue of Gibraltar (cf. chap. 6), wanted a Third Pillar legal basis for nearly all the provisions of the Schengen *acquis*, and maintained this position until the very end of negotiations.[24]

With regard to substantial issues, the Council hardly discussed provisions concerning police cooperation and judicial cooperation in criminal matters, which found their legal basis in the new Third Pillar. In contrast, the allocation of the articles of the Schengen Implementation Convention dealing with border controls, free movement, and visas was rather contentious, notwithstanding their communitarization by virtue of the Amsterdam Treaty. The choice for a First Pillar legal basis for these provisions was accompanied by a series of statements and declarations in line with the security preoccupation of certain Schengen member states.[25] The most divisive case concerned the allocation of the Schengen Information System. The Luxembourg presidency initially proposed to distribute the SIS between the First and the Third Pillar (on one hand, the management and structure of the system, and third for the management of personal data). The Council Legal Service and the Commission supported this position. Various national delegations (Austria, France, Italy, Portugal, and Spain) were opposed. They were worried about the uncertainty it would create (with effects on its practical application) and about the interference in the national police affairs. They therefore suggested a legal basis entirely in the Third Pillar.

The debate over the SIS continued during the winter and spring of 1999. In this period it was still unclear whether consensus could be achieved before the entry into force of the Amsterdam Treaty (which, after the completion of the ratification process, was set for May 1999). Thanks to the activism of the German presidency, which was chairing both the EU and the Schengen Group,[26] political agreement was reached in the General Affairs Council in April 1999. This agreement offered a compromise solution

23. On this point, see the testimony of Adrian Fortescue of the European Commission in House of Lords, *Select Committee on European Communities—Seventh Report*, 1999, pt. 30; Den Boer and Corrado 1999: 400.

24. *Agence Europe*, no. 7202, April 16, 1998; *Agence Europe*, no. 7452, April 23, 1999 and no. 7454, April 17, 1999; Den Boer and Corrado 1999: 406; Monar 1999: 12.

25. The list of the statements and declarations is included in Council Decision 99/436/EC, annex A.

26. The Schengen regime's institutions continued their work until the ratification of the Amsterdam Treaty. The final Schengen Executive Committee meeting was held in the German city of Mannheim on April 28, 1999.

to counter the Spanish objections on principle linked to the dispute over the status of Gibraltar; however, no agreement was reached on the SIS, and therefore the provisions related to this item (articles 92–119 of the Schengen Implementation Convention) were provisionally allocated to the Third Pillar. The agreement was sealed in two Council decisions issued on May 20, which specified the definition and the determination of the legal basis of the Schengen *acquis*.[27] After a long and tortuous route, Schengen's new life in the EU had officially begun.

27. "Council Decision 1999/435/EC of 20 May 1999 concerning the definition of the Schengen *acquis* for the purpose of determining, in conformity with the relevant provisions of the Treaty establishing the European Community and the Treaty on European Union, the legal basis for each of the provisions or decisions which constitute the *acquis*"; and "Council Decision 1999/436/EC of 20 May 1999 determining, in conformity with the relevant provisions of the Treaty establishing the European Community and the Treaty on European Union, the legal basis for each of the provisions or decisions which constitute the Schengen *acquis*," *Official Journal* L 176 (July 10, 1999).

EIGHT

Consolidating the New Culture of Border Control: Schengen in the European Union

The European Union's external borders are . . . a place where a common security identity is asserted. The absence of a clearly stated vision and common policy on external borders would entail major political and strategic risks. Those could ultimately block the expression of a viable Union policy on Justice and Home Affairs.[1]

The Union has practically no other *acquis* concerning external border control than the Schengen *acquis*.[2]

The Meaning of Schengen's Consolidation

The Schengen regime's formal incorporation into the European Union was a fundamental stepping stone in the establishment of Schengen as the new culture of border control in Europe. Its assumptions and practices were now inserted in a legitimate and coherent institutional framework. Thanks to the predictability and stability that this framework offered, Schengen was able to consolidate its dominant position in the border control domain.

This process of consolidation manifested itself in two parallel developments affecting Europe's border control community. The first is the expansion of Schengen's underlying assumptions and practices within this policy field and beyond. Official discourses and practices—from debates within

---

1. Commission of the European Communities, "Towards integrated management of the external borders of the Member States of the European Union" (COM [2002] 233 final, May 7, 2002).

2. EU Enlargement Working Group, 12148/01.

the border control community about how to realize the new "area of free-dom, security and justice" envisioned in the Amsterdam Treaty, to their practical application in policy initiatives both inside and outside Europe—reproduced the culture's tenets more consistently and coherently. The con-sequence of these dynamics was that the discursive space within the border control domain was progressively "filled" by the new culture.

The second development characterizing the border control domain is the progressive internalization of Schengen's assumptions by Europe's bor-der control community. As one commentator put it, in the late 1990s "the policy of free circulation of persons in the Schengen area has been success-ful to such an extent that the reimposition of an old style, person-by-person control [at the internal borders] is not feasible any more today" (Thränhardt 1999: 46). The very idea of going back to "old" nationalist practices was dismissed as unreasonable. Alternative approaches to border control (e.g., the communitarian approach favored by the European Commission) were also sidelined. Similarly, the questioning of Schengen's underlying assump-tions significantly subsided. Some of its earlier critics, such as the European Parliament and the European Commission, toned down their concerns over Schengen after its communitarization.

The objective of this chapter is to support the claim that Schengen is indeed consolidating. For this purpose, the analysis focuses on some key policy developments that characterized the EU justice and home affairs field from the period that preceded the entry into force of the Treaty of Amsterdam (May 1999) to the end of the transitional period when all the treaty provisions could take effect (May 2004), a date that coincided with the official accession of ten new member countries to the EU. The first issue addressed is that of the "internal" dynamics within this field. This section considers the debate within the EU over the features and priorities defining the "area of freedom, security and justice" mentioned in the Amsterdam Treaty. Then it turns to new policy initiatives that stemmed from this de-bate, focusing on one of the most controversial examples, namely, the pro-posal to create a European border agency.

The following two sections trace the evolution of the external dimen-sion of EU policy regarding border control in the post-Amsterdam period. As in previous chapters, the relations that the EU and its member states had with Europe's "near" and "far" abroad are explored. The first topic examined is the European Neighbourhood Policy (ENP)—the new EU initiative for the countries that after the last wave of enlargement found themselves at the Union's edges—paying special attention to the aspects of this policy that have a more direct bearing on the issue of border control. The argument then moves to the set of practices that have characterized the relations between the EU and regions beyond the European continent. One of the most noticeable developments in this area is the expansion of "remote control" policies that the EU adopted vis-à-vis third countries to tackle potential threats at their source. After presenting some of the key tenets of this new form of foreign policy, two case studies are elaborated more in detail, namely, the external processing of refugee claims and the establishment of Immigration Liaison Officers (ILOs) outside Europe. The chapter concludes by examines how the consolidation of Schengen has involved the border control community. It will be shown how, through their interaction and participation in common practices, its members, and especially those affiliated with the Commission and the Council, reproduced the core tenets of the Schengen culture, and in so doing reinforced its dominant position in Europe's border control policy domain.

Implementing the Area of Freedom, Security, and Justice: The Case of the European Border Agency

At the end of the 1990s a number of political and institutional developments created a favorable context for a reformulation of the way the European Union managed its external frontiers. On one hand, European policy makers became increasingly concerned about the implications of EU enlargement for border control. New member states would have eventually taken over the responsibility of guarding the EU frontiers. Questions were raised about their capacity to successfully accomplish this task and more generally about their reliability in guaranteeing Europe's security. On the other hand, with the Amsterdam Treaty the EU had acquired new powers in the border control field. These elements put pressure on EU institutions and existing member states to devise a more coherent and effective approach to dealing with the frontiers of the Union.

The Amsterdam Treaty, however, only set a broad framework for EU policies in the newly named "area of freedom, security and justice." Both the European Commission and EU member states felt that a clearer set of priorities and an agenda were required. A chance to advance these objectives came with the Tampere European Council—the first council entirely dedicated to justice and home affairs. At this summit, which took place in October 1999, European heads of state and governments wanted to put JHA issues at the top of the EU agenda. The intention was to treat this domain as a political priority in the same way that the original customs union, then the internal market, and more recently the common currency had been. Expectations for the Tampere summit were therefore high. While the Amsterdam Treaty had created the *legal* possibility to go beyond the previous institutional and political weaknesses of the JHA field (i.e., its intergovernmental approach based on unanimity and lack of democratic control), the discussion taking place at Tampere had the potential to open the *political* door to achieve this goal (Pastore 2002b; Elsen 1999).

The main themes on the summit's agenda were a Union-wide fight against crime, mutual recognition of judicial decisions, and asylum and migration policy. The last of these issues occupied center stage at the meeting. There was agreement among the participants on the need for a comprehensive approach to migration that addressed political, human rights, and development issues in countries and regions of origin and transit (Niessen 1999: 494; see more below). During the meeting, however, a great emphasis was put on more familiar securitarian themes. As the British delegation, led by prime minister Tony Blair, bluntly put it, the purpose of the summit was "to tackle illegal immigration and allow no hiding place for criminals."[3] This stance found an echo in the mostly intergovernmental and security-oriented political guidelines and practical objectives that characterized the program of action agreed upon at the summit.[4]

The so-called Tampere Program became the policy framework for EU policy in the post-Amsterdam period, and its implementation the principal goal of the Union in the short and medium term. Some of the initiatives proposed for this purpose addressed the internal functioning of the area of freedom, security, and justice, while others dealt with its external dimension. Among the "internal" initiatives (the external will be examined in the second part of this chapter), arguably the most far-reaching and controversial was the proposal to set up a European border agency. The debate over this project and the reactions it stimulated are illustrative of how the Schengen culture of border control was consolidating among Europe's border control policy community. The next section is devoted to the evolution of this proposal.

3. Tampere Special European Council, UK Position Paper, Oct. 5, 1999.

4. "Presidency Conclusions—Tampere European Council, 15 and 16 October 1999," Council of the European Union (October 12, 2004), 200/1/99, section A-D. This plan was, to a large extent, built on a text prepared for the Vienna Council held in December 1998 (the Vienna Plan); "Council and Commission Action Plan of 3 December 1998 on how best to implement the provisions of the Treaty of Amsterdam on the creation of an area of freedom, security and justice," *Official Journal* C 19 (Jan. 23, 1999).

Toward a European Border Agency

The Tampere Program explicitly called for the formulation of a more coherent and effective approach to managing Europe's external borders. With this objective in mind, the European Commission and EU member states started to ponder possible solutions that took into account the new post-Amsterdam political and institutional scenario. The central theme in these discussions was the setting up of a common border guard responsible for EU external frontiers. Those in favor of such a move (among them, the most vocal was the Commission) claimed that it would provide an instrument of solidarity for sharing the burden of controlling external borders in the enlarged Union and allow for the better use of personnel and technical resources as well as available expertise, while at the same time also marking a step forward in the route to political integration.[5] Some member states, including the United Kingdom, agreed that more cooperation on external border issues was needed but expressed reservations about establishing a supranational border police force.

In December 2001, the Laeken European Council arrived at a carefully worded compromise on cooperation on external border issues, which gave the Council and the Commission a mandate to work out "arrangements for co-operation between services responsible for external border control and to examine the conditions in which a mechanism or common services to control external borders could be created."[6] The term "European Border Police" or "European Border Guard," although already used by some member states' governments, did not appear in the mandate (Monar 2003a: 3).

On these premises, in May 2002 the European Commission presented to the Council and the European Parliament a communication that examined the case for "an integrated management of external borders."[7] In this document the Commission proposed mechanisms for cooperation at the European Union level that would permit practitioners to coordinate their

---

5. In testimony for the British House of Lords, Mr. Faull, the director general for Justice and Home Affairs at the Commission, compared border control of people with customs controls. Since the European Community is a customs union that operates with a unified customs code, its common frontiers should receive the same treatment (29th report, Select Committee on the European Union, "Proposals for a European Border Guard, With evidence," House of Lords, Session 2002–3, HL paper 133, July 2003. par.66. For an early statement of the Commission's position on the border agency, see "Communication on Illegal Immigration" (COM [2001] 672 final, Nov. 15, 2001).

6. "Presidency's Conclusions on Justice and Home Affairs," par. 42, Laeken, Dec. 17, 2001.

7. Commission of the European Communities, "Towards integrated management of the external borders of the Member States of the European Union" (COM 233 final, May 7, 2002).

operational actions in the framework of an integrated strategy.[8] Under the heading "common coordination and operational co-operation mechanism," the Commission proposed the creation of an "External borders practitioners common unit."[9] The unit would be composed of border guard heads and national high-level practitioners, and institutionally built on the existing meetings of border control heads within the Council's Strategic Committee on Immigration, Frontiers and Asylum (SCIFA).[10] The common unit would have mainly a practical role in coordinating the management of border control across the EU. Yet one of the possibilities that the Commission advanced was that it would supervise a newly created European border guard corps. This point was arguably the most controversial of the entire plan, as it provided a supranational entity with the possibility of presiding over an army not directly controlled by individual national governments.

The official rationales given by the Commission to justify the need for a European border agency are couched in functionalist terms. A common framework is needed because it addresses a common concern of all member states.[11] Parallel to this traditional "communitarian" argument, a securitarian orientation also seemed to guide the proposal for the border agency. As the quotation at the beginning of the chapter suggests, the Commission argued that a common approach to border control would foster a "common *security identity*" and that a "coherent, effective common management of the external borders of the Member States of the Union will boost *security* and the citizen's sense of belonging to a shared area and destiny."[12] Moreover, in presenting its plan the Commission acknowledged the need for a flexible and gradual approach in the development of a common policy for management of the external borders. This might entail allowing initiatives by small groups of member states to prepare the ground for future Union action in an intergovernmental fashion.

The Commission made an effort to satisfy both the advocates and the opponents of such a project. Its reception was therefore overall positive (Monar

8. Ibid., par. 6, p. 5
9. Ibid., par. 27, p. 13. A common coordination and operational cooperation mechanism is one of the plan's five "mutually interdependent components" (the others being a common corpus of legislation; a common integrated risk analysis; staff trained in the European dimension and interoperational equipment; and burden-sharing between member states); "Towards integrated management of the external borders of the Member States of the European Union," par. 20, p. 12.
10. When meeting in this expanded form, the committee would be known as SCIFA+.
11. Commission of the European Communities, "Towards integrated management of the external borders," 3.
12. Ibid., p. 2; emphasis added.

2003a: 4). Yet, despite the cautious approach adopted by the Commission, several member states did not agree with the view that integrated border management should ultimately lead to the creation of a European border guard corps. This different assessment was reflected in an Italian-led feasibility study on the creation of a European border police, which was presented at a ministerial conference in Rome on May 30, 2002.[13] Although partly overlapping with the Commission's communication both in terms of content and approach (the two proposals had a similar time frame, and the envisioned common policy framework was based on flexibility and an evolutionary approach), the study differed from the Commission's plan in some important respects. It advocated a complex network of national border police forces that would be linked by a number of common elements, including the following: a series of "centres" based in the territory of member states, each specializing in specific areas of border security and which would serve as "knots" of the network; common units for special tasks (e.g., a "rapid response unit"); a common risk assessment; financial burden sharing; and a common training curriculum. Despite some reservations,[14] the majority of member states favored the network system proposed by the Italian delegation over the more traditional communitarian option advanced by the Commission.

In the meantime, the Council had come under pressure to deliver on the subject of Europe's external borders. In the run-up to the Seville European summit (summer 2002), in a joint letter issued on May 16, the British and Spanish prime ministers Tony Blair and José Maria Aznar called for the summit to give "a remit for urgent action to strengthen the EU's borders."[15] The proposal for the creation of a common border force was given a warm welcome. Gerhard Schröder, the German chancellor, confirmed that enhanced cooperation was a mere stepping stone to the corps, and that the "creation of a common police force to guard our border remains the long-term goal."[16] Some delegations, however, opposed the move. Jack Straw, the

13. "Feasibility Study for the Setting Up of a European Border Police," *Final Report*, Rome, May 2002. The other countries involved in the project were Belgium, France, Germany, and Spain. Available at http://www.statewatch.org/news/2005/may/eba-feasibility-study.pdf.

14. Some member states criticized the study as lacking in clarity and forceful central ideas (Monar 2003a: 4). Still others, such as the United Kingdom and Finland, preferred a more informal type of cooperation. The British government emphasized *operational cooperation* rather than centralization. Finland advocated a system of external border security that places the main emphasis on efficient cooperation with border guards on the other side of the border rather than the creation of common EU structures (ibid.).

15. "Blair suffers a double defeat on asylum seekers at Seville summit," *Telegraph*, June 23, 2002.

16. Ibid.

British foreign secretary, argued that "such is the opposition to the principle of a European Union border police that it will not feature except as an acknowledgement that a discussion took place."[17]

In Seville, the European Council agreed on a plan for the management of the external borders.[18] Although the plan took up most of the analysis and the proposals in the Commission communication, it also added some of the elements of the Italian-led feasibility study (such as the idea of creating a network structure). Moreover, it left the member states with a wide margin to maneuver in its implementation and did not commit them to any particular model of a European border guard. It also adopted the cautious, evolutionary approach suggested by the Commission. Thus, though the plan was agreed upon, it remained unclear whether the long-term aim was to establish an operational force or a less ambitious arrangement (Monar 2003a: 8).

The European Council returned to the issue at Thessaloniki in June 2003. It invited the Commission to examine the necessity of creating new institutional mechanisms, including a "Community operational structure, in order to enhance operational cooperation for the management of external borders."[19] This appeared to be a reference to the possibility of an operational European border guard without actually using the term. Later in the year the Commission responded to the Council's call by issuing a draft regulation on the establishment of "a European Agency for the Management of Operational Co-operation at the External Borders."[20] This long-awaited proposal was presented by the Commission as the basis for the long-term development of an EU border police. It systematized the various ideas that had been hitherto advanced on the subject and specified the legal foundations, tasks, and financial coverage of the project. This proposal took into account the experiences of cooperation between the member states in the framework of the common unit. The border agency in fact would take over the unit's responsibilities (viz., coordination of operational cooperation). In addition, it was given the task of "coordinating and organizing return operations of member states and identifying best practices on the acquisi-

17. Ibid.

18. "Plan for the management of the external borders of the member states," 10019/01, Brussels June 14, 2002.

19. Council of the European Union, "Presidency Conclusions. Thessaloniki European Council, 19 and 20 June 2003," April 20, 2005, 11638/03.

20. Commission for the European Communities, "Proposal for a Council Resolution establishing a European Agency for the Management of Operational Co-operation at the External Borders" (COM [2003] 687/2, Nov. 20, 2003).

tion of travel documents and removal of third-country nationals from the territories of the member states."[21]

On the basis of the Commission's communication, the Council started working to lay the legal foundations for the new border agency. In October 2004 it adopted a regulation establishing the new agency.[22] The European Agency for the Management of Operational Cooperation at the External Borders of the Member States of the European Union (also known as "Frontex") was formally inaugurated on June 30, 2005. The main tasks of Frontex include the following:

- coordinating operational cooperation between member states in the field of management of external borders
- assisting member states in the training of national border guards, including the establishment of common training standards
- carrying out risk analyses
- following up the development of research relevant for the control and surveillance of external borders
- assisting member states in circumstances requiring increased technical and operational assistance at external borders
- providing member states with the necessary support in organizing joint return operations.

The idea of providing the agency with a border guard corps was momentarily put on the back burner to await a resolution of the deadlock over the European Constitution (see chap. 10). The project was nonetheless still on the EU agenda, ready to be discussed when the appropriate political moment arrived.

In commenting on the proposal to establish a European border agency, a report submitted to the British House of Lords argued that this is "one of the most ambitious [proposals] which has so far appeared in the context of EU justice and home affairs."[23] The eagerness to advance the project shows how EU institutions and member states have been willing to experiment

21. Ibid., p. 4. According to some critics, the addition of these new powers signals the emergence of an "expulsion agency in disguise." Hayes 2003; "The proposed Regulation: an EU Expulsions agency in disguise?" *Statewatch* (Nov. 2003).

22. "Regulation establishing a European Agency for the Management of Operational Cooperation at the External Borders of the Member States of the European Union" (10827/04 + 12553/04 ADD 1; Oct. 25, 2004).

23. Twenty-ninth report, Select Committee on the European Union, "Proposals for a European Border Guard, With evidence," House of Lords, Session 2002–03, HL paper 133, July 2003. par. 48.

with the creation of common structures and to enhance operational cooperation at their common borders. Crucially, the underlying tenets of these
experiments are consistent with those of the Schengen culture of border
control. If we look at the content of the initiative, we can see that it follows the diffused and networked (that is, no longer territorially fixed and
delimited) approach characteristic of Schengen. As not all member states
are participating equally in these initiatives, more integrated border guard
structures might initially only involve some of them. The possibility thus
exists for this intergovernmental cooperation to take place outside the am-
bit of the EU treaties, which would lead to a fragmentation of the EU into
different subsystems of external border controls with major differences in
standards and procedures.

In terms of method, the border agency's proponents chose a pragmatic
and evolutionary approach to policymaking. They advanced the project despite the resistance and the obstacles it entailed. As one commentator put it,
"there is little consensus about precisely what it means and whether such a
common force is actually needed, and even those supporting it have different ideas about its shape, task organisation and the time-frame for achieving it" (Monar 2003a: 14). This pragmatic approach is reflected in the fact
that, while the formal features of the agency were debated, its practical implementation was already under way. We have already noted how the common unit (the precursor of the border agency) had been active even before
the agency was formally established. The same could be said for some of
the activities that the agency would have to coordinate. Cooperation among
member states at EU external borders was in fact already in full swing well
before 2005.[24] As had occurred with Schengen, the proponents went ahead
with the project despite the lack of a clearly defined legal framework and
the involvement of democratically elected bodies, in the hope that practical
achievements could provide the necessary legitimacy to the project.

---

24. In January 2003, for example, France, Italy, Spain, Portugal, and the United Kingdom
launched Operation Ulysses, which involved joint patrols in the Mediterranean and Atlantic
Ocean. The project was presented by Spanish interior minister Angel Acebes as "an advance
toward the creation of an EU border police force within an area of freedom, security and justice
in which we all want to live," quoted in El País, Jan. 28, 2003. Although politically significant,
the initial results of the project were disappointing. A combination of adverse weather and mis-
communication (the participants had failed to agree on a common language), led the British
and Portuguese to pull out and prevented the Italians from even leaving port. Elizabeth Nash,
"Europe's first migrant patrol founders on the rocks of incomprehension," Independent, March
11, 2003.

Pragmatism might in turn explain the decision to limit (at least in the preparatory stages) the democratic input and oversight of the project. European and national parliaments were consulted on the agency's legal personality. This consultation, however, concerned an operational body that had already been established and excluded parliamentary involvement in its further development. In this sense, the main purpose of bringing elected bodies into the policymaking process was to build ex post facto political legitimacy into the new agency. The story of the emergence of the Schengen regime seemed to repeat itself. After all, since this intergovernmental and unaccountable method of policymaking had been successful in the past, why shouldn't it work again with the border agency?

Projecting Schengen in the Near Abroad: From Enlargement to the European Neighbourhood Policy

After the signing of the Amsterdam Treaty, EU leaders recognized that the external aspect of the Union's action in the border control domain was going to take on "a new and more demanding dimension."[25] In recognition of its growing relevance, foreign policy was therefore named as one of the "essential" components of the comprehensive approach to dealing with migration and border control issues that were outlined in Tampere.

The reasons for this emphasis on the external dimension of border control stemmed from some relevant developments that affected Europe at the turn of the millennium. Institutionally, the advances introduced by the Amsterdam Treaty had strengthened the Union's role as an active player on the international stage, both bilaterally and in multilateral forums. In geopolitical terms, this period was characterized by the continuing instability around the European Union (e.g., the former Yugoslavia) and the mounting migratory pressure coming from across the Mediterranean Sea. One of the events that had the most direct effect on the European Union's foreign policy on border control, however, was the completion of the process of EU enlargement.

Between the summer of 2001 and the fall of 2002, the negotiations over "Freedom of Movement" and "Justice and Home Affairs" (chaps. 2 and 24

---

25. "Council and Commission Action Plan of 3 December 1998 on how best to implement the provisions of the Treaty of Amsterdam on the creation of an area of freedom, security and justice" (*Official Journal* C 19 [Jan. 23, 1999]: par. 22).

of the accession treaties, respectively) were concluded.[26] In the Copenhagen European Council in December 2002, it was agreed that free movement within the EU would be granted to citizens from the new member states. There were different approaches, however, regarding the timing of this liberalization. France and Germany were the most reluctant, calling for a period of transition, whereas the Netherlands, Sweden, Spain, Ireland, and the United Kingdom stated that they would opt to open their borders to the new EU countries upon accession. No common position was found, but all delegations attending the Copenhagen council nonetheless agreed on a package for the admission of ten new member states to the Union. The accession treaty was signed in Athens on April 16, 2003, and the new member states were slated to join the EU on May 1, 2004, once the accession treaty was ratified.

Enlargement had important "internal" implications not only for the European Union but also for the relations with its new near abroad, namely, countries that were previously distant and that would soon have shared borders with the EU. Before the conclusion of the accession negotiations, EU institutions and governments started to debate more explicitly the prospects of the Union's relations with its future neighbors. The first concrete result of this discussion came in January 2002 in the form of a letter from the British foreign minister Jack Straw to the Spanish presidency.[27] This document envisioned a comprehensive approach to dealing with some EU neighbors (Belarus, Moldova, and Ukraine). The approach was similar to the one adopted by the EU toward the western Balkans (viz., closer integration) but without the added enticement of future EU membership, one of the central pillars of EU foreign policy in the previous decade. The Straw letter was followed by a

26. European Commission, "Report on the results of the negotiations on the accession of Cyprus, Malta, Hungary, Poland, the Slovak Republic, Latvia, Estonia, Lithuania, the Czech Republic and Slovenia to the European Union," January 2003. Negotiations with Bulgaria and with Romania ended only in December 2004. One of the most contentious issues in the discussion over chapter 2 was the request of the Czech Republic for better protection of its national labor market, if market access restrictions in Germany and Austria massively diverted workers from other new Eastern EU members to the Czech Republic. A compromise was found in October 2001 as a common negotiating position which accepted Prague's demand (*Uniting Europe*, no. 160, Oct. 8, 2001). The final agreement on chapter 24 introduced a two-stage approach in the implementation of the Schengen regime in new member states: the application of the EU *acquis* immediately after accession, and the lifting of internal borders later, following a separate decision by the Council (in turn based on an evaluation conducted by the Commission to establish whether all legal, organizational, operational, practical, and technical preconditions are fulfilled).

27. Letter from Jack Straw to Josep Piqué, Foreign and Commonwealth Office, London, Jan. 28, 2002

Swedish initiative, the "Lindh-Pagrotsky letter,"[28] which suggested a broader geographical scope to the policy (its expansion to Mediterranean countries) and an emphasis on free trade and economic development.

The European Commission took up these ideas and in March 2003 drafted a plan in which it outlined the guiding principles of the new European Neighbourhood Policy (ENP).[29] The ENP was officially adopted by the Thessalonica European Council in June 2003. A year later, the Commission issued a strategy paper[30] that set out the principles, geographical scope, and methodology for the implementation of this policy.

The main principles of the ENP are summarized by then president of the European Commission Romano Prodi: "My aim is giving them [EU's neighbors] incentives, injecting a new dynamic in existing processes and developing an open and evolving partnership. This is what we call our proximity policy, a policy based on mutual benefits and obligations, which is a substantial contribution by the EU to global governance."[31] The incentives Prodi is referring to are a stake in the EU's Common Market and further integration and liberalization to promote the free movement of persons, goods, services, and capital.[32] This access does not, however, mean formal membership in the EU. What is offered is "everything but institutions."

The ENP refers to a variety of policy domains where partnership between the EU and its neighbors should be fostered. One of them is justice and home affairs. When addressing this domain, the Commission calls for closer cooperation on issues such as border management; migration; the fight against terrorism; trafficking in human beings, drugs, and arms; organized crime; money laundering; and financial and economic crime. It also considers the question of the movement of people. The possibility for citizens the neighboring countries to obtain easier access to the EU is one of the main incentives the ENP offers. In the 2003 communication there is indeed a reference to possible "perspectives for lawful migration and movement

28. Letter from Ms. Anna Lindh (minister of foreign affairs) and Mr. Leif Pagrotsky (minister of international trade) to Josep Piqué, Regeringskansliet, Stockholm, March 8, 2002.

29. The plan was included in a communication to the Council and the European Parliament and was entitled "Wider Europe—Neighbourhood: A New Framework for Relations with our Eastern and Southern Neighbours" (COM [2003] 104 final, March 11, 2003).

30. Commission of the European Communities, "European Neighbourhood Policy: Strategy Paper" (COM [2004] 373 final, May 12, 2004).

31. Romano Prodi, "A Wider Europe—A Proximity Policy as the key to stability," speech delivered at the Sixth ECSA-World Conference, Brussels, 5–6 December 2002.

32. Commission of the European Communities, "Wider Europe—Neighbourhood: A New Framework for Relations with our Eastern and Southern Neighbours" (COM [2003] 104 final, March 11, 2003), 10.

of persons." The practical implementation of these objectives is in turn addressed in the ENP's action plans.[33]

At first glance, the European Neighbourhood Policy seems to be a promising development in the EU's foreign policy. It represents a comprehensive and progressive approach to dealing with the implications of enlargement and with the challenges and opportunities that Europe's new neighbors raise. It is based on a quid pro quo relationship between the EU and its neighbors, which should have positive implications for both sides. In this sense the ENP appears as the latest application of Europe's "civilian" foreign policy model (Rosencrance 1996). Yet a critical analysis of the form and content of the initiative suggests that, in many respects, the ENP is not really consistent with the benevolent spirit underlying this model.

The first element that stands out in the ENP is the central role that security issues, such as illegal migration, drug trafficking, and terrorism, play in the initiative. These elements were already present in the early formulations of the policy. In his letter to the Spanish presidency, for example, Jack Straw portrayed a rather bleak picture of the EU's neighbors:

> Within three years, Ukraine and Belarus will border the EU—with all the attendant problems of cross-border crime, trafficking and illegal immigration. Moldova will not be an EU neighbour until later . . . but it already faces grinding poverty, huge social problems and mass emigration.[34]

This securitarian orientation is reproduced in the commission's documents. In a 2003 communication, "stability and peace" around the EU's borders are presented as two of the ENP's main objectives. Clearly, these terms are code words for "security" and, more specifically, "European security." Stability and peace in the neighborhood are in fact mentioned in the European security strategy paper, which was issued only a few months after the Commission's communication.[35] This document outlines the key security challenges the region faces in the new millennium and what measures the EU

33. Action plans are policy documents outlining the overarching strategic policy targets and benchmarks that each neighbor should achieve. They contain a set of jointly agreed-upon key priorities in selected areas. Besides justice and home affairs, these areas are political dialogue and reform, economic and social development and reform, regulatory and trade-related issues, and people-to-people contacts (COM [2003] 104 final).

34. Letter from Jack Straw to Josep Piqué.

35. "A Secure Europe in a Better World—European Security Strategy," Brussels, Dec. 12, 2003. For a critical commentary, see Toje 2005.

should take to address them. Although it is not explicitly mentioned in the text, the similarities with the ENP in terms of approach and objectives (and in some instances, even the wording in the proposal) are evident.

The emphasis put on the issue of security in the ENP is not problematic per se. Security can be complementary to other more traditional "economic" goals that characterize EU's foreign policy. And indeed, in the vision of its creators, the ENP should foster both prosperity *and* security. Yet if we look closer at the ENP, this complementarity is seriously put into question. The section on the initiative dealing with movement of people is a good case in point. The offer to ease the access of citizens of countries that border the EU is not in fact as generous as it at first seems. With respect to visa policy, for example, there is the possibility of facilitated procedures for short-stay visas for some countries, but this is a small minority (Guild 2005). More generally, in regard to legal migration, there is no substantial expansion of the already limited number of provisions included in the existing bilateral agreements between the EU and its neighbors. Significantly, any reference to access to the EU's "four freedoms," including freedom of movement, is dropped in the Strategy Paper and substituted with much more vague language. Now what the EU can offer are just "measures preparing partners for gradually obtaining a stake in the EU's Internal Market."[36]

The ENP not only fails to improve access to the Common Market, but, more problematically, it includes new measures that, if applied, would impose further restrictions on the EU's neighbors. In the ENP there is recognition that all parties have a stake in ensuring that the new external borders are not barriers to trade, social and cultural interchange, or regional cooperation. Through effective border management, the ENP seeks to contribute further to joint prosperity and security: "Facilitating trade and passage, while securing the European Union borders against smuggling, trafficking, organised crime (including terrorist threats) and illegal immigration (including transit migration), will be of crucial importance."[37]

In reality these are more than just compensatory measures. On the grounds of security, cooperation is in fact extended beyond freedom of movement. The ENP requires the EU's neighbors to reinforce controls and security in order to avert threats before they reach the heart of the Continent. The EU proposes to its partners "intensified co-operation to prevent

36. "A Secure Europe in a Better World—European Security Strategy," p. 3.
37. COM (2003), 104, p. 5.

and combat common security threats."[38] Regarding border management, the role of neighboring states is to keep out of the EU third-country nationals that the member states consider personae non gratae. Neighbors thus should become buffer zones between the EU and what are considered the original sources of potential threats (e.g., sub-Saharan Africa in the case of illegal immigration).

One of the consequences of the securitization of the relationship between the EU and its neighbors is that in the name of an alleged future "friendship" with Europe, neighbors run the risk not only of losing domestic support (as governments will be required to take coercive actions against their own nationals), but also of tarnishing the relations among themselves and with third countries. It should also be kept in mind that some of the ENP's provisions require EU's neighbors to tighten controls not only at their outer borders, but also at those with the EU itself. This obligation reinforces the idea that neighbors are a potential threat and thus part of the problem the ENP is attempting to "fix." The securitization of border control could therefore work against one of the alleged objectives of the initiative, strengthening and rendering more effective political dialogue (both bilaterally and multilaterally) between Europe and its neighbors.[39] Instead of reinforcing solidarity in the region, the unintended consequence of the ENP would be to cause more instability and conflict.

What the language of the ENP omits is as revealing as what it expresses. Although the countries involved in the project are often referred to as "partners," the term "partnership" is in fact not mentioned.[40] The very idea of creating a "ring of friends" around Europe suggests that the goal is not the establishment of a "horizontal" system in which each of the actors interacts on an equal plane, but a "concentric" one where Europe is the hub and the neighbors the various spokes. This arrangement reinforces, rather than challenges, the existing disparities between the two camps in terms of population, wealth, and power. The Commission has tried to counter this perception of

---

38. Ibid.

39. The ENP mentions the importance of this dialogue with regard to foreign and security policy issues. It also stresses that the EU and partner countries should work together on effective multilateralism, so as to reinforce global governance (COM [2004] 373 final).

40. The term is reserved only for Russia. In recognition of Moscow's participation in the initiative, the original name of the ENP's main financial instrument was changed from European Neighbourhood Instrument (ENI) to European Neighbourhood *and Partnership* Instrument (ENPI). For an analysis of the role of Russia in the ENP, see Tassinari 2005.

the EU imposing its agenda on the neighbors.[41] Its qualifications, however, do not dispel the sense that it is a top-down, asymmetric initiative.

Despite claims of avoiding new barriers between the EU and its neighbors, the ENP is sending a series of contradictory signals. On one hand, the initiative promises more access to the EU and an equal partnership; on the other, it contains an unprecedented emphasis on security, which in practice not only limits the capacity of the EU to meet the expectations generated by its offer, but also opens the door for imposing further restrictions and a set of onerous obligations on its neighbors. At the same time, both the content and the form of the initiative reinforce the asymmetry between the two sides. If we take all these elements together, we can clearly notice parallels between the ENP and some of the core tenets of the Schengen culture of border control. Read against the grain, the ENP gives the impression that some of the policies adopted in the context of the Schengen culture have just been "repackaged" and then "delivered" to the neighboring countries.

What characterizes the relation between the ENP and the Schengen culture is not, however, just a series of correspondences. I contend that the Schengen culture has in fact "spread" to the ENP as an unintended consequence of its consolidation. This consolidation was, in turn, the result of the evolution of Europe's border control community practices in this period. In order to account for the Schengenization of the ENP, it is therefore necessary to examine more closely the developments within the community that had a direct bearing on the ENP.

The European Commission and the European Council were the two main driving forces behind the initiative. In its formulation, different units within these institutions participated—sometimes in competition with each other—in the policymaking process. The most relevant were, on one hand, the Commission's Directorates-General (DGs) for External Relations (Relex); for Enlargement; and for Justice, Liberty and Security. On the other were the various member states' national delegations acting within the European Council, and the Council's General Secretariat. The birth and early developments of the ENP can be seen as the story of the dialectical relation between these actors. By examining their interaction over time it is thus also possible to understand how the initiative was "Schengenized."

41. The 2004 strategic paper discusses the issue of joint ownership: "Joint ownership of the process, based on the awareness of shared values and common interests, is essential. The EU does not seek to impose priorities or conditions on its partners. . . . There can be no question of asking partners to accept a pre-determined set of priorities. These will be defined by common consent and will thus vary from country to country" (COM [2004] 373 final), 8.

The securitarian orientation of the ENP was already apparent from the initiative's early steps, as the Straw letter to the Spanish presidency attests. Yet when the Commission started to work on the ENP file, other than some general guidelines there were still no precise details about the content and organization of the initiative (especially who should be in charge of it: a "Wider Europe" task force within the Commission was not instituted until July 2003). The DG Relex took up most of the work. Other DGs, however, played an important part in shaping the policy. Members of the DG Enlargement were particularly active in the ENP and often struggled with their Relex colleagues over this file (Goujon 2005). Less apparent yet equally relevant was the influence that the DG for Justice, Liberty, and Security (JLS) exerted within the Commission (Jeandesboz 2006: 34–35). The DG JLS is one of the so-called line DGs invited to participate in the policymaking because of its competence and expertise. As the ENP became more clearly defined, the DG JLS claimed more space in its planning, and its involvement increased over time. Because of the subject matters it deals with and the fact that it has contacts with the Ministries of Interior of the various member states, this DG tends to reproduce a more securitarian orientation than other DGs. And indeed, it vigorously advocated the insertion of asylum, illegal immigration, and trafficking at the top of the ENP agenda. This stance clashed with that of the DG Relex, which considered these issues as only one element in the overall policy (ibid., 25). Thanks to the DG JLS activism, the securitarian dimension of the ENP in the Commission's proposals acquired a more visible profile, especially in the action plans devised for the neighboring countries.

The decisive push toward a more securitarian outlook of the ENP, however, did not come from the Commission but from its institutional counterpart, the Council. Since the initiative's launch in 2002, the Council had been less directly involved, leaving the Commission in charge of defining policy details. After the issuing of the 2003 communication on "Wider Europe," the Council began to reassert its role and exert increasing political pressure on the Commission. The main reason for the Council's move stemmed from the belief that the Commission was overstepping its powers, especially when it started direct negotiations with some of the neighbors on the action plans. To counter this trend, the Council decided to oversee more of the Commission's activities and to have a say on the content of the ENP, especially if the issue was politically relevant or it entailed questions of foreign policy. This change of approach toward the ENP was expressed in the Council's decision to take upon itself the job of designating and opening formal negotiations with neighboring states.

The effect of the Council regaining control over the ENP was apparent in the 2004 Strategy Paper. Here, as we have seen, the Commission "purged" some of the most progressive elements of the Communication on Wider Europe (such as the offer to enjoy the benefits of freedom of movement across the Continent). Whatever the rationale for this stance (pragmatism, socialization, or arm-twisting by the Council), by including these securitarian items in the ENP, the Commission not only reproduced some of the Schengen culture's core tenets, but it also helped further legitimize its underlying discourse. In this sense, the ENP can be considered the latest "victim" of the Schengen culture's spread into new areas of EU policy.

Europe's Far Abroad and the Expansion of "Remote Control" Policies

The combination of security risks and economic opportunities emanating from neighboring regions in the 1990s led the European Union and its member states to focus most of their attention and resources to the areas directly east and south of the EU, to the detriment of African, Asian, and Latin American countries.[42] This geographically skewed policy became more noticeable at the turn of the millennium, when the EU was moving toward enlargement. The treatment that differentiated between "near" and "far" abroad did not, however, significantly affect the border control domain. On the contrary, in this period the EU actually expanded its relations with regions beyond Europe on subjects related to the management of frontiers. The reasons for this development stem, to a large extent, from the new competences that the European institutions had obtained with the Amsterdam Treaty. These powers gave more impetus to the Union's action. The EU could also exploit the advantage it had in terms of political neutrality over its member states (the latter in many instances representing former colonial powers).

At the October 1999 Tampere summit, EU leaders had agreed to advance a comprehensive approach to border control that relied on bi- and multi-lateral cooperation with third countries and that addressed the structural factors causing poverty and instability. Despite these claims, the expansion

---

42. The declining interest in developing countries was reflected in the decrease of EU development funds going to African, Caribbean, and Pacific (ACP) countries. Between 1987 and 1995, ACP's share of total aid disbursements fell from 62.8 percent to 41.5 percent. At the same time, the share of Mediterranean countries rose from 8.3 to 10.5 percent, while that of the CEECs and the Commonwealth of Independent States (CIS) reached 17.1 and 11.6 percent, respectively, of the budget (Boswell 2003: 19).

of EU external action in border control issues in the post-Amsterdam era was not translated into a parallel transformation toward a comprehensive foreign policy. Similar to what was occurring with the near abroad, EU relations with third countries remained mostly intergovernmental and asymmetric and became progressively more aggressive and security-oriented. These features became even more acute after the terrorist attacks of September 11 in the United States. In the aftermath of these events, a more proactive border control policy was in fact seen as a central aspect of the fight against terrorism.[43]

The Schengenization of EU foreign policy was apparent in the policies that EU governments and institutions formulated in this period. This is the case, for example, for readmission. This policy had been used since the early 1990s to expel unwanted individuals and to induce the countries of origin or transit to reaccept them (see chap. 6); yet until then these measures were not always applied in a consistent fashion and lacked an effective enforcement mechanism. This state of affairs changed in the post-Amsterdam era. In the various proposals dealing with illegal immigration and trafficking of human beings in the European Union, return and readmission policies were identified as "integral and vital components."[44] The main innovation of this period was the introduction of readmission agreements, which became part of the EU's broader strategy for combating illegal immigration. Such agreements involved reciprocal undertakings by the European Union and third-country partners to cooperate over the return of illegal residents to their country of origin. They also contain a "readmission clause." Similar clauses existed even before the signing of the Amsterdam Treaty (cf. the "standard clause" mentioned in chap. 6). They did not, however, constitute readmission agreements in themselves, but could only establish a framework for negotiating them in the future. According to the new arrangement, signing the agreement created an obligation to negotiate a supplementary treaty with the entire Community, not just individual member states. Moreover, such clauses became mandatory, and thus the EU would no longer sign any

---

43. The nexus between foreign policy and the protection of the EU external frontiers was explicitly made in the action plan on illegal migration, which the European Council adopted in February 2002. See "Proposal for a comprehensive plan to combat illegal immigration and trafficking of human beings in the European Union" (*Official Journal* C 142 [June 14, 2002]).

44. "Council Proposal for a comprehensive plan to combat illegal immigration and trafficking of human beings in the European Union," 6621/1/02, Brussels, 27 Feb. 2002, JAI 30, FRONT 19, MIGR 10, VISA 29.

association or cooperation agreement unless the other side agreed to these new obligations.[45]

Despite the language of cooperation and partnership that characterized the discussions over the issue of readmission, the EU approach was based on the imposition of its will rather than a real dialogue. Consultation to establish the willingness of the third party to enter negotiations with the EU was generally limited. The revision of the Lomé Convention is exemplary in this regard (cf. chap. 3). Soon after the conclusion of the Tampere European Council, EU officials turned their attention to the final stages of the negotiation of the convention on aid and trade between the EU and seventy-seven African, Caribbean, and Pacific (ACP) states. The October 1999 meeting of the ACP-EU Joint Assembly adopted a resolution on immigration. This resolution called for a consistent EU policy that addressed the root causes of forced migration and that included measures in the fields of home affairs (Niessen 1999: 490). At the last minute, the EU demanded the insertion of a clause on readmission and repatriation and that this clause be included in the negotiations on the revision of the Lomé Convention.[46] The ACP states argued that there was no basis in international law for such a demand but eventually they had to give in to EU demands. The new Lomé convention (known as the "Cotonou Agreement") was signed in February 2000. Article 13 of the agreement requires ACP states to "accept the return and readmission of any of its nationals who are illegally present in the territory of a member state of the European Union, at that member state's request and without further formalities."

In the Cotonou Agreement, and more generally in the readmission agreements that the EU was negotiating, there was no explicit reference to the possible consequences of a country's lack of cooperation. The controversial proposal of introducing a "retaliatory clause" and making aid dependent on efforts to combat illegal immigration was brought forward by EU ministers of interior and justice and put on the agenda of the Seville EU summit (July 2002) by the British and Spanish governments. The EU declared its willingness to offer financial assistance to third countries in managing migratory flows and assisting with the readmission of illegal immigration. Yet it also warned that "failure of those countries to adopt such

45. Since 1999, most EU association and cooperation agreements have included the updated readmission clause. Between 2000 and 2002, the Council authorized the Commission to negotiate Community readmission agreements with eleven third countries (Morocco, Sri Lanka, Russia, Pakistan, Hong Kong, Macao, Ukraine, Albania, Algeria, China, and Turkey). The first readmission agreement to be signed was with Hong Kong in November 2002.

46. *Guardian*, Feb. 5, 2000.

measures without good reason may give rise, in particularly serious cases, or for repeated minor incidents, to appropriate early political response."[47] Although the proposal was eventually withdrawn because of the opposition of some delegations,[48] the broad support it achieved among EU delegations confirmed that the underlying securitarian principles that sustained it had indeed pervaded the EU's foreign policy.

Readmission policies were not the only mechanism through which the EU and its member states dealt with its neighbors on the issue of border control in the post-Amsterdam era. What we witness in this period is an intensification of the set of practices directed toward the prevention of potential threats at their source, also known as "remote control" (Zolberg 1999). These practices can take different forms (e.g., visa regimes, carrier sanctions, interdiction policies) and involve a multiplicity of international and national actors (e.g., EU institutions, consulates, airlines, security agencies, immigration officers). These practices and actors are deployed in new sites to respond more effectively and efficiently to changing constraints and opportunities in the border-control field (Lahav and Guiraudon 2000: 58).

Remote control is not a new phenomenon. Early examples of these practices date back to the beginning of the twentieth century.[49] It is only in the 1980s, however, that they gained prominence as a foreign policy tool, becoming an integral part of the Schengen culture of border control. What characterizes the post-Amsterdam phase is the expansion of these practices and their higher degree of sophistication. Remote control techniques were included in the overall strategy of the EU toward its near and far neighbors. Moreover, unlike the previous period, they benefited from the already well-established network of relations that the EU had with third countries.

Table 8.1 lists the main policies falling under the category of "remote control" that were either developed *ex novo* or significantly expanded in the post-Amsterdam era (the list includes visa regime, carrier sanctions, and

47. European Council, "Council Conclusions on measures to be applied to prevent and combat illegal immigration and smuggling and trafficking in human beings by sea and in particular on measures against third countries which refuse to co-operate with the European Union in preventing and combating these phenomena," 10017/02, Brussels, 14 JAI 142 RELEX 122 MIGR 57, June 2002, par. 33.

48. France and Sweden argued that denying financial support would increase poverty and emigration ("A Meeting of Minds," *Time–Europe*, June 23, 2002).

49. This is the case, for instance, of carriers as instruments of immigration control. At the 1919 Paris Conference, airspace was placed under state sovereignty. Hence, airlines had to comply with state rules. With the 1944 Convention on International Civil Aviation, a set of guidelines compelled transport companies to assume the role of international immigration officers under the threat of hefty fines (Lahav and Guiraudon 2000: 63).

Table 8.1 Toward an integrated management of EU external borders: key initiatives (1999–2004)

Type	Initiative	Objectives
Programs	Programme Argo	Support of administrative cooperation in the fields of external borders, visas, asylum, and immigration
	Focal Point Offices program	Create local border guard departments in charge of border control in a defined area, with support guest officers
	Immigration Liaison Officers (ILOs) Network	Post officers from member states in a nonmember state to facilitate the measures taken by the EU to combat illegal immigration
Projects and joint operations at sea borders	Project Deniz	Take enforcement action in Turkey as a major source and transit country for illegal maritime migration (leader: UK)
	Ulysses	Reinforce operative systems used to prevent illegal immigration at sea borders (leader: Spain)
	Operation Triton	Produce concrete operational results on tackling illegal migration by sea (leader: Greece)
	Operation RIO IV	Improve the systems and procedures used at border controls in designated ports (leader: Spain)
	Operation Orca	Develop control routines at sea borders (leader: Norway)
Projects and joint operations at air borders	Operation VISA	Investigate the possible misuse of visas (leader: Denmark)
	International Airports Plan	Set up common standardized control procedures for international airports (leader: Italy)
	Rational Repatriation Procedures Project	Rationalize expulsion measures by means of group flights (leader: France)
Projects and joint operations at land borders	Operation at the Eastern External Land Borders	Monitor the variations of the migration flows: test the effectiveness of border control; promote cooperation between competent authorities (leader: Greece)
	IMMPACT Project (I & II)	Tackle people smuggling; provide specialist immigration training and advice to local border guards in Bosnia and Herzegovina; Serbia-Montenegro (leader: UK)

Table 8.1 (*continued*)

Type	Initiative	Objectives
Ad hoc Centers	Centre Land Borders	Test, coordinate, and evaluate operational cooperation in the practical management EU land borders
	Centre of Excellence Dover	Strengthen the EU external border by using modern search technology to combat illegal immigration
	The Risk Analysis Centre	Develop resources for gathering, analyzing, and disseminating information and data and recommending specific joint actions

Source: Author's elaboration of EU documents.

immigration liaison officers [ILOs], and asylum processing). As an illustration of the trends characterizing the EU foreign policy in this period, the next section takes into consideration two recent EU-sponsored proposals in this policy field: the external processing of refugee claims (ILOs).

Helping Refugees Out: The Case of Asylum's "External Processing"

The Tampere European Council established a general policy framework regarding policies on asylum. A key element in this plan was the creation of the Common European Asylum System. This system would guarantee a uniform asylum procedure and a similar set of rights for refugees valid throughout the Continent. Tampere also called for the organization of partnerships with immigrants' countries of origin, as part of the comprehensive approach the EU had proposed to tackle the root causes of unregulated population movements.

As was made apparent at Seville, EU member states were particularly worried about the perceived lack of cooperation from countries considered to be the main sources of illegal immigration. One of the solutions to this problem was elaborated by the British government. In March 2003, Prime Minister Tony Blair sent a proposal to create "external asylum processing centres" to the EU presidency, requesting that the issue of "better management of the asylum process" be added to the agenda of the next European Council.[50] The

50. Blair-Simitis letter, March 10, 2003, Prime Minister Office. The title of the paper attached to the letter is "New international approaches to asylum processing and protection." Available at: http://www.statewatch.org/news/2003/apr/blair-simitis-asile.pdf.

document envisaged the development of a system that guarantees "protection in the region" for refugees. The first stage of this project would see the "immediate transfer upon arrival anywhere within the territory of EU member states . . . all asylum seekers from the designated countries of origin" to "closed reception centres" located in one or two member states where they would be processed under a fast-track procedure. Those found in need of protection would be distributed around the EU, while "economic migrants" would be immediately sent back to the country of origin under EU-imposed readmission agreements or to detention centers in the region.

The proposal constituted the catalyst for an intense debate. Some NGOs and EU member states voiced their concerns about its principles and implications. An unexpected boost to the initiative came from the United Nations High Commissioner for Refugees (UNHCR), the agency responsible for the protection of refugees.[51] The following European Council (spring 2003) in its conclusions "noted" the British letter and invited the Commission to explore these ideas further. Responding to the invitation of the Council, the Commission drafted a communication on the issue of asylum, addressing the question of external processing.[52] In this document, the Commission examined the "serious and structural deficiencies" of the existing international protection system and concluded that there was a clear need to explore new avenues to tackle the issue. The Commission therefore embraced the main elements of the British proposal, that of protection in the region and resettlement. Such an approach would lead to "a more accessible, equitable and managed asylum system." It would enable persons in need of international protection to access such protection as soon as possible and as closely as possible to their needs, "*therewith reducing felt needs and pressures to seek international protection elsewhere.*"[53]

At the Luxembourg meeting of the Justice and Home Affairs Council (June 5–6, 2003), the issue of asylum "processing centres" was introduced by JHA Commissioner Vitorino, and it obtained a positive reception. Only the Swedish government voiced opposition. The Netherlands, Denmark, and

51. Shortly after the issuing of the British paper, the UNHCR presented a proposal for a new approach to processing asylum claims ("UNHCR's Three-Pronged Proposal," UNHCR Working Paper, Geneva, June 2003, mimeo). In this document the UN agency suggested measures to improve protection and solution arrangements in regions of origin, and an EU-based approach to dealing with essentially manifestly unfounded applications. In terms of general guidelines, this proposal followed those of the Blair project.

52. Commission of the European Communities, "Towards more accessible, equitable and managed asylum systems" (COM [2003] 315 final, June 2003).

53. Ibid. Emphasis added.

Austria, together with the United Kingdom, were strongly in favor. The controversial proposal to offshore asylum beyond Europe's borders, although still in its early stages, seemed to have achieved a solid basis of consensus, demonstrating once again how the new securitarian culture of border control was taking hold among Europe's border control community.

Immigration Liaison Officers: Pillars of an Emerging "Security Community"

Immigration liaison officers (ILOs) are government-appointed civil servants posted in selected third countries whose job is to obtain and exchange information on illegal immigration and related issues (e.g., illegal flows of immigrants, clandestine immigration networks, operating methods, use of false documents), to assist, advise, and train consular and diplomatic staff as well as airline companies, and to cooperate with the authorities of the host country. The establishment of ILOs was suggested at the Tampere European Council. The idea was not new. Since the mid-1980s, there already existed a tightly knit community among EU countries' liaison officers abroad. Until the 1990s, however, the status and mandate of ILOs were not clearly defined. Moreover, the policy framework in which they worked was largely informal.

After the signing of the Amsterdam Treaty, EU leaders decided to expand the ILO program and render it more coherent and structured. Its value in achieving the area of freedom, security, and justice was explicitly emphasized. By 2000, all the member states (except for Luxembourg and Ireland) already had liaison officers in other member states and/or third countries.[54] At the June 2002 JHA European Council meeting, EU ministers of interior and justice adopted the plan drawn up by the Spanish presidency for the management of EU external borders, which, among other things, called for the creation of ILOs. The move from an informal to a formal network of liaison officers was presented as "a progressive road towards enhanced co-operation and ever closer teamwork." The Seville European Council approved the plan and requested the creation of a network of member states' immigration liaison officers before the end of 2002. In July of the same year, the Strategic Committee on Immigration, Frontiers and Asylum, meeting with

---

54. "Note from the Secretariat to CIREFI, reporting on the number and features of existing Immigration Liaison Officers/Airline Liaison Officers" (7717/1/00, REV 1 CIREFI 17 COMIX 331 LIMITE).

the participation of the Heads of Border Control Services (SCIFA+), reached an agreement on the initiation of a network of liaison officers.[55]

As indicated, informal liaison between national officials from European governments and local authorities in other countries has occurred for some time. What is novel about recent developments is that liaison is now accorded a strategic significance and official status as part of the EU's quest for further integration. Unlike national bodies of customs, immigration, and police officers who manage a nation's borders, liaison officers foster cooperation *between* national agencies. Moreover, member states may bilaterally or multilaterally agree that ILOs are to look after the interests of one or more other member states. They may also decide to share certain tasks among themselves. As one report put it, ILOs could be considered the foundation of a "European security community,"[56] a community that extends beyond the geographical confines of the Schengen area.

The emergence of this community reinforces the trend toward the strengthening of what Bigo (2000a) calls an "archipelago of police," endowed with sweeping powers and little democratic control. By deploying this network, the EU and its member states are extending their surveillance over third countries and limiting the freedom of movement of their citizens. The EU has obtained the consent of the host countries to deploy ILOs. Yet non-EU countries are given little room to refuse. This program, like other remote control policies, therefore de facto represents an encroachment on their sovereignty.

"Schengen is not dead": The Dynamics of Europe's Border Control Community after Amsterdam

While the debate over the future of the area of freedom, security, and justice was under way, a less visible yet equally important "battle" was taking place within Europe's border control community over the control of the policymaking process in the justice and home affairs field. As for the policies described in the previous sections, the political dynamics characterizing this power struggle were clearly marked by Schengen tenets. The way this contest

55. 10917/1/02 REV 1 FRONT 69 CIREFI 42 COMIX 452. For an overview of the developments regarding the ILO program in this period, see the note from Presidency to SCIFA "The establishment of ILO network in third countries" (7462/03 LIMITE CIREFI 10 MIGR 20 COMIX 170, Brussels, March 14, 2003).

56. "Building a security community": the immigration liaisons officers (7717/1/00, REV 1 CIREFI 17 COMIX 331 LIMITE).

played out over time is thus another piece of evidence that, in the post-Amsterdam era, the Schengen culture of border control was consolidating.

Thanks to the Amsterdam Treaty, all the major EU institutions had been given a more prominent role in justice and home affairs matters. The Commission was the one that, in principle, should have gained more in terms of visibility and power. A review of its performance in the post-1999 period indicates that the Commission indeed exploited the complexity and incoherence of the JHA policymaking structure (it should be recalled that the Commission had to share the right of initiative with the Council in these matters for a five-year transitional period). At the Tampere Council, for example, the member states asked the Commission to make exclusive use of its initiative right on asylum issues, five years ahead of schedule. Subsequently, the Commission started working intensely on various initiatives, including two directives on temporary protection and minimum asylum standards. This was the first time that a binding Union policy instrument was being drafted by the Commission. Aware of its new responsibilities, the Commission quickly realized that the existing Task Force for Justice and Home Affairs in the Secretariat-General was insufficient to meet the requirements of the treaty and to carry out its constitutional mandate effectively. Soon after the new Prodi Commission was sworn in, one of the president's first moves was the creation of the new Directorate-General for Justice and Home Affairs (DG JHA), with greater power and staffing than its predecessor (Uçarer 2001: 11–12).

Despite this activism, the Commission's attempts to carve a leadership role for itself in this field were by and large unsuccessful. The Commission did not manage to offer a valid counterbalance to the Council. Not only did it have to give way to its institutional counterpart in the EU, but it also seemed to steer the direction of its policy initiatives more closely toward that of the Council. In its work on JHA issues, the Commission's involvement was in fact accompanied by a move toward more securitarian themes. In this sense, the Commission was "effectively recruited among the enemies of free movement, and while its role in this field has indeed expanded, rather than a promoter of the values of freedom it has become a coordinator of Interior Ministries' will" (Bigo and Guild 2003). This is the case, for example, for the imposition of readmission clauses to third countries. By repeatedly linking this policy issue to the broader "problem" of illegal immigration, it bought into the Council's securitarian discourse. Representative of this attitude is the suggestion, hinted at in a key communication on illegal immigration, that the EU "should also use its political weight to encourage third countries which show a certain reluctance to fulfil their readmission obligations."[57] In numerous occasions, the Commission has tried to defend its position on this subject.

> The sensitivity to crises, such as the tragic events of September 11, 2001 and March 11, 2004, have sometimes given rise to criticism that progress is made in an unbalanced way overemphasising security aspects. While this is the impression that may be given by certain media reports, European integration in this area is based on a rigorous concept of the protection of fundamental rights, and the Commission has always been at pains to ensure balance between the freedom, security and justice aspects. In addition, the Union must guarantee a high level of security so that the freedoms can be exercised to the full.[58]

Its rebuttals have not, however, completely dispelled the charge that the Commission could have been more vocal in emphasizing the "freedom" aspect of the EU project.

While the Commission was progressively stepping away from its traditional role as advocate of a comprehensive and liberal approach to border control, the European Council acquired more and more of the features and modus operandi that characterized the Schengen regime in the 1990s. Telling in this regard is the fact that the long-standing battle between the Ministries of Foreign Affairs and Interior that characterized the Schengen regime resurfaced within the EU institution. Tampere had given visibility to foreign ministers in justice and home affairs issues. Unlike their counterparts in the Interior Ministry, Foreign Affairs Ministers were present at the summit and actively participated in its organization. In the run-up to this event, the ministers of interior did not hide their disappointment about being excluded from participating in the event.[59] Despite this setback, the ministers of interior's involvement in diplomatic forums grew in this period (Guiraudon 2003: 272).[60] Their ascendancy within the EU meant that the

---

57. Commission of the European Communities, "Communication from the Commission to the Council and the European Parliament on a common policy on illegal immigration" (COM [2001] 672 final, Nov. 15, 2001), section 4.8.

58. Commission of the European Communities, "Area of Freedom, Security and Justice: Assessment of the Tampere programme and future orientations," staff working paper (COM [2004] 4002 final, June 6, 2004).

59. On this point, see the debate at the Luxembourg JHA Council of October 4, 1998.

60. For instance, in February 2000, during the negotiations of the revision of the fourth Lomé convention between the EU fifteen and seventy-one African, Caribbean, and Pacific countries, interior ministers insisted that a clause of readmission of illegal migrants be included in the final text and threatened to block the agreement (Guiraudon 2003: 272).

tug of war with the Foreign Ministries, albeit at a low intensity, continued to characterize the political dynamics within the border control domain.

Schengen-like features were also presented in the various working groups active within the European Council. The Commission tried to infuse the idea that Schengen was "dead"; yet the message was difficult to get across. For most participants in the Council's meetings there was a sense that they could adopt the same informal and pragmatic style that had defined the Schengen regime.[61] This attitude was hard to eradicate, partly because some of the EU officials and members of national delegations in these groups were actively involved with Schengen before the regime was incorporated into the EU. For instance, Charles Elsen, the then director of the Council's DG JHA, before being appointed to this position, for many years represented Luxembourg in the Schengen Executive Committee.

This "Schengenized" worldview among Council officials was in turn translated into the organization and functioning of new working groups. The High Level Working Group on Asylum and Migration is a good case in point. The group was created after Amsterdam to give more clout to the Council's foreign policy. Despite the progressive elements present in its mandate (namely, devising a comprehensive approach to border control), the group clearly had a securitarian orientation. Among its stated aims, it had to devise policies directed at curbing migratory flows toward Europe.[62] Its presence also created tension with the Commission. The group was acting under the auspices of the Council and thus outside the normal Commission structures for formulating and implementing foreign policy. As such, it generated problems of consistency and coordination with other EU external relations activities (Boswell 2003: 21).

The dispute involving the High Level Working Group on Asylum and Migration was a symptom of a deeper tension between the Council and the Commission over issues of competence in the JHA field. It is on this subject that in July 2001 the Commission commenced legal proceedings before the European Court of Justice against the Council, seeking to annul two regulations passed that year that gave authority to member states to examine visa

---

61. Author's interview with Commission official, formerly in Working Group Visas, July 10, 2004.

62. "Terms of reference of the High Level Working Group on Asylum and Migration." See also "Modification of the terms of reference of the High Level Working Group on Asylum and Migration (HLWG)," from COREPER to Council: 9433/02 2002 JAI 109AG 20 ASIM 18, Brussels, May 30, 2002.

applications and to carry out checks at EU external borders.[63] The Commission argued that the measures were too generic to be lawful and that they would reserve implementing powers to the Council, not allowing member states to exercise those powers independently. The Court found in favor of the Council.[64] In its judgment it stressed the role of the five-year transitional period as a phase that allowed flexibility in the management of borders. Moreover, considering the political sensitivity of the subject matter, the enhanced role of the member states in respect to visas and border surveillance "are such as to show clearly the grounds justifying the reservation of powers to the Council."[65]

Assessing Border Control after Amsterdam: Schengen Still Going Strong[66]

Since the ratification of the Amsterdam Treaty, the justice and home affairs domain has been one of the most dynamic within the EU, taking up a big part of the legislative work within the Union. In this period, the EU Council adopted between eighty and one hundred texts—most of which were legally binding—per year (Monar 2003b: 2). This activism invested all aspects of the border control domain, from immigration, asylum, and visa policy, to rules regarding the management of borders. In evaluating the work accomplished in this period, the Commission claimed that progress in most areas of justice and home affairs was "undeniable and tangible."[67] Other commentators seem to agree. According to Monar, the pace of progress had been "impressive, especially if compared to the nineties" (Monar 2003b: 2). Yet five years after its launch, only a small part of the treaty objectives and the items of the Tampere agenda had been implemented. As the European Commission recognized, it was not always possible to reach European-level agreement for the adoption of "certain sensitive measures relating to policies

---

63. "Regulation 789/2001 reserving to the Council implementing powers regarding certain provisions and practical procedures for examining visa applications" and "Regulation 790/2001 reserving to the Council implementing powers with regard to certain detailed provisions and practical procedures for carrying out border checks and surveillance." For an analysis of this case, see Guild 2006.

64. C-257/01 *Commission v Council*, 18 Jan. 2005.

65. Ibid., par. 52.

66. The title of this section is borrowed from Den Boer 2000.

67. Commission of the European Communities, "The Area of Freedom, Security and Justice: assessment of the Tampere programme and future orientations," Staff Working Paper (COM [2004] 4002 final, June 6, 2004).

which remain at the core of national sovereignty," such as asylum and immigration policy.[68] The original ambition was "limited by institutional constraints, and sometimes also by a lack of sufficient political consensus."[69]

If the final evaluation of the success in achieving the Tampere goals is mixed, seen from a cultural evolutionary perspective the developments within Europe's border control domain since the incorporation of Schengen into the EU instead indicate a trend toward the consolidation of the newly selected culture of border control. Indeed, if we look closely at the evolution of discourses and practices in this field we can notice how Schengen's assumptions (i.e., an overemphasis on security matters, the central role of governments, flexibility as the preferred working method, limited judicial and democratic control) have been progressively internalized by members of the border control community and expanded to new policy realms. Since the turn of the millennium, there has been less debate on the core foundations of the new governance system (e.g., What is the meaning of the "common external border"? Is an intensive transgovernmental approach consistent with the goal of European integration? Why should security be the premise to achieve freedom?). Discussions have instead switched to concrete proposals to advance and extend the new type of governance. At the same time, despite the greater involvement of EU institutions, border control has turned into a full-fledged Schengenized domain. Attempts to further communitarize it have generally been unsuccessful. On the other hand, thanks to the formal incorporation of its *acquis* into the EU institutional framework, Schengen's assumptions and practices have spread throughout this policy domain, influencing areas that hitherto had been only tangentially affected, such as the relations with the Union's neighbors. Even traditionally fierce opponents, such as the United Kingdom, softened their stance against Schengen and opted in to a growing number of its provisions and programs.[70]

68. Ibid.

69. Ibid.

70. The Schengen Information System, for example, became partially applicable in the United Kingdom on December 22, 2004. A government official summarized London's stance on Schengen in testimony to the House of Commons: "We take a close interest as we believe a strong Schengen border is in our interests as is a strong UK border in the interests of the EU as a whole" (182 Ev 133; p.66) House of Commons, Home Affairs Committee, *Justice and Home Affairs Issues at European Union Level: Third Report of Session 2006–07*, vol. 1, *Report, together with formal minutes* (London: Stationery Office Limited, 2007). The British government has not, however, become a full-fledged Schengen member because it maintains its reservation on the abolition of national border controls.

Schengen's consolidation was not, however, an inevitable development. As the experience of the creation of an EU-based justice and home affairs policy domain in the early 1990s showed, the communitarization of border control in itself was not sufficient to guarantee the survival of the new culture. Schengen could still have become irrelevant or could have even folded. It therefore had to be actively sustained and reproduced by members of the border control community in order to maintain its dominant position. At the same time, it had to counter challenges to its newly established dominant position. Supporters of alternative approaches (viz., communitarian and nationalist) were still active among the border control community. External threats, such as international terrorism and other cross-border crimes, also frequently put to the test the culture's resilience.[71]

These developments, however, did not substantially change the course of Europe's border control domain. On one hand, supporters of communitarian and nationalist approaches have been relegated to the margins of the policymaking process, and their impact has been limited. On the other, border control was already going along the securitization path, and threats such as terrorism simply accelerated this trend. From a political perspective, in the post-9/11 world the prioritization of security over other concerns was in fact legitimized, becoming a new, unchallengeable dogma. In turn, the "comprehensive" response to the terrorism adopted by EU governments and institutions has contributed to the further blurring of the distinction between internal and external security and to the deemphasis of the importance of national borders to guarantee Europe's security. These developments have therefore had the effect of reinforcing, rather than challenging, the ongoing process of consolidation of Schengen as the new dominant culture of border control in Europe.

71. On the impact of the recent wave of terrorism on the justice and home affairs field in Europe, see Guild 2003.

NINE

Beyond Europe: Toward a New Culture of Border Control in North America?

I think that if we had policies on immigration and refugee status that were more common, we could establish this perimeter to protect the United States and Canada, and I think that is where we should be headed.

—Paul Cellucci, US ambassador to Canada, 2001

When you say "perimeter," people think the European model where you erase the internal borders. That is not what we are talking about.

—Elinor Caplan, Canadian immigration minister

The challenge for us, now, is that [the US-Canada friendship] needs to be continually reinvigorated and reenergized in the midst of this culture change where there really does need to be a border, and there really do need to be protections back and forth, and we really do need to think about how that's going to work so that it does not unduly impact all of the trade that must be able to flow back and forth.

—Janet Napolitano, US secretary of homeland security

Transatlantic Flights: Cultural Evolution and North American Borders

No other region in the world has achieved Europe's level of political and economic integration in recent times. Having gained this unique (some would say "exceptional") status does not mean, however, that insights drawn from the European experience cannot be cogently applied to other contexts. In this chapter, I intend to demonstrate that a pragmatist cultural evolutionary model can indeed "travel" beyond Europe and be used to examine instances of epochal change in the border control domain in other parts of the world. North America is the region where this analytical framework seems particularly promising. Europe and North America's political worldviews and policies are often at odds with each other, and these differences are reflected in their approaches to border control. (North American governments, for instance, have not established a border-free regime like their European counterparts.) Despite these differences, there are important parallels with the recent history of this policy field in Europe that warrant the application of a cultural evolutionary model of policy change across the Atlantic. The most relevant is that, in the last decade, North America has undergone a similar epochal change with regard to border control. After the terrorist attacks on American soil on September 11, 2001, North American policy makers—mainly in the United States but, to a certain extent, also in Canada and Mexico—have introduced a series of policy initiatives that have radically transformed the way territoriality is managed in the region. Although not in the same manner as their European counterparts, they too have moved away from traditional territorial models and embraced a "post-Westphalian" approach to border control, an approach that is based on a new conceptualization of territory, security, sovereignty, and international relations.[1]

If indeed in North America there has been an epochal change in border control policy, how can a cultural evolutionary account explain this development? The premise of this line of inquiry is that, at any given time, in North America the border control domain is characterized by a set of assumptions and practices that inform the way policy makers go about their everyday management of borders. The emergence of a new approach to border control in the region can therefore be conceptualized as being the result of the evolution from a long-standing nationalist culture (a North American version of Westphalia) to a "neonational" one, a culture which I call

---

1. Admittedly, the case for an epochal change in North America's border control domain is less apparent than for Europe's. Indeed, some commentators discard this idea altogether (see, for example, Rudolph 2005). These commentators point to the degree of continuity between the pre- and post- 9/11 systems and to the fact that, unlike Europe, North America has not witnessed the same unprecedented event that is the abolition of national border controls and, more generally, the same level of regional integration. While these arguments are factually correct, those who use them to support their skeptical views tend to conflate the idea of European-style political integration with epochal change in a given policy field. There are equally valid alternative scenarios to these types of transformations, as the events in North America described in the following paragraphs can attest.

the *Washington culture of border control.*[2] Here I will explain this evolution, starting with the challenges to the Westphalian model of border control in the latter part of the twentieth century, and then turning to the post-9/11 emergence of the Washington culture of border control, its pursuit, and its (still unfinished) selection.

Challenging Westphalia: A North American Perspective

Whether directly (through colonization) or indirectly (as influential template to emulate), Europe has been the inspiration for the development of the modern territorial state in North America. Since becoming independent political entities, the United States, Canada, and Mexico have adopted different institutional arrangements to protect their territories. Canada, and to a certain extent the United States, has relied on the British model, while Mexico was influenced by the Continental European tradition. These arrangements were adapted to the particular geopolitical situation these countries faced. Most borders in the region were not "settled" until late in the nineteenth century; indeed, in this period we can talk about "frontiers," rather than clearly marked and patrolled "borders," to describe these states' outer limits.

It is only at the turn of the twentieth century that the foundations of the Westphalian model were consolidated. This phase coincided with the crystallization of the national territory and a greater assertiveness of central governments over the states' borders. New and larger, albeit not always well-coordinated, bureaucracies were established to manage and protect the national territory and its borders.[3] The first official immigration policies were implemented, passports were introduced, and border controls were beefed up.

As in Europe, the Westphalian model of border control in North America was never perfectly practiced. Until recently, for example, the policing of the

---

2. As for previous examples, this geographical reference is meant to be evocative of the culture's spirit. "Washington," in this context, does not refer solely to the US city, but to a particular way of dealing with borders, which is indeed US-driven but has been, by and large, adopted by Canada and Mexico. This approach, as we will see, is still government-centric—hence the reference to the US capital as site of government—but is more fragmented than in earlier times and has a significant foreign policy component.

3. Unlike its northern neighbors, after independence Mexico instituted a European-style ministry of interior ("Secretaría de Gobernación"), which was the lead agency responsible for the management of borders. The United States and Canada only recently created the equivalent of such a ministry (see below).

US-Canada border was relatively "light," deserving the title of "world's longest undefended border." Yet, until the second part of the twentieth century, these "quirks" did not represent a serious threat to the model's foundations. Recent geopolitical developments both within and outside the region, however, began to change this state of affairs. The most serious was the growing migratory pressure that has affected North America since the 1970s. The United States and Canada have been the favorite destinations of migratory flows in the region, while Mexico has been their main source. The response of the US government, and to a lesser extent Canada's, has been to follow the traditional nationalist route, with the creation of ever-higher barriers and the introduction of stricter immigration policies. The failure of these measures, however (illegal migration in the region has actually increased over the years), has put into question the validity of this approach among pragmatic policy makers. Economic globalization is another important factor challenging statecentric approaches to border control in North America. The trend toward greater economic liberalization has put pressure on governments to ease their grip on borders to facilitate the flow of goods and people. The creation of the North American Free Trade Agreement (NAFTA) between the United States, Canada, and Mexico in the 1990s was an attempt to address this issue. While opening up borders for goods and services, the agreement did not entail the complete lifting of barriers to the cross-border movement of people across the continent. As in the European case, the economically driven calls for the easing of border controls have clashed with the growing anxiety over the security implications of cross-border illegal activities. The tension between freedom of movement and security, which was brewing in the 1990s, exploded in full force in the new millennium, shaking to the core the Westphalia edifice in North America.

The events of 9/11 were the catalyst for this development. It was not the first time that North America was the target of terrorist attacks.[4] Until then, however, terrorism was not a top priority on the region's political agendas, and it was not considered an issue directly affecting North America's territorial security. The lack of political urgency meant that no systemic reorganization of national security apparatuses took place. That all changed

---

4. Al Qaeda had already struck American targets in the 1990s (New York's Twin Towers, and the US embassies in Kenya and Tanzania). In the same decade, the United States had also witnessed homegrown terror, the most notorious being the 1995 Oklahoma bombing. Canada suffered a major terrorist attack in the mid-1980s with the downing of an Air India plane flying over the Atlantic Ocean, an attack planned in British Columbia by a local terrorist cell. Mexico was less directly affected by international terrorism, although the violence related to drug trafficking could be construed as a sort of domestic "terror."

after the attacks by al Qaeda. Their magnitude was unprecedented and their impact devastating, affecting all fields of North American life. With it, the myth of the region's insularity was shattered. Policy makers in Washington and in other national capitals became more aware of their countries' territorial vulnerability. Borders in particular acquired an unprecedented political relevance.

In this politically charged environment, North American policy makers were compelled to question existing approaches to border security and to search for new solutions to address the shortcomings that had rendered 9/11 possible. As the "9/11 Commission," the group of experts set up by the US government to bring to light the weaknesses of the existing system of homeland protection and to give recommendations on how to improve it, put it:

> The United States faces a sudden crisis and summons a tremendous exertion of national energy. Then, as that surge transforms the landscape, comes a time for reflection and reevaluation. Some programs and even agencies are discarded; others are invented or redesigned . . . Now is the time for that reflection and reevaluation. The United States should consider *what to do*—the shape and objectives of a strategy. Americans should also consider *how to do it*—organizing their government in a different way.[5]

This strategic rethinking started soon after the debris of the attacks had settled, sowing the seeds of a new culture of border control in the region.

The Birth of the Washington Culture of Border Control

In its final report, the 9/11 Commission listed a damning series of shortcomings of existing US policies in the homeland security field, from lax borders and poor communication among agencies inadequate funding, and called for a fundamental reformulation of the entire approach to domestic and international security in the United States.[6] Albeit narrower in scope, the Canadian and Mexican governments followed the American example and launched internal reviews of their security policies. This policy review process led to the drafting of new legislation (e.g., the US Patriot Act and Canada's Antiterrorism Act and Immigration and Refugee Protection Act)

---

5. *The 9/11 Commission Report: Final Report of the National Commission on Terrorist Attacks upon the United States*, official government edition (Washington, DC: US GPO, 2004), 361.

6. *The 9/11 Commission Report*, 339 et seq.

and strategic plans of actions for homeland security (the 2002 National Homeland Security Strategy in the United States; the 2004 National Security Policy in Canada). Taken together, these documents outline a relatively coherent set of new assumptions and practices that should regulate North American borders and guide policy makers in the everyday management of homeland security in the post-9/11 era. These assumptions and practices constitute the foundations of the emerging Washington culture of border control.[7]

Table 9.1 shows the culture's key tenets. This culture, like its European counterpart, is regional and is characterized by a set of assumptions about the meaning of "borders," their management, the policy community responsible for it, the community's practices, and internal dynamics. The new culture is *neonational*, for the state as sovereign territorial unit remains the main term of reference. The object that should be protected and the means to accomplish this task are, however, substantially reformulated. To capture the object that should be protected, a rarely used term is resumed: "homeland."[8] The term has an explicit territorial connotation. The protection of the "land," however, is not restricted to the national territory proper. While homeland security "is a concerted national effort to prevent terrorist attacks *within* the United States, reduce America's vulnerability to terrorism, and

7. Unlike the European case, in North America there was only one major alternative to the existing Westphalian model of border control. One of the options put on the table by some scholars and policy makers was that of a "North American Community," which would have involved a deeper degree of integration of various sectoral fields, including homeland security and an advanced regional institutional framework (Pastor 2001). This option is similar to the "Brussels" initiative as described in previous chapters. The idea had been flagged in the past, but, as we will see shortly, it was put on the back burner in the aftermath of 9/11, in favor of more "securitarian" measures to protect the North American homeland. Although there has been renewed interest in recent times (see, for example, "Building a North American Community," the 2005 Report of the US Council of Foreign Relations–sponsored task force chaired by John P. Manley, Pedro Aspe and William F. Weld), North American governments have not officially endorsed the initiative, and thus its underlying culture was never formally pursued. For this reason, this initiative is not treated as an alternative culture of border control for the purpose of a cultural evolutionary argument.

8. Since 2001, "homeland" and "homeland security" have become common terms in US public and official discourse to define the new policy field. Canada and Mexico have generally shied away from using this terminology. Canadian officials prefer talking about "public safety," while Mexico has stuck with the more traditional "internal security." In practice, however, the two countries' approach to territorial protection has converged toward the American model; see more on this point below. It should be noted that the US does have a "Department of the Interior." Unlike its European homonyms, however, this ministry's mandate is not securitarian but "ecological," namely the management and conservation of land owned by the federal government.

Table 9.1 Washington culture of border control: key tenets

Time frame	2001–2010+
Borders	Semilinear; "smart"/filter, extensible, layered (national and extranational), partially unbundled (only security), homeland's outer limits
Border control	National and extraterritorial, governmental, limited pooling, securitized, policing function, asymmetric responsibilities, virtual/technological
Type of practices	Transgovernmental, bi-/multilateral, asymmetric, flexible, informal

Border control community:
    Identity
    Composition
	
	National
	Officials from national governments (ministries of interior, experts)

Relevant texts	9/11 Commission Report; 2002 US National Strategy for Homeland Security; national strategies of Canada and Mexico

minimize the damage and recover from attacks that do occur,"[9] if necessary, the homeland's boundaries can be stretched beyond their physical location. Indeed, the US National Homeland Security Strategy is largely based on policy proposals to "push U.S. borders out" (Flynn 2000) beyond US territorial boundaries. The goal is to "extend our zone of security outward, so that American seaports and borders become the last line of defense, not the first."[10] These "extraterritorial" borders are the homeland's outer limits and coexist with national borders; they are not linear, but "a continuum framed by land, sea, and air dimensions."[11] To some extent, Canada and Mexico have embraced this new vision of territoriality. One feature of Canada's "comprehensive approach" to border control, for instance, is "applying the smart borders principles internationally."[12] In the United States, however, these changes, especially the extraterritorial dimension of border control, are a more central component of the border strategy and their implications more wide-ranging.

9. Office of Homeland Security, "National Strategy for Homeland Security" (July 2002), 2. Available at http://www.dhs.gov/xlibrary/assets/nat_strat_hls.pdf.

10. Remarks by Secretary Tom Ridge at the Port of Newark, New Jersey, June 12, 2003. Available at http://www.dhs.gov/xnews/speeches/speech_0118.shtm.

11. Office of Homeland Security, "National Strategy for Homeland Security" (July 2002), 22.

12. "National Security Strategy 2004," 46.

This reconceptualization of borders is reflected in the formulation of a new approach to their management. Border controls are explicitly linked to the issue of security and, more specifically, to the protection against terrorism. In the US and Canadian homeland security strategies, border and transportation security is a "critical mission area" that should contribute to the prevention of new attacks, the reduction in vulnerability, and the minimization of damage from such attacks. Such an area requires the upgrading and integration of border controls, which should become "smart," that is, allow desirable people and goods in and leave out the unwanted.[13] Advanced technology tracking the movement of people and goods by land, air, and sea should accomplish this task. These activities should start at the source of potential threats, since "the border of the future must integrate actions abroad to screen goods and people prior to their arrival in sovereign US territory."[14]

In the emerging culture, national governments are still the primary authority responsible for border control. Unlike the European case, no regional supranational or intergovernmental agency is envisioned. As in Europe, however, there are calls for the expansion and diversification of the border control policy community. The organization of the border security apparatus was a legacy of the Cold War and was understood to make little sense for dealing with the new problem of transnational terrorism.[15] The proposed solution was to create a dedicated governmental agency that would put the hitherto scattered agencies dealing with border issues under a single leadership and institutional umbrella. The new Department of Homeland Security ("Public Safety and Emergency Preparedness" in Canada) would be working side by side with other governmental actors traditionally responsible for border issues (e.g., ministries of foreign affairs, immigration, transportation, and finance).

The revamped border control policy community should be more heavily and aggressively involved in foreign affairs. Indeed, one of the implications of the externalization of border control is that external relations in this field would become paramount. International cooperation is actively encouraged, even in countries where unilateralism is deeply rooted, such as the United States. As the 9/11 Commission put it,

---

13. "Office of Homeland Security, "National Strategy for Homeland Security" (July 2002), viii.
14. White House fact sheet, "Border Security," Jan. 25, 2002.
15. *The 9/11 Commission Report*, 428.

The US government cannot meet its own obligations to the American people to prevent the entry of terrorists without a major effort to collaborate with other governments. We should do more to exchange terrorist information with trusted allies, and raise U.S. and global border security standards for travel and border crossing over the medium and long term through extensive cooperation.[16]

The areas indicated for this cooperation include emergency preparedness, intelligence, law enforcement, and land, sea, and air border security, and it should involve neighboring and overseas countries and international organizations (e.g., the International Maritime Organization and the International Civil Aviation Organization).[17] Since homeland security is still considered primarily a national prerogative touching upon issues of sovereignty, intergovernmental relations are still characterized by competitiveness, especially vis-à-vis partners beyond North America.

As the key role in border control policymaking is placed upon governmental agencies (especially the homeland security departments), the expectation is that relations among countries in the region and beyond should involve mainly these policy actors. As in Schengen, the border control governance mode in North America is therefore a sort of "intensive transgovernmentalism." While multilateral efforts are encouraged both within the region and abroad, there is no explicit call for the institutionalization of these relations, which remain mainly informal. Bilateral and informal contacts are still considered the primary means of solving collective problems. Unilateral action, however, is not completely abandoned and is still considered a valid option if other methods fail. As part of its "national vision," the United States is thus "sensitive to treaty and other obligations; however, where we find existing international arrangements to be inadequate or counterproductive to our efforts to secure our homeland, we will work to refashion them."[18]

Taken together, the set of assumptions about borders and their management that were elaborated in North America after 9/11 represented the foundations of the emerging culture of border control that have since guided policy makers in the region.

16. *The 9/11 Commission Report*, 390.
17. Office of Homeland Security, "National Strategy for Homeland Security" (July 2002); Canada National Security Policy 2004: 37–40.
18. Office of Homeland Security, "US National Strategy for Homeland Security" (2002), 59.

The Pursuit of Washington Culture: "Pushing Borders Out"

The reformulation of the approach to border control in North America in the wake of 9/11 had become unavoidable. Whether the type of response envisaged by the homeland security strategy plans presented in this period would have been successful, however, was far from certain. Paraphrasing US defense secretary Donald Rumsfeld's notorious quip, there were too many "known unknowns" in this policy domain. For some critics, the planned bureaucratic build-up was a recipe for inefficiency and failure. In some apocalyptic scenarios, the entire North American economic and transportation system would be disrupted as a result of the shutting down of borders. An ever more powerful "big brother" government would infringe on individual citizens' rights through the extensive use of electronic surveillance at borders and beyond. Moreover, the extraterritorial nature of the new approach would inevitably lead to tension both within the region and beyond.

As their European counterparts experienced when establishing the Schengen border regime, North American policy makers were embarking on a difficult journey in their quest for a post-Westphalian approach to border control. As a result, this pursuit had to be justified with a convincing argument to support this "leap into the dark." The official narrative that was elaborated in the United States and that reverberated throughout the region was based on the theme "Never Again!"—that is, never again would there be a terrorist attack on North American soil. The reference to 9/11 thus became a sort of trump card that could be deployed to defend controversial decisions that would hitherto have been unimaginable. The protection of the nation was paramount.

While preventing new attacks became the overarching theme in the construction of the new homeland security domain (see, for example, the US National Strategy for Homeland Security), more specific arguments were used to legitimize the pursuit of border-related initiatives. This was particularly the case for one of their most controversial aspects, namely, their extraterritoriality. If threats are global, the argument went, so border controls should be global. The idea of addressing a problem at its source was inspired by the military doctrine of *preemption*. This doctrine was resumed in this period to justify military interventions in Afghanistan and Iraq and was then applied by imitation to a nonmilitary domain such as homeland security. Preemption allows governments to maintain the initiative by setting the agenda and directly controlling a policy and its implementation. Unlike the military doctrine, however, preemption in homeland security does not involve overt prevarication, for third parties willing to accept a limitation of their sovereignty are needed for the policy to be successful. This explains the repeated reference to international cooperation that characterizes North American homeland security strategies developed in this period.

The United States clearly set the tone of the arguments used to pursue the new culture of border control in North America. In the early stages of the emerging Washington culture of border control, the Canadian and Mexican governments had little influence on the process. Despite their reservations about some of the implications of the new policies, the two governments agreed on the key principles underlying the new culture, especially the fact that a more aggressive stance regarding border security was necessary in the post-9/11 world. Pragmatically, they also realized that pursuing the new initiative would help maintain a working relationship with their powerful neighbor. The stage was therefore set for a new phase in the Washington culture's evolutionary process.

Selecting Washington: From "Smart Borders" to Transatlantic Dialogues

The first concrete steps toward the selection of the Washington culture of border control took place in the months that followed the events of 9/11. From early 2002, the US administration started to address some of the requests made by Congress to increase the security of the country's land, sea, and air borders. The new measures included the Container Security Initiative (CSI), which entailed a series of agreements between American and foreign port authorities to permit American inspectors to prescreen shipping containers destined for the United States; the collection of passenger name records (PNRs) on US-bound flights; and a rule that foreigners entering the United States hold biometric passports. These provisions had serious practical implications both for the United States and for its regional and international partners, for they added new security requirements to the flow of goods and people into and within North America. Some of these measures were contentious and created political tensions between the US government and its regional and transatlantic partners. All parties involved, however, had compelling political and economic reasons to find a solution to these problems. The United States also needed other governments' support for the new measures to be effective.

The interactions between the United States and its regional and international partners took the form of ongoing negotiations and "dialogues" among senior policy makers from relevant ministries (mainly homeland security and foreign affairs), supported by the work of experts. These diplomatic practices, and the policy outcomes they produced (agreements, new policy measures), represented the first applications of the emerging Washington culture of border control, and they functioned as a training ground toward its final selection.

In the next sections I consider three instances of the Washington culture's selection process as it has unfolded in the last decade. I begin with dynamics within North America, focusing on the debate between the United States and Canada over the project of a "North American Security Perimeter." I then turn to the Security and Prosperity Partnership of North America (SPP), a trilateral initiative aimed at expanding the security perimeter to Mexico. Finally, I examine the selection process's external dimension, addressing some of the thorniest disputes to recently characterize the relations between North America and Europe over issues of homeland security.

Playing It Smart: The United States, Canada, and the North American Security Perimeter

Because of their geographical proximity and high level of interdependence with the United States, Canada and Mexico were the countries that felt more directly the effects of their neighbor's new border policies. The tightening of controls indeed seriously hampered the movement of people and goods across their common frontiers, becoming a source of contention in the relations among the three North American governments. It is in this context that the idea of a North America security perimeter was put on the table. Presented as a way to strike a balance between the often clashing needs of security and freedom of movement, a security perimeter entails the coordination of entry controls for visitors arriving in the region so that less scrutiny would be needed at land borders.

Although the idea had been flagged in the past (Noble 2005), it was only after 9/11 that it gained political traction. The debate focused primarily on a perimeter around Canada and the United States, since Mexico was deemed unsuitable for such a project (see more on this point below). Policy makers and the business community in the US and, at least initially, Canada, enthusiastically endorsed the project. From a Canadian perspective, a North American perimeter could have deepened the already existing military arrangement with their southern neighbor (centered on the North American Aerospace Defense Command [NORAD]) into a more comprehensive security perimeter that would enhance physical and economic security. Senior Canadian officials, however, were nervous about any policy that would leave them open to charges of compromising Canadian sovereignty. The Canadian government therefore quietly distanced itself from the notion of "perimeter" in their public statements. The new buzzword became the more politically neutral "zone of confidence." As one Canadian official put it, "We were the ones who started using the word perimeter and it started to resonate in the U.S. But all of a sudden, it became a dirty word in Canadian circles."[19]

Despite this shift in tone by the Canadian government, discussions on the implementation of the security perimeter continued behind the scenes. Throughout the fall and winter of 2001, teams of Canadian and American bureaucrats met regularly in Washington and Ottawa to discuss a wide variety of concerns.[20] Canada's foreign affairs minister, John Manley, who was the lead figure in this file in the cabinet, and his American counterpart, homeland security secretary Tom Ridge, exchanged views and assured each other of their commitment to the project. The change in terminology notwithstanding, the security perimeter was "really what these Manley-Ridge discussions amount(ed) to."[21] It is in this period that the United States and Canada hammered out the first practical steps toward the creation of such a zone. The institutional framework that formalized and gave coherence and political direction to this initiative was the Canada-US Smart Border Declaration.[22] The declaration, signed by Manley and Ridge on December 12, 2001, set out the principles of the initiative and its objectives. The action plan that accompanied the declaration outlined the practical steps necessary to achieve these goals. The list of proposed measures included the development of common standards for biometrics and the adoption of a compatible technology for reading them; an integrated approach for processing truck, rail, and marine cargo away from the border; the sharing of customs data; a bilateral arrangement to eliminate "asylum shopping" by refugee applicants; consultation on visa policy, sharing advance passenger information and passenger name records concerning high-risk travelers; and

19. Allan Thompson, "It's time for homeland hardball"—Ridge warns that the tough part is about to begin. Entry-exit registry will be next major sticking point, *Toronto Star*, 22 Dec. 2002.

20. For example, Canadian officials were talking about cooperating with US authorities on a system for dealing with the entry of third-country nationals, in effect, a common policy for visitor visa requirements (ibid.).

21. Thompson, "It's time for homeland hardball."

22. "The Smart Border Declaration: Building a Smart Border for the 21st Century on the Foundation of a North American Zone of Confidence," Ottawa, Dec. 12, 2001.

the development of compatible immigration databases to facilitate regular information exchanges.

Even if it is not explicitly referred to in terms of security perimeter, the agreement and the plan of action contain *in nuce* the project's key components,[23] components that are consistent with the emerging Washington culture of border control. While the US-Canadian border is reinforced, it is more layered, and it is expanded beyond the national territory. By taking the first steps toward the harmonization—or, at least, an advanced coordination—of border practices, the United States and Canada's external borders are de facto becoming the outer limits of a "North American homeland." Despite the new bilateral regime's limited institutionalization, the ongoing convergence of border practices means that the US and Canadian governments are indeed pooling some of their sovereignty. Moreover, by emphasizing the "smart" nature of these practices, the two governments are attempting to strike a new balance between security and freedom of movement across their common border.[24]

The declaration and the new vision of US-Canadian border control it entailed was an important stepping stone in the evolution of the Washington culture of border control. Its successful implementation in fact contributed to the culture's institutionalization in the region. One of the most visible achievements in the aftermath of the initiative's launch (coinciding with the end of the first Bush Administration in the United States) was the creation of special regimes for cross-border travelers. Following a recommendation of the 9/11 Commission, the US Congress passed new border security legislation that mandated the implementation of an entry-exit system, now called United States Visitor and Immigrant Status Indicator Technology (US-VISIT). To render this system "smarter," the United States negotiated with Canada a series of programs to facilitate traffic for preregistered passengers (the Nexus program) and truckers (FAST). Security measures at the common border were also improved. The Integrated Border Enforcement Teams (IBETs), a multiagency law enforcement teams targeting cross-border criminal activity, were revamped. Originally established in 1996 along the

23. Some commentators go as far as to argue that a security perimeter in North America has already been in place for some time in the military field, and thus debates about its existence are "sterile" (Noble 2005: 461). Today the perimeter is "steadily being strengthened in other fields in light of the changing nature of the security threats to North America" (ibid.).

24. The position of the two governments differed over this balance. The United States was clearly more interested in the security dimension, whereas Canada was concerned about the economic side. Despite the key role that Canada played in the drafting of the declaration—it was the Canadian government that presented US negotiators with the first draft of the agreement—security concerns remained paramount.

border in the western region of Washington State to combat drug smuggling and illegal immigration, these teams were expanded across the entire US-Canada border. The two governments also tackled the issue of asylum seekers crossing the border. Under a bilateral agreement reached in June 2002, known as the Safe Third Country Agreement, if an alien seeks to travel from the United States to Canada (or vice versa) through a land border port of entry to apply for asylum, he or she will be sent back to the first of the two countries in which the alien traveled. The justification for this move was that both are parties to the protocol relating to the status of refugees and thus considered to be "safe."

The change in leadership over this file in both the United States and Canada, especially in the Homeland Security Department in the second Bush administration (which was more hawkish and unilateralist than the previous one) took away the political impetus that the Manley-Ridge partnership had hitherto provided, thus slowing down the pace of the implementation of the Smart Border Declaration. The concrete results obtained in the early stages of the initiative, however, persuaded the two sides of the viability and the added value of the project of a security perimeter around North America, even if it had to be achieved by small incremental steps. It is on these grounds that a discussion began about the expansion of the regime to Mexico.

The SPP: Expanding the North American Perimeter?

Although discussion about the North American security perimeter was mostly restricted to the United States and Canada, some of the bilateral measures proposed in the Smart Border initiative were put into practice with Mexico as well. The Favored Travelers initiative between the United States and its southern neighbor (known as SENTRI) is a good case in point. The Mexican government had lobbied for a regional approach to border control in the past. After the signing of the Canada-US Smart Border Declaration, calls for the expansion of the North American perimeter became louder. The issues at stake were not just about its "widening" (whether it should include Mexico), but also about its "deepening" (whether it should provide for both physical and economic security and for the full mobility of labor), and also about the steps required to achieve it (whether it could be constructed as part of a comprehensive "strategic bargain" or through a "moderate" or "aggressive" incrementalism [Noble 2005: 461]).

Both the United States and Mexico seemed to favor a trilateral vision of North American homeland security. In a January 2003 bilateral meeting, Tom Ridge and his Mexican counterpart discussed the possibility of a future regional arrangement on trade and security with officials from Mexico, Canada, and the United States. The idea of a trilateral approach to homeland security became more concrete when it was linked with the ongoing Partnership for Prosperity initiative.[25] With the infusion of a security dimension, in March 2005 the initiative became the Security and Prosperity Partnership of North America (SPP).

The SPP is built on existing bilateral and trilateral arrangements in the region—including the Smart Border Declaration—and was meant to provide a forum for ongoing dialogue, priority setting, collaboration, and action on a variety of economic and security issues. The areas of cooperation considered include border facilitation, the environment, food and product safety, and economic competitiveness. The SPP's most innovative aspect is that it is based on the principle that security and prosperity are mutually dependent and complementary. Indeed, the attempt to go beyond security was a primary motivator of the initiative. A trilateral approach was also seen as a way to engage traditionally "unilateralist" countries such as the United States, but also skeptics of trilateralism such as Canada.[26]

Judging from its practical achievements, the SPP's record in meeting its stated goals has been mixed. On one hand, its first years in existence seem to suggest that the process has pushed the respective bureaucracies toward greater understanding of one another's positions on parts of the agenda. It has also made strides in overcoming bureaucratic inertia, thanks to its agenda-setting features and its role in facilitating the exchange of information. With each leaders' summit, priorities have in fact been reaffirmed and set, motivating cabinet-level work on specific policy items.[27] On the other

25. The Partnership for Prosperity was launched in September 2001 by the US administration as an attempt to spur further regional economic integration. This initiative was in a revision of the more ambitious project for a "North American economic community" that the American president had proposed in his first trip to Mexico right after taking office.

26. Canadian officials have longstanding doubts about trilateralizing their relationship with the United States. A major concern is that Mexico has not taken part in regional security arrangements in the past, and thus its integration with the other two partners might be difficult, dilute the initiatives' potential (both in the economic and security tracks), and slow down cooperation with the United States on this file. Another issue raised by Canadian officials is the difference between the problems at the US-Canadian border and those at the US-Mexican border (illegal immigration and drug and arms trafficking). From a practical perspective, the addition of a new partner could have therefore rendered existing informal cooperation more cumbersome. Persuaded that the SPP could after all have some positive impact on the increasingly inflexible US stance toward its northern border (and regain political capital with the US administration lost during the Iraq crisis), the Canadian government temporarily put its doubts aside and decided to participate in the initiative.

27. Christopher Sands and Greg Anderson, "Trilateral dialogue is worth the effort; Partnership tackles continent's economic, security needs," *Edmonton Journal*, April 19, 2008.

hand, progress on its agenda has been uneven among the three countries. While the partnership is "trilateral in concept," the framework is de facto "dual-bilateral" (Pastor 2005). Political will also seems to be lacking. In the last part of the Bush administration, there were attempts to revive the initiative, but with few results. For the new Obama administration, deeper American cooperation does not seem to be one of its foreign policy priorities. The consequence of this shift in focus is that the SPP, at least in its current form, has been momentarily shelved.

From a cultural evolutionary perspective, a possible explanation for the initiative's bumpy ride stems from the fact that it has been too ambitious. The attempt to merge the economic and security realms is not consistent with one of the main tenets of the Washington culture of border control, namely, the trumping of security over economic considerations. Moreover, the emphasis on bilateral rather than regional relations characterizing this culture means that the attempt to regionalize the policy was bound to encounter obstacles. Ebbing political will has heightened these problems further, dampening its chances of success. Conversely, the initiative's lackluster performance might spur a return to the Washington culture's securitarian roots, and with it, the possibility revamping of the project of an "enhanced" North American perimeter.

Transatlantic Encounters: North America, Europe, and Border Control after 9/11

The externalization of US policies did not reach only its neighbors in North America. Given the level of economic and political enmeshment with its partners across the Atlantic, Europe was affected as well. In the post-9/11 politically charged environment, the transatlantic agenda became increasingly dominated by questions concerning the security of the North American homeland. Issues such as border control, visas, data exchange, and antiterrorism more generally became a central feature of bilateral meetings between, on one hand, the US and Canadian governments, and on the other, individual European governments and the European Commission.[28] The policy makers involved in these meetings agreed on the importance of border security, and more generally, in working together to achieve this goal.

---

28. This shift affected Canada mostly indirectly. Canada participates with the United States in some EU working groups on homeland security. Most of the partnership with the European Union, however, is bilateral. It is in these interactions that Canada felt the "echo" of the discussion going on between the EU and the United States. Mexico did not take part in this cooperation, since for diplomatic purposes it is not part of the EU's North American desk.

However, US actions were the source of increasing tension in transatlantic relations. The situation became particularly difficult during the acrimonious rift over the Iraq war. What had previously been a relatively technical and primarily economic process of bilateral customs cooperation had become heavily securitized and politicized (Peterson 2005: 50).

The awareness of the potential for conflict convinced all parties involved to figure out ways to avoid confrontation and to engage in proactive cooperation to achieve common goals. Indeed, in this period, interactions between North American and European officials—from ministerial to working-group levels on police, judicial, and border control policy matters—increased substantially. The most relevant transatlantic forums dealing with border issues established after 9/11 have been the Dialogue on Transport and Border Security and the EU-US justice and home affairs meetings. In these forums, senior officials have laid out the basic outline of bilateral agreements, leaving out only the most hotly contested political issues for the EU-US summits, while preliminary work was carried in specialized working groups (e.g., visa, data privacy). An intensive dialogue was initiated on issues such as travel document security, visa policies, information sharing on lost and stolen passports, and other border control and migration-management issues. Most of these discussions were friendly and relatively unproblematic and were quickly followed by the signing of cooperation agreements (e.g., 2001 and 2002 US-Europol agreements; US-EU 2003 agreement on extradition; 2005 EU-Canada Passenger Name Record Agreement). In some instances, however, the issues on the agenda turned out to be much more politically contentious.

The most controversial of these cases were related to the US requests for more security on containers directed to its shores, information on incoming passengers traveling by air, and tighter rules for citizens of countries that did not require a visa to enter the United States. In all three circumstances, US actions raised a series of political and legal issues with the EU. In the case of the Container Security Initiative (CSI), one of the post-9/11 measures taken by the United States to tackle the perceived terrorist threat of container transport, Washington began negotiating bilateral agreements with individual European countries—European ports being among the most important for the United States in terms of volume of traffic—to allow the stationing of US custom agents in their ports to identify and examine maritime containers before the containers were shipped to the United States. This move, however, violated the established rule (sanctioned by EU law) that customs issues are a matter of Community competence. The dispute over Passengers

Name Records (PNR) was sparked in autumn 2001 when the US Congress passed the Aviation and Transportation Security Act, which requires that airlines with US-bound international flights electronically submit such data to the authorities. Failure to comply would have resulted in fines for the airlines and enhanced security screenings for passengers. These requirements, however, raised concerns regarding their compatibility with EU, in particular with regard to data protection. Congress legislation was involved also in the third major EU-US dispute in this period. The US Visa Waiver Program (VWP), introduced before the fall of the Berlin Wall, allows nationals of selected countries to enter the United States without a visa for a stay of up to ninety days. Post-9/11, Congress passed provisions designed to increase its security. The stricter requirements of the Enhanced Border Security and Visa Entry Reform Act meant that most new EU members were deemed not ready to be included in the program.[29] This created a serious political problem for the EU, for some of the excluded could have been tempted to invoke an EU "solidarity" clause that would require all member states to back them in a visa dispute with the United States.

The diplomatic practices that characterized the negotiations over these disputes represent the external component of the ongoing "trials" of the emerging Washington culture of border control. Their dynamics—especially the dialogical relation between the United States as the initiatives' main proponent and the European Commission as recalcitrant party—shaped the trajectory that the culture's selection process took since 9/11. As for the case of the North American security perimeter and its expansion, these negotiations were characterized by initial disagreement among its participants, followed by instances of compromise and progress, which were made possible by practical results in terms of agreement achieved and policies effectively implemented.

In the case of the Container Security Initiative, the European Commission objected to the attempt to step over its competence in the custom policy area and in early 2002 began infringement proceedings against a number of EU member states. US officials, however, continued to claim that the problem was an internal EU issue and decided to move on with the initiative, signing bilateral agreements with more European countries. With regard to the Passenger Name Records program, the United States and the EU clashed over the issue of privacy in the handling of sensitive data. The United States

29. At the time, the program included all fifteen EU member states except Greece and included only Slovenia from the ten new EU member states.

believed that their system guaranteed sufficient privacy to travelers, and in any case it was its right to control who was entering its soil. In Europe, privacy is considered one of the basic values of human life, and it is enshrined as one of the fundamental rights of EU citizens. European officials also did not accept the unilateral nature of US actions. In the case of the Visa Waiver Program, the transatlantic spat stemmed from the fact that, despite the EU's call to exclusively negotiate with the Union's representatives on this issue, the US authorities continued with their bilateral approach with individual European countries, which involved the signing of memorandums of understandings requiring these countries to introduce new security measures in order to join the program.

Despite these early diplomatic clashes, in the months that followed the new initiatives' launch, the two sides managed to elaborate compromise solutions to solve the most contentious issues on the negotiating table. To overcome the impasse over the CSI, in November 2003 the European Commission reached an interim agreement with the United States to expand the 1997 EC-US agreement on custom cooperation and mutual assistance in custom matters. The purpose of this new agreement was to enable the Container Security Initiative to be extended to all EU ports meeting the relevant requirements and, consequently, to permit the infringement proceedings to be halted. In the case of the PNR issue, after a year of negotiations, the Commission reached an interim agreement in February 2003 with the US government in which the EU agency adopted a so-called adequacy decision expressing that the United States would ensure an adequate level of data protection, allowing the transfer of data from EC member states to the US. With regard to the Visa Waiver Program, in March 2008, the EU unblocked the stalemate by agreeing to pursue a twin-track approach with the United States, whereby bilateral negotiations between the United States and the EU member states continued on issues that, under EU law, fell within the competence of the member states, while simultaneously the United States would discuss issues under EU community competence with the EU Commission.

The new compromises immediately led to some concrete movement toward the initiatives' adoption. With regard to CSI, in November 2004 the EU and the United States approved the first joint measures to assist maritime transport security measures based on the new framework agreement for transatlantic custom cooperation. A decision was made to set up an information exchange network and identify "best practices" for security inspections in international trade. While negotiations over the PNR were ongoing, the Commission advised the EU data protection authorities not to impose fines on air carriers transmitting data to the US authorities. The threat of disruption of transatlantic air traffic was therefore momentarily avoided, and flights continued as usual. Regarding the EC-US dimension of the VWP's twin-track approach, in April 2008, the Council adopted a mandate for the Commission to negotiate an agreement between the European Community and the United States whose purpose was to satisfy US legal requirements falling under EC competence for entry or continued participation in the VWP.

The trajectory of these transatlantic negotiations was not linear. Early successes were followed by setbacks and new compromises between the two sides. Although the 2004 CSI agreement solved the most pressing political differences between the US and the EU, the issue of container security was not completely settled. Again, it was a US bill that sparked the dispute. This bill required all containers shipped to the United States be scanned by custom agents at the port of departure. This bill provoked fierce opposition from the European Commission, which threatened to retaliate. The Commission claimed that the rule would require large infrastructural investments, have a negative impact on EU-US trade, and "could be interpreted as a negative signal" for transatlantic relations generally.[30] In late 2008, however, the Department of Homeland Security (DHS) came forward with an alternative approach. The proposed rule is that, rather than the proportion of containers scanned, the amount of data that carriers and US importers have to send the DHS should be increased. Under this rule, twenty-four hours before the cargo is loaded, the importer would have to transmit the identity of the seller, buyer, manufacturer, and country of origin.

In June 2004, the European Parliament sought the annulment of the PNR agreement before the European Court of Justice (ECJ). The ECJ agreed with the EP and annulled both the EU-US agreement and the Commission's adequacy decision in its judgment of May 2006. The annulment was based on the grounds that subject of these instruments fell outside the scope of existing EU data protection law. Following the annulment by the European Court of Justice, in the second part of 2006 the European Commission tried to find an arrangement that could put a legally sound framework in place for the transfer of PNR data to the United States. After having concluded an interim agreement in October 2006, the EU and the US Department of Homeland Security signed a final agreement on the use of PNR in July 2007

30. "100% Container Scanning Rule Arouses Commission Ire," *Europolitics*, 7 March 2007.

and exchanged "Letters," including further details and commitments with regard to the use of PNR.[31]

While engaged in negotiations on the EU track over the VWP, the United States signed bilateral memoranda of understanding with seven EU member states. The European Commission, however, threatened to take action over these agreements. It also complained that no additional member state has joined the VWP, as it had promised. In light of the above, the Commission threatened retaliatory measures in order to expedite progress toward full reciprocity. In the meantime, the Czech Republic, Estonia, Hungary, Latvia, Lithuania, and Slovakia agreed with the United States to share information about threats, use tamper-proof biometric passports, and register with the Electronic System for Travel Authorization. Thanks to these practical arrangements, in October 2008 President Bush announced that these countries had indeed met the requirements for admittance into the US Visa Waiver Program.

Institutionalizing the Washington Culture of Border Control: The Road Ahead

The drafters of the US Homeland Security Strategy, written when the memory of 9/11 was still vivid, claimed that the future of border management would be "radically different from today's."[32] This prediction was correct. A decade later, border control in North America has indeed gone through sweeping transformations. Traditional statecentric notions of territoriality have given way to new assumptions and practices about how to best protect the North American "homeland." North American policy makers have pursued this new culture of border control with the elaboration of new border initiatives both within the region (e.g., the Smart Border Declaration and the Security and Prosperity Partnership) and with international partners (e.g., agreements with the EU and European governments over container security, passenger name records, and visa waivers). The implementation of these policy initiatives has functioned as a training ground for this emerging

---

31. Besides adopting a new legal basis compatible with EC law, the new agreement addressed some of the criticized sections of the 2004 text. For example, it includes nineteen types of data to share compared to thirty-four under the old one. The new arrangement was also based on a "push" system, whereby airlines only supply data to the US authorities following a specific request, as opposed to US authorities having their own access to airline reservation systems (a "pull" system).

32. Office of Homeland Security, "National Strategy for Homeland Security" (July 2002), 22.

culture and contributed to the internalization of its assumptions among an increasingly coherent regional border control policy community.

This process of cultural selection was not without challenges. Disagreement over the correct courses of action to undertake was common, with some policy makers calling for the return to a more orthodox nationalist approach to border control. Relations within North America's border control policy community and with the community's international partners have been characterized by recurrent diplomatic crises, which have tarnished long-standing partnerships and required laborious efforts to put bilateral negotiations back on track. Some of the initiatives' results have also been disappointing (e.g., the SPP). These setbacks have slowed down but not stopped the emerging culture's progress toward its final selection. Compromises among policy makers have eventually been found on most contentious issues, leading to the successful implementation of numerous border initiatives. New border practices introduced in this period (e.g., the policy measure that created "smart borders" between the United States and its southern and northern neighbors) have become more routinized. Policy makers and practitioners in the newly created homeland security bureaucracies have deepened their cooperation and exchange of information and made some (albeit timid) steps toward institutionalizing the relations with their North American partners. There are even signs of the Washington culture's "spreading" beyond North America. One example is the reproduction of some of its most representative border control practices in other regions. The European Commission, for example, after clashing with its transatlantic partners on the exchange of passenger data, is currently working on a similar arrangement for Europe (a "European PNR"), and it has advanced proposals for an entry-exit system and a favored traveler program along the lines of those introduced in North America. Recently, some border security practices elaborated in North America (e.g., cargo security, biometrics) have also been endorsed by international organizations such as International Civil Aviation Organization, the World Customs Organization, and the G8.

Given the element of path dependency that characterizes a cultural evolutionary process, we could expect—at least in the medium term—a further consolidation of the Washington culture of border control. The Obama administration has signalled that the path taken by its predecessor with regard to border control will not be radically modified in the near future, to the dismay of some of those (especially in Canada and Mexico) who were hoping for a more "liberal" stance in this policy domain. Public statements by US officials and the first border-related measures adopted (e.g., the implementation of the US-VISIT program and the beefing up of security at the border with Canada) seem to confirm that the new "border culture," which the incoming homeland security secretary Janet Napolitano refers to in the epigraph to this chapter, is indeed taking roots in North America.[33]

Despite these developments, the final selection of the Washington culture of border control has not occurred yet. Most of the new border practices introduced in the last decade have not been institutionalized into a formal policy regime, as has been the case in Europe with the incorporation of Schengen into the European Union. More problematically, despite the resolution of the most contentious issues affecting relations among governments in the region and with partners across the Atlantic, there are still some outstanding issues on the border control agenda that might again stir up tensions. Canada, for example, is not pleased with the new US administration's increased scrutiny of the two countries' common border. The US Congress is still adamant that all US-bound cargoes should be checked (the so-called 100 percent rule), a position Europeans oppose, favoring a more risk-based approached to security screening. Some European policy makers (especially in the European Parliament) also complain that the 2007 PNR agreement has not satisfactorily addressed concerns over privacy, and, more generally, the handling of passengers' data. Finally, not all EU countries are in the Visa Waiver Program yet and access to the program is not guaranteed. These unsolved issues could jeopardize the future evolution and final selection of the Washington culture of border control. The culture's evolutionary journey is clearly far from over.

33. Janet Napolitano, quoted from the transcript of the conference "Toward a Better Border: The United States and Canada," held at the Brookings Institution, Washington, DC, March 25, 2009.

TEN

Conclusion: After Schengen

At the time of the signing of the Treaty of Amsterdam, the fear was that the integration of the Schengen *acquis* into the European Union framework would mark the end of this co-operation, which has been praised for its flexibility and effectiveness. Fortunately, this has not occurred at all.

—Franco Frattini[1]

I just sometimes wonder what the map of Europe will quite look like and what the politics of it will be in twenty or thirty years' time, because we have lived for so long with a sharp frontier of freedom across our continent. Now, I think that that will become less sharp.

—Margaret Thatcher[2]

The least simple, the least natural, the most artificial, that is to say, the least fated, the most human and free in the world, this is Europe . . .

—Jules Michelet, 1831

The Tale of a Success Story

In June 2005, delegates from EU member states and the European Commission gathered in Luxembourg to celebrate Schengen's twentieth anniversary. During the event, Luc Frieden, president of the Justice and Home Affairs Council, proudly proclaimed that Schengen had become a symbol of

1. Franco Frattini, "20 years since the signing of the Schengen," European Commission, SPEECH/05/318, June 2005.

2. Margaret Thatcher, from TV interview for *BBC2 Newsnight*, COI transcript, June 3, 1988, Thatcher Archive.

"freedom, security, and European success."[3] This remark reflects a common belief among most European policy makers and, increasingly, EU citizens as well. Although it is difficult to accurately determine the current popular support for Schengen across the Continent,[4] EU citizens' views on border-related policy issues (e.g., asylum and immigration) and on the role of EU institutions in these matters—both proxies for the regime as a whole—seem to back up this claim.[5] If we add anecdotal evidence of European citizens' overall satisfaction with the newly acquired freedom to travel across the Continent without border controls, it could be inferred that today Schengen enjoys a remarkable popularity.[6] There is also general agreement among policy makers on the fact that Schengen represents one of the most significant achievements in recent European politics. This initiative has accomplished what for a long time the European Union, and the European Communities prior to it, aspired to, namely, a "Europe without frontiers." In this perspective, it is not surprising that Schengen was awarded an honor generally reserved only to "historical" events: the erection of a monument on its name, evocatively located along the banks of the river Moselle, in the same location where the regime was officially born.

The journey that began two decades ago on the cruise ship the *Princesse Marie-Astrid* has not been smooth and straightforward. Dramatic geopolitical shifts (the fall of the Berlin wall, EU enlargement) and recurring threats to peace and security caused by terrorism and other cross-border criminal activities have seriously put to the test the idea of creating an area of free movement across the Continent. Fluctuations in political will have periodically threatened to bring the initiative to a halt. Coming from different

3. Luxembourg presidency, press release,, "Twentieth anniversary of the signing of the Schengen Agreements," June 2, 2005. Available at http://www.eu2005.lu/en/actualites/communiques/2005/06/02schengen/index.html.

4. The European Commission conducted two opinion polls (known in EU parlance as "Eurobarometers") on the topic at the time of the Schengen regime's entry into force in the mid 1990s (see below, p. 293 fn. 291). However, a specific question about Schengen was not present in following surveys.

5. In a poll conducted in December 2003, a large majority of European citizens (80 percent) declared themselves to be in favor of strengthening checks on non-EU citizens at Europe's external borders and of a common policy on asylum and immigration (see "Justice And Home Affairs: Opinion Poll Shows Demand For Tighter Border Controls," *European Report*, March 10, 2004). These data confirm the results of previous surveys.

6. These findings do not mean that the regime lacks detractors. Besides the still consistent political opposition in places like the United Kingdom (often, it must be said, the result of more general anti-EU sentiment rather than dislike of Schengen per se), there are patches of vocal resistance to some of Schengen's most securitarian components and to its negative implications for the rights of both non-EU and EU citizens. On this point, see below.

political perspectives, critics have contested its very rationale and methods. For some, the abolition of internal border controls would reduce the security of European countries and the Continent as a whole. For others, it would instead create a "wall around Europe" and seriously curb the rights of non-EU citizens.[7] For still others, its development outside the EU was a powerful drawback, not only for the initiative and its legitimacy but also for the Union itself, since it would have weakened the coherence of the entire project. Yet what rendered it more challenging was the fact that Schengen involved a fundamental shift in the assumptions and practices defining border control, and that it questioned the nationalist common sense that for a long time had shaped this policy domain in Europe and beyond. The idea of European countries "pooling" their sovereignty over such a sensitive issue was therefore daring, and pursuing it was a political bet that few thought could be won.

Despite the obstacles and widespread skepticism, the vision underlying the Schengen initiative has demonstrated a surprising resilience over the years, and today its central tenets have become part of the political landscape in Europe. Checks at internal borders have been almost completely abolished across the Continent. In December 2007, the regime expanded to nine new members,[8] and as a result the area of free movement has expanded eastward and includes territories that not long ago were protected by the Iron Curtain. Although it is still formally possible to reinstate border controls within the Schengen area, this option has only been used in exceptional circumstances (e.g., in the aftermath of the March 2004 Madrid bombings; G8 summits, sport events such the 2004 Olympic Games held in Athens). Moreover, in all these cases the reinstatement of national border checks has been temporary and geographically limited, and with the consent of all the other Schengen partners (Groenendijk 2004). In turn, external borders are now de facto European, since their management is shared among EU governments and coordinated by an EU agency, Frontex. At a symbolic level, Schengen's "signs" are now a ubiquitous presence at Europe's external frontiers (e.g., EU flags and preferential lines for EU citizens at international airports).

Its impact does not stop at Europe's confines, either. Schengen projects itself beyond the Continent thanks to the common visas issued by member

---

7. On the debate over whether Europe is a "fortress" or a "sieve," see Bigo 2000b.

8. The new Schengen members are the Czech Republic, Estonia, Hungary, Latvia, Lithuania, Malta, Poland, Slovakia, and Slovenia. All of them became EU members in 2004. Romania and Bulgaria (EU members since January 1, 2008) are scheduled to join the regime in 2011.

states to non-EU citizens and valid throughout the Schengen area. The ultimate testament of Schengen's growing fame is the fact that it has turned into a recognizable item of popular culture. A hotel in Shangai and a British rock band are named after it; in the Congolese capital Kinshasa, *schege boys* are the street kids whose dream is to join their parents and co-nationals working in Europe (Biaya 2000: 20). All these developments clearly indicate that Schengen is now fully entrenched in everyday political and popular discourses. In other words, it has become common sense.

Schengen beyond Schengen: The Promise of a Cultural Evolutionary Analytical Framework

The fact that Schengen was a success story has rendered the (re)telling of its origins and development worthwhile. But what justifies the type of story told here? In other words, why is a cultural evolutionary account needed to explain this event? The claim advanced in this work is that an analytical framework based on the concept of culture of border control and its evolution captures the specific features and dynamics of Europe's border control domain. As Monar puts it:

> [I]n the Justice and Home Affairs domain, the challenge (is) different in nature from those in other EU policymaking areas and more sensitive because the area of freedom, security and justice that is supposed to be set up is, in essence, a developing common zone of internal security. Internal security is an essential public good and a highly sensitive one of immediate concern to citizens . . . and voters. (Monar 2003b: 2)

Using culture as analytical prism allows the foregrounding of the social and intersubjective underpinnings that define border control as an autonomous policy field. This field is not just about formal policies and rules of governance resulting from the bargaining among individual state actors with competing interests. It is also, and more importantly, about a discrete set of taken-for-granted assumptions shared by members of a policy community and the routinized practices instantiating these assumptions in the everyday life of the community. These elements constitute the backbone of the three cultures of border control that I have identified as characterizing the European experience in the last fifty years, namely, Westphalia, Schengen, and Brussels.

If a more nuanced account is necessary to examine the everyday functioning of border control as a policy domain, *a fortiori* this should be the case for transformations within it. Since the domain is characterized by entrenched assumptions and routinized practices, going beyond the existing order will be difficult. Rationalist accounts that look at materially based interests of powerful actors, such as France and Germany, and at contextual geopolitical shifts (e.g., the fall of the Berlin Wall), are unable to capture the nature and implications of the fundamental break that the emergence of a postnational approach to border control has represented, above all if these variables are treated in an uncritical manner (i.e., as direct causal factors). Works adopting a normative shift hypothesis are more sensitive to Schengen's ground-breaking character. Yet, by relying on sudden worldview shifts to explain the regime's trajectory, these accounts miss the dialogical and practical dimensions that defined the transition from a nationalist to a postnationalist approach to border control in Europe.

A cultural evolutionary framework, on the contrary, places these aspects at the forefront, thereby offering a more nuanced interpretation of this process. While recognizing the "rupture" represented by Schengen's appearance on the European political scene and that its pursuit was a "leap into the dark," this framework highlights how this leap was not a completely irrational act, for it required both faith *and* planning on the part of the European policy makers who were behind this groundbreaking initiative. The hypothesis of considering Schengen's pursuit (and, at least in the initial stages, Brussels's as well) as a "reasonable gamble" can explain why members of Europe's border control community managed to overcome the odds of launching such a politically audacious project—a decision that could not have been justified on strict cost-benefit terms (given the lack of reliable information on its chances of success)—and account for the initiative's resilience in spite of the turbulent political context in which it took place. If we turn to the issue of how Schengen was eventually adopted as the official approach to border control in Europe, by pointing at practices as the central mechanism of selection, a cultural evolutionary framework can explain why, despite sharing the same objective, Schengen and its main alternative (Brussels) were elaborated in parallel initiatives and did not directly clash with each other, as would be expected in a contest between competing political projects. It was in fact these projects' performance that determined their ultimate success or failure. An evolutionary account based on performance also explains why the creation of a postnational approach to border control in Europe was a work in progress, which took shape as it was deployed, and which was completed only after a long gestation punctuated by periodical setbacks. Because of their cognitivist bias (i.e., the emphasis on actors' reasoning capacity or on collective mental structures), both the logical response and normative shift hypotheses do not cogently account for the role that practices played in the establishment of Schengen.

Overall, when observed from a cultural evolutionary perspective, the emergence of Schengen appears as the result of a combination of elements often in opposition with one another, such as insight and instinct, creativity and bureaucratic control, long-term planning and contingency, collective effort and individual entrepreneurship. Framed in this fashion, Schengen represents a truly *pragmatist* enterprise. And it should be apparent that the term "pragmatism" as it is used here is not synonymous with "expediency" or "instrumentalism," as is often the case in common political parlance; rather, it refers to, and takes its clues from, the philosophical tradition championed by authors such as Charles Sanders Peirce, or what we might call a pragmatism with a capital "p."[9]

Thus, by addressing the specific traits defining Europe's border control domain, a cultural evolutionary framework can explain (and do it better than other accounts) the conditions that made possible the emergence of Schengen. This framework's added value does not end here. By tracing the recent (and still ongoing) evolution of the "Washington culture of border control" in North America, I have shown how a cultural evolutionary approach can be employed to account for other cases of regional border cooperation outside Europe. This approach can also offer relevant insights into current and future political dynamics affecting Europe's border control and make sense of developments occurring beyond this policy domain. First, it can provide a plausible explanation for certain "anomalies" in the way border control issues are dealt with across Europe, such as the continuing popularity of Schengen-like intergovernmental models of governance outside the EU and the resurfacing of "Schengenized" assumptions in plans outlining the future of the Union. Second, it can shed light on what various critics have described as major shortcomings in the Schengen model, and assess their significance and implications. Finally, a culturalist account can offer a novel perspective on the debate over the future of Europe as political project, a debate that pits those who envision Europe as a "super-state in the making" against those who think of it as a "neo-medieval empire." Taken together, these lines of inquiry seem to sketch a promising research agenda. In the remainder of this chapter, the content of this agenda is elaborated in more detail.

---

9. On the distinction between pragmatism with or without a capital "p," see Albert and Kopp-Malek 2002.

Schengen Redux: From New "EU Laboratories" to the EU Constitution and Its Reformulations

The model of policy innovation that characterized Schengen in its early stages is still alive today, even though the border control domain is currently part of the EU governance system. The resilience of the Schengen model is evidenced in the experience of recently launched intergovernmental initiatives dealing with internal security in Europe. Their features and activities in fact bear striking resemblances with their illustrious predecessor. One of them is the "G6" group (originally "G5"). The G6 was created in 2003 by a small circle of EU countries (France, Germany, Italy, Spain, and the United Kingdom; Poland joined them in March 2006). It is an informal forum where interior ministers meet and discuss issues related to their field of competence and plan for cross-border cooperation. Although it acts outside the EU institutional framework, the G6's stated goal is to work as policymaking "laboratory" for the Union as a whole, and membership is open to all EU countries.

Similar features characterize another ad hoc intergovernmental forum that has sprung up in Europe in recent years, namely, the "Prüm group." This group, which initially included five members (Belgium, Netherlands, Luxembourg, Germany, and Austria) and was joined by France, Spain, and Italy, was formed with the aim of elaborating and expanding the scope of the Schengen *acquis*. Discussions within this group have led to the drafting of the Treaty of Prüm, also known as "Schengen III," which was signed in May 2005.[10] The objective of this treaty is to advance police cooperation in the field of security. Besides its content, which clearly confirms and strengthens the trend toward the securitization of the justice and home affairs field in Europe,[11] there are other similarities with the Schengen experience. Despite being conceived and elaborated outside the EU institutional and legal

10. Council of the European Union, "Convention between the Kingdom of Belgium, the Federal Republic of Germany, the Kingdom of Spain, the French Republic, the Grand Duchy of Luxembourg, the Kingdom of the Netherlands and the Republic of Austria on the stepping up of cross-border co-operation, particularly in combating terrorism, cross-border crime and illegal migration." Prüm is the town in the German land of Rhenania-Palatinate where the agreement was signed. On the treaty's political and legal implications, see Balzacq, Carrera, and Bigo 2006.

11. Among its main provisions, the treaty requires the contracting parties to establish a pool of DNA profile databases, which all members can access upon request, and a system to match fingerprints of suspected criminals and terrorists; it regulates the deployment of air marshals on commercial flights and of immigration liaison officers (ILOs) in third countries, and authorizes joint deportations. The convention also grants police officers from partner countries executive powers to carry out cross border arrests and to engage in other police activities in the host country.

framework, its proponents' ultimate goal is the eventual incorporation of its *acquis* into the Union (art. 1[4]). Other willing and capable countries can sign the treaty, but they have to do so by accepting the existing *acquis* in its entirety (art. 1[2]). The intergovernmental nature of this initiative also implies that the European Parliament cannot oversee its activities, and it will likely only have a limited role when its *acquis* is communitarized. In turn, national parliaments have to ratify the treaty without much prior information on its content and power to amend it, while the contracting parties can continue to work multilaterally on the technical measures necessary to implement it. The result is a general lack of transparency and accountability.

The activities of the G6 and the Prüm groups are thriving, and their membership is expanding. Talks about the incorporation of their *acquis* into the EU are already at an advanced stage.[12] The method that was so successful with Schengen still seems to be popular, thus confirming that its underlying culture is very much alive.

The trend toward the further consolidation of Schengen is evidenced not only by what is occurring outside the EU institutional framework but also in some of the Union's plans outlining the future of the border control policy domain. This is the case, for example, of the provisions of the (now defunct) Constitutional Treaty on the European Union dedicated to justice and home affairs and their reformulations in the Lisbon Treaty, the document that has replaced the constitution after the latter's failed ratification. Since the Lisbon Treaty by and large reproduces the content of the constitution with regard to border control issues, it is appropriate to start a review of the recent developments in the JHA field with the analysis of this document. In 2001, European heads of government established the Convention on the Future of Europe to prepare a single treaty to replace the patchwork of exiting treaties defining the EU's legal framework and to render the EU more coherent and legitimate. The reform of the area of freedom, security, and justice was among the topics discussed by the convention.[13] The result of this discussion was the inclusion in the final text of the constitution of

12. The seven original signatories of the Prüm Treaty and five of those who have notified their intention to join it have proposed a draft council decision, which reproduces, with few differences, the provisions of the Prüm Treaty. See "Draft Council Decision on stepping up cross-border co-operation, particularly in combating terrorism and cross-border crime" (6002/07, Brussels, 6 Feb. 2007); see also "Note by the Presidency of the Council: Integration of the Prüm Treaty into the Union Legal Order" (6220/07).

13. See the "Final report of the Working Party X ("Freedom, security and justice")," December 2002, available at www.statewatch.org/news/2003/apr/wpX.pdf.

five articles and four protocols dealing with issues of border control, immigration, and asylum policy.[14]

The expectations regarding the EU constitutional treaty were high. However, the document encountered serious obstacles at the ratification stage, which was required before its provisions could become fully operational. Popular support for this initiative was very low across the Continent, and the negative results of the referendums held in France and the Netherlands brought its implementation to an abrupt halt. Discussions over a possible resurrection of the constitution continued. Various options were put on the table, ranging from minor "restyling" to more serious "cuts" of its most controversial parts. None of these options, however, envisioned a radical transformation of the way the different policy areas are organized, including justice and home affairs.

Eventually, at the European Council held in Brussels on June 2007, EU leaders agreed to get rid of the term "constitution" and rely on a less ambitious treaty arrangement. A new ICG to determine the content of the new treaty met in the fall of 2007. On October 19 an agreement on a "Draft Treaty amending the Treaty on European Union and the Treaty establishing the European Community" was reached at an informal summit in Lisbon. Although the Lisbon Treaty was swiftly signed by European leaders on December 13, 2007, its ratification among member states was delayed because the Irish voters initially rejected it in a referendum held in June 2008 (Ireland, it should be noted, was the only EU country that held a popular vote on the subject). Only after much political wrangling and some concessions to reassure the Irish public, the "yes" prevailed in a new referendum held a year later, paving the way for the Lisbon Treaty's official entry into force on December 1, 2009.

Despite their difficult gestation, the EU Constitution and its successor, the Lisbon Treaty, remain important political documents, for they are representative of the existing consensus among Europe's border control community over JHA matters, a consensus that does not seem have been shaken by the growing unpopularity of EU-based initiatives among the Union's

14. A draft of the constitutional treaty was agreed upon in July 2003 and signed by all EU heads of government and three candidate states on October 29, 2004. The articles dealing with justice and home affairs are found in part 3 of the treaty ("The Policies and Functioning of the Union"). For the full text of the convention's sections dealing with border control and immigration, see "The European Union Constitution on Border Checks, Asylum, and Immigration," *Population and Development Review* 30, no. 4 (Dec. 2004): 789–792.

citizens and some of its member states' governments.[15] Taken together, the Constitutional Treaty and the Lisbon Treaty strengthen the EU's role in Justice and Home Affairs and signal a converging movement toward a reinforced Community method. The constitution envisaged the abolition of the pillar structure and the creation of a single operational and legal framework under which this policy domain would operate. Thanks to the new arrangement, it offered for the first time a legal base for the EU to control its external borders, thus setting the foundations for "the gradual introduction of an integrated management system for external borders" and for the development of a common immigration policy.[16] The Lisbon Treaty maintains the constitution's approach on this topic, although toning down its more "communitarian" language.

Despite the new elements introduced by the EU Constitution and the Lisbon Treaty, these two legal documents seem not to represent a decisive policy shift in the area of freedom, security, and justice. Overall, these texts reproduce some of the core assumptions of the Schengen model. Security and the prevention of potential threats affecting Europe and its borders were undoubtedly on the mind of the drafters of the EU Constitution and the Lisbon Treaty. The European territory is in fact organized through border controls, jurisdictional limits and a concern with territorial integrity and sovereign rights. The "common immigration policy" that is signaled in article III-267 of the EU Constitution is yet to be shaped, and the treaty offers few hints of what it may look like. A reluctance on the part of member states to cede sovereignty in the area of immigration is seen also in the retained right of all members to restrict non-EU labor migrants (art. III-267, par. 5) and to conclude bilateral agreements on border crossing with non-EU states (protocol 21). Heiner Busch was therefore not off the mark when, commenting on the draft constitution's provisions regarding justice and home affairs, he argued that this domain was turning out to be "an area of security, security and security."[17] In the draft constitution and the Lisbon Treaty there is therefore a tension between a vision of Europe

15. It should be kept in mind that European citizens' skepticism over the Constitution and the Lisbon Treaty was not specifically directed at the proposed reforms of the JHA field (which few people were actually familiar with), although some concerns about Europe being invaded by low-wage and dangerous immigrants were raised.

16. The EU Constitution also introduces qualified majority voting, expands the role of the European Parliament and the jurisdiction of the European Court of Justice in JHA-related issues, incorporates the Charter of Fundamental Rights, and brings the European law enforcement agency (Europol) within the EU's legal framework.

17. Quoted in Tony Bunyan, "The creation of an EU Interior Ministry—for the maintenance of law and order, internal security and external borders," *Statewatch*, April 2003.

that aims to transcend existing territorial divisions and notions of territory, particularly those associated with the nation-state, and one whose objective is the establishment of a secure environment in a territorially defined space (Bialasiewicz, Elden, and Painter 2005). This tension is clearly reminiscent of the one that has affected Schengen since its very beginnings.

Making Sense of Schengen's Contradictions

Some of the major criticisms leveled against Schengen are that it has been a top-down model lacking democratic control and input, its flexible method has damaged the EU's institutional coherence, it overemphasizes security over freedom, it has a negative impact on Europe's neighbors and non-EU citizens, and its expansionary drive can lead to overstretching.

Seen through a culturalist prism, these features acquire a special meaning. The fact that Schengen is an élite-driven and undemocratic enterprise has prevented an open discussion about the actual meaning of "European border" from taking place. When the Westphalia culture of border control was predominant, the legitimacy of the system was based on the protection of citizens *qua* nationals. Now, it should be based on shared protection, but the current arrangement lacks a genuine sense of solidarity and shared identity of the protected.[18] This shared identity must emerge for the peoples of Europe to fully accept a common external frontier and the abolition of police controls on frontiers between them (Anderson 1996: 178–179). Since the regime's inception, Schengen's popular support has grown.[19] This

18. This is the case not just for the population at large, but also for Europe's border communities. In their empirical analysis of the role of "Europe" in border communities' narratives across the Continent, Armbruster, Rollo, and Meinhof (2003) note the absence of Europe or "Europeanness" as a self-chosen category of identification.

19. In an opinion poll conducted before the entry into force of the Schengen regime (spring 1995), the citizens of the European Union (then composed of fifteen member states) were evenly divided between those who thought that the removal of border controls between the signatory states was "a good thing" (43 percent), and those who believed it was "a bad thing" (42 percent). When the regime did enter into force a year later, the proportion of respondents in favor had risen to 48 percent, while those against had gone down to 38 percent. Not surprisingly, in both surveys there were differences in terms of distribution of support across Europe. These differences, however, did not necessarily reflect the stance of the national governments representing their people. Among the countries whose population viewed Schengen favorably, for example, we find Ireland (the others being Spain, Portugal, Belgium, Austria, Germany, Ireland, Greece, Italy), while on the skeptical front, side by side with the United Kingdom, we find a list of odd bedfellows such as France, Luxembourg, Finland, Denmark, the Netherlands, and Sweden. See "Results of 'Continuous Tracking' surveys of the European Union—(April to June 1995)," *Europinion* 5 (July 1995); and "Results of 'Continuous Tracking' surveys of the European Union—(January to March 1996)," *Europinion* 8 (April 1996).

support, however, has been mainly passive, and based on practical results of the policies introduced. Its relative shallowness is reflected in the fact that popular opinion has fluctuated depending on the issue at stake and the mood of the moment.[20] This condition seriously weakens Schengen's legitimacy, and it could hurt the long-term success of the initiative.

If the lack of popular support has prevented Schengen from gaining greater legitimacy, its reliance on flexible methods has created political and legal fragmentation in the policymaking process. The result has been increased complexity and diminished transparency. These issues were a source of concern before Schengen was incorporated in the EU, and they remain so today, given the undiminished appeal of "enhanced cooperation" arrangements in the area of justice, security, and freedom.

Even more worrying is the potentially self-destructive dynamic stemming from Schengen's "internal security dilemma." According to this logic, security is a necessary precondition for the establishment and expansion of freedom in a given community. The quest for security, however, can never be completely fulfilled, since this is an inherently subjective and unstable condition. As a result, security feeds more security, and the process can potentially go on ad infinitum. One of the side effects of this "hypersecuritization" is that the policies it entails become almost exclusively repressive, since they are aimed at sealing off Europe from potential threats. This explains why Schengen has been opposed by civil libertarian groups in current member states and has created widespread suspicion and resistance among Europe's neighbors.[21] It also explain why it has been fiercely contested by feminist and other critically oriented activists who consider Schengen a vehicle for the imposition of a particular gendered, racialized and classed vision of reality (Raj 2006).

The prospect of the new EU member states becoming fully integrated into the Schengen space represents another serious challenge to the regime's future viability. The quest for expansion was part of this project since the very beginnings and this feature was maintained with its incorporation in the EU. A potential implication of this "bigger is better" logic is that the system may become overstretched and eventually lose momentum and effectiveness (not to mention its function as laboratory for the EU). For

---

20. The same could be said for the early stages of the Schengen regime in the late 1980s and early 1990s. The popular view of the role of borders was in fact ambiguous; on one hand, favorable regarding lifting of national borders; on the other, still strongly nationalistic in tone (Anderson 2002: 241).

21. On the impact of rebordering practices on the EU's new neighbors and their populations, see Grabbe 2000; Krok-Pasazkowska and Zielonka 2000; Amato and Batt 1999.

Monar, the EU's main postenlargement challenges stem from the increased political, structural, and implementation capability diversity that the new members will bring (Monar 2003b). All these differences will remain after enlargement, rendering common decision making in the JHA area more problematic.

Steps have indeed been taken, or at least discussion is ongoing, to address some of these shortcomings. So far there have been proposals to make the policymaking process in justice and home affairs more transparent.[22] Ideas to expand and render more meaningful EU citizenship are going in the direction of creating a sense of solidarity and shared identity among Europeans. The European Commission has been the most vocal in ensuring that concerns over security do not overshadow the "freedom" and "justice" objectives of the EU, thus guaranteeing a better balance in the delivering of these public goods (Monar 2003b: 17–18).

Despite these attempts, addressing Schengen's shortcomings will be difficult. The main reason is that these elements in the Schengen experiment are, ironically, also some of its major assets. These features were instrumental in allowing the border control policy community to go beyond the nationalist common sense.[23] In terms of participation and democratic control, opening up the debate over Schengen would have weakened the community's effort in pursuing it. Flexibility was one of Schengen's major strengths, since it allowed European policy makers to avoid getting bogged down in legal and bureaucratic wrangles or vetoing by individual countries, as often occurred in the EU. The emphasis on security, especially at Europe's external borders, was aimed at soothing popular anxieties that the lifting of internal frontiers was believed to create. Limiting the rights of neighbors and non-EU citizens has become the price paid in order to expand the rights of EU citizens, and more generally a way to externalize the negative implications of the newly created area of free movement. Finally, the continuing expansion of the regime, now including the new EU members, represents a politically expedient means to solidify the regime and to guarantee its survival.

22. These discussions have focused on increasing transparency through better information on objectives and progress to parliaments, the media and the citizens, as well as more effective parliamentary control (Monar 2003b: 17–18).

23. The main focus on this work is on how policy makers embraced a postnational approach to border control. Part of the success of Schengen (especially its current consolidation) is due to the fact that European citizens as well have accepted it as part of the new common sense. I have mentioned in passim that practical results might have played a role in creating popular support for Schengen. A cultural evolutionary approach can therefore give some clues to answer this question. Given its relevance, this line of inquiry would gain from a more in-depth exploration than is offered here.

The tensions within Schengen have so far been contained, because the culture of border control in which the regime is embedded is today on an ascendant path in terms of strength and coherence. It might, however, create problems in the long term and open up the possibility for alternative cultures to challenge its predominance. I will return to this point below.

Schengen beyond Border Control: The Debate over the Future of Europe

Locating Europe's boundaries and defining their nature have practical repercussions on the region's internal and external development, for it influences the degree of political integration, the operations of its institutions, and the extent of policy harmonization (Anderson 1996: 179). The debate over borders in Europe is thus firmly intertwined with the broader discussion over the future of Europe as a political project.

Defining such a project is no simple task. "Europe" is an elusive idea that continues to baffle policy makers and pundits alike. As Walker puts it, Europe "often is not where it is supposed to be" (Walker 2000). Despite its unpredictability, there have been numerous attempts to pin down what the European project actually represents and where it might (and should) be going. Besides those—currently a minority—who foresee a return to a purely intergovernmental system of governance with the EU stripped of its main powers, two of the most influential visions refer to Europe as either a "super-state in the making" or a "neo-medieval empire" (Morgan 2005; Walters 2002; Zielonka 2001; Waever 1997).

Those who support the idea of Europe as a "super-state" point out that its current political arrangements present in embryonic form most of the key features of the classical state model: a functioning government, a territory, a population, and the capacity to enter diplomatic relations with other political entities. There are clear parallels with the nation-state building process as well. First, in the same way that in the past city walls became secondary to the new state borders, what we are witnessing today is the downgrading of existing national borders and the transfer of their most important functions to Europe's external frontiers (Walters 2002). This new common border is also greatly fortified (or at least the aspiration is that this border becomes "hard") to allow "domestic" (viz., regional) political, social, and economic processes to be further institutionalized. For those who support the analogy, enlargement is not stopping this development, since what Europe is searching for in this process is its ultimate border (Fischer 2000; Zielonka 2001: 510).

Other signs indicate that Europe is, or at least it is moving toward, a spatial organization different from the modern nation-state. According to Caporaso, Europe's emerging "form of state" is "abstract, disjointed, increasingly fragmented, not based on stable and coherent coalitions of issues or constituencies, and lacking in a clear public space within which competitive visions of the good life and pursuit of self-interested legislation are discussed and debated" (Caporaso 1996: 45). Some commentators draw a parallel between these "postmodern" elements and the structures characterizing Europe's medieval empires (Waever 1997).[24] In a neomedieval model, the various legal, economic, security, and cultural spaces across the region are bound separately, creating a "maze" (Christansen and Jørgensen 2000: 74). Borders are progressively delinked from territory. Controls are applied to persons not on the basis of their physical position but more and more on the basis of their nationality and individual characteristics. In a neomedieval perspective, Europe is becoming "less territorial, less physical and less visible" (Hassner 2001).

The "super-state" and "neo-medieval" models foreground relevant features and dynamics characterizing contemporary Europe. Yet they do not completely capture what is occurring in the region. On one hand, if it is becoming a state, the EU is definitely a sui generis one. Currently Europe has no common army, proper government, fixed territory, cultural identity, or *demos*. And it is not clear whether the existing embryonic statelike traits will evolve into a fully developed entity analogous to the modern state. On the other, the present political system is more regulated and "bordered" than the neomedieval model would suggest. In medieval empires, borders were porous, and there was no structured and widespread surveillance system in place. Imperial influence is today less visible and militaristic than in the past, although its disciplining power over its subjects is arguably greater (Waever 1997: 70).

It is apparent that the political reality in Europe today is a mix of the two models. Europe's system of governance is geographically flexible, but still territorially based; it involves the interpenetration between interior and exterior; it is based on surveillance of the population, although this control is diffused and selective. The supporters of the "super-state" and "neo-medieval" visions of Europe do not deny this state of affairs. However, they seem to suggest that this condition of uncertainty is temporary, and due to the current state of flux of European politics. In their view, Europe will eventually

24. The EU has been compared to other historical examples of empire, such as the Austro-Hungarian (Farago 1995), the Roman (Brague 1993), and the Mesopotamian (Waever 1997).

settle for the proposed model, or at least it *should* go in that direction. The argument is in fact often couched in normative terms.[25]

Seen from a cultural evolutionary perspective, however, Europe's existing hybrid form of governance is more coherent and stable than is generally portrayed. Its apparently clashing features not only coexist, but also *thrive* together. Using the language previously applied to the border control domain, they are in fact evidence of an emerging new "governance culture." This culture can be defined as "neoterritorial" since it is based on the modern principle according to which freedom can only flourish in a clearly demarcated political space. This is the idea Hannah Arendt had in mind when she described the predicament of refugees in postwar Europe:

> Freedom, wherever it existed as a tangible reality, has always been spatially limited. This is especially clear for the greatest and most elementary of all negative liberties, the freedom of movement; the borders of national territory or the walls of the city-state comprehended and protected a space in which man could move freely. Treaties of international guarantees provide an extension of this territorially bound freedom for citizens outside their own country, but even under these modern conditions the elementary coincidence of freedom and a limited space remains manifest. (Arendt, quoted in Apap and Carrera 2003)

Yet this enclosed political space does not necessarily require the entire legal and institutional paraphernalia of the modern state, especially the exclusive and indivisible control over a homogenous territory and population. It can instead be based on a "pooling" of sovereignty and be spread out over a larger and more heterogeneous area than the traditional nation state. This neoterritorial vision by and large reflects that of the European project today.[26]

---

25. This is especially the case for those who support the neomedieval model. In their view, this model should be implemented because it would be "the best suited for a post-modern environment" (Zielonka 2001: 508–509) and because it may establish "a new type of relation between center and periphery, allowing the expansion of the existing area of peace and security across the region" (Hassner 2001: 40). The state model, on the other hand, is "unduly excessive, impractical and at odds with EU's major strategic objectives" (Zielonka 2001: 518).

26. Since border control and territoriality are so strictly interrelated, we could take this line of reasoning a step further and argue that the new trend toward the reterritorialization of Europe is actually the result of a "spill over" of assumptions and practices from the border control domain. In other words, what we are witnessing is a process of *Schengenization* of European politics. This hypothesis is intriguing and is therefore worth pursuing in more depth. For an attempt in this direction, see Zaiotti 2007.

Into the Future: From Border Fixation to Pragmatism?

The Schengen model is today in a phase of consolidation and expansion. Its prospects seem bright. The cultural evolutionary framework proposed here, however, warns against teleological accounts. Given its focus on contingency and agency, this framework suggests that the future of Europe's border control is (at least potentially) open-ended. Alternative projects about how to deal with borders might in fact emerge as potential challengers to Schengen.

At this point, no new proposal is the object of explicit discussion within Europe's border control community. There is the possibility, however, that "old" projects might be reconsidered. Indeed, cultures that have not been selected (or were just superseded by others) may remain dormant and then be resumed at a later stage, adjusted to the new circumstances. A potential trigger for change could come from some of the problems Europe is currently facing in managing its external borders. This is particularly true with regard to the enlargement of the European Union to new members. When Schengen becomes fully operational in these countries, its capacity to effectively secure its frontiers might be questioned. In this context, some members of Europe's border control community might call for a return to an intergovernmental approach to border control free from the EU's legal and institutional constraints, and even the reestablishment of national border checks.

Given the current level of integration and interconnectedness among European countries, a return to a system of hard borders among competing states is unrealistic (Anderson 1996: 249). A more plausible scenario entails the reemergence of a "communitarian" approach to border control along the lines of the "Brussels" initiative originally launched in the 1980s, albeit updated and bolder in scope. This approach would resemble a federal model, involving the delegation of power over Europe's external borders to a supranational agency, the establishment of European border police, and more democratic and judicial control in the policymaking process. The European Commission, together with some traditionally prointegration European governments, is actively supporting this option.[27] Given the unpopularity of the EU project, its appeal is currently very low. In promoting this proposal, the Commission is using a lot of caution, aware of the fact

---

27. Its call for the creation of an EU border guard force under the management of the newly created EU border agency, which would gain a more substantial degree of independence from member states (cf. chap. 8), would be included in this vision.

that the majority of member states and public opinion are not (yet) ready for this new "leap into the dark."

There is a much more difficult obstacle to surmount, however, before this vision can become a reality. It is the persistence among European policy makers and the population at large of what can be defined as "border fixation." (Williams 1996: xx) Despite claims that borders and territory are "passé" (Rosencrance 1996) and we have reached the "end of territoriality" (Badie 1995), borders have not lost their appeal. For some commentators, this fixation is baseless. First of all, advocates of hard borders tend to exaggerate the demand for them.[28] Moreover, borders cannot (and arguably never did) effectively achieve one of the main goals they are established for, namely, preventing unwanted entries into a territory (Anderson and Den Boer 1994; Walker 1998; Jacobson 1996). These arguments are well founded, but they do not take into consideration that the appeal of borders does not stem (or at least not solely) from their "material" functions; instead, it is based on the powerful psychological need for order and stability in a community (Bigo 1999). The leap required to go beyond this border fixation would therefore entail embracing a new type of "post-territorial" governance where this need is addressed in a different fashion. This possibility does exist. According to Ruggie, politics is about rule, and the most generic attribute of any system of rule is the "legitimate dominion over a spatial extension" (Ruggie 1993: 148). Although the social dimension of any spatial extension involves some mode of differentiating human collectivities from one another, "these systems of differentiation need not be territorial, nor fixed" (ibid.).

Some authors have attempted to show how this new post-territorial vision might be realized (Maier 2001; Zielonka 2001: 530; Breuilly 1998; Guéhenno 1995). Given the existing inward-looking political climate in Europe, the conditions to overcome the long-lasting fascination with borders do not seem ripe. European politics is nevertheless not new to far-reaching and "unimaginable" transformations. Europe is a constant work in progress, an open-ended experiment that can be readjusted in light of new events or circumstances. It is therefore truly "artificial" in the sense that Michelet uses the term in an epigraph to this chapter. This artificiality, however, does not

---

28. A good case in point is Western Europe's fear of mass migration from the east after the fall of the Iron Curtain. From 1989 until 2000, Eastern Europeans were only 15 percent of the total migrants in the EU (6 percent of foreign workers) and 0.2 percent of the workforce (Thränhardt 1996). If we include illegal immigrants, the percentage would probably double, but the numbers are still far from alarming.

have to assume the Jacobin characters (viz., radical and hyper-rationalist) that Margaret Thatcher so strongly despised in the European project:

> [L]ook at the architecture of the last fifty years—look, in particular, at the architecture that went beyond the modern to the futuristic. It was certainly a very dramatic architecture but the one thing it no longer expresses is the Future. What it expresses is yesterday's vision of the future. C'est magnifique, mais ce n'est pas la politique.[29]

As the Schengen experience has shown, "dramatic" projects in European politics can be conceived and realized in a pragmatic and evolutionary fashion and be able to successfully withstand the future. Although she would probably object to the idea, not least because it applies to initiatives that foster European integration, the way these projects are put into practice actually comes very close to the essence of *la politique* as the Iron Lady envisioned it.

---

29. Margaret Thatcher, "Europe's Political Architecture," speech in The Hague, May 15, 1992, Thatcher Archive.

REFERENCES

Adler, E. 1991. "Cognitive Evolution: A Dynamic Approach for the Study of International Relations and their Progress." In *Progress in Postwar International Relations*, ed. E. Adler and B. Crawford. New York: Columbia University Press.

———. 1997. "Seizing the Middle Ground: Constructivism in World Politics." *European Journal of International Relations* 3, no. 3: 319–363.

———. 2005. *Communitarian International Relations. The Epistemic Foundations of International Relations*. London and New York: Routledge.

Adler, E., and M. Barnett, eds. 1998. *Security Communities*. Cambridge: Cambridge University Press.

Adler, E., and V. Pouliot, eds. Forthcoming. *The Practice Turn in International Relations*. Cambridge: Cambridge University Press.

Agnew, J. 1994. "The Territorial Trap: Geographical Assumptions in International Relations." *Review of International Political Economy* 1, no. 1: 53–80.

———. 2002. "The 'Civilisational' Roots of European National Boundaries." In *Boundaries and Place: European Borderlands in Geographical Context*, ed. D. H. Kaplan. Lanham: Rowman & Littlefield.

Albert, M., and T. Kopp-Malek. 2002. "The Pragmatism of Global and European Governance: Emerging Forms of the Political 'Beyond Westphalia.'" *Millennium: Journal of International Studies* 31, no. 3: 453–471.

Albert, M., D. Jacobson, and J. Lapid, eds. 2000. *Identities, Borders, Orders: Rethinking International Relations Theory*. Minneapolis: University of Minnesota Press.

Allen, D. 1992. "European Union, the Single European Act and the 1992 Programme." In *The Single European Market and Beyond. A Study of the Wider Implications of the Single European Act*, ed. D. De Swann. London and New York: Routledge.

Amato, G., and J. Batt. 1999. *Final Report of the Reflection Group on the Long Term Implications of EU Enlargement: The Nature of the New Border*. Florence: Robert Schuman Center and Forward Studies Unit, EC.

Anderson, B. 1983. *Imagined Communities: Reflections on the Origin and Spread of Nationalism*. London: Verso.

Anderson, D. R. 1986. "The Evolution of Peirce's Concept of Abduction." *Transactions of the Charles S. Peirce Society* 22, no. 2: 145–164.

Anderson, J., L. O' Dowd, and T. M. Wilson, eds. 2003. *New Borders for a Changing Europe: Cross-border Cooperation and Governance*. London: Franck Cass.

Anderson, M. 1996. *Frontiers: Territory and State Formation in the Modern World*. Cambridge: Polity Press.

Anderson, M., and E. Bort, eds. 1998. *The Frontiers of Europe*. London and Washington: Pinter.

Anderson, M., and J. Apap, eds. 2002. *Police and Justice Co-Operation and the New European Borders*. The Hague: Kluwer Law International.

Anderson, M., et al. 1996. *Policing the European Union*. New York: Oxford University Press.

Andreas, P., and T. J. Biersteker. 2003. *The Rebordering of North America: Integration and Exclusion in a New Security Context*. London: Routledge.

Andreas, P., and T. Snyder, eds. 2000. *The Wall around the West: State Borders and Immigration Controls in North America and Europe*. Lanham: Rowman & Littlefield.

Ansell, C. K. 2004. *Restructuring Territoriality: Europe and the United States*. Cambridge: Cambridge University Press.

Apap, J., and S. Carrera. 2003. "Maintaining Security within Borders: Towards a Permanent State of Emergency in the EU?" *CEPS Policy Brief* 41 (Nov.): 1–18.

Appadurai, A. 1996. "Sovereignty without Territoriality: Notes for a Postnational Geography." In *The Geography of Identity*, ed. P. Yaeger. Ann Arbor: University of Michigan Press.

Armbruster, H., C. Rollo, and U. H. Meinhof. 2003. "Imagining Europe: Everyday Narratives in European Border Communities." *Journal of Ethnic and Migration Studies* 29, no. 5: 885–899.

Badie, B. 1995. *La fin des territoires*. Paris: Fayard.

Balzacq, T., Bigo, D., Carrera, S. and Guild, E. 2006. "Security and the Two-level Game: The Treaty of Prüm, the EU and the Management of Threats." Working Document no. 234, CEPS, Brussels.

Barnett, M. 1999. "Culture, Strategy and Foreign Policy Change: Israel's Road to Oslo." *European Journal of International Relations* 5, no. 1: 5–36.

Bates, R., A. Greif, M. Levi, J.-L. Rosenthal, and B. Weingast. 1998. *Analytical Narratives*. Princeton: Princeton University Press.

Bauer, H., and E. Brighi, eds. 2008. *Pragmatism in International Relations*. London and New York: Routledge.

Berg, E., and H. Van Houtum, eds. 2003. *Routing Borders between Territories, Discourses and Practices*. Aldershot: Ashgate.

Bernstein, R. J. 1992. "The Resurgence of Pragmatism." *Social Research* 59: 813–840.

Bernstein, S. F. 2001. *The Compromise of Liberal Environmentalism*. New York: Columbia University Press.

Bialasiewicz, L., S. Elden, and J. Painter. 2005. "The Constitution of EU Territory." *Comparative European Politics* 3, no. 3: 333–363.

Biaya, Tshikala K. 2000. "Jeunes et culture de la rue en Afrique urbaine." *Politique Africaine* 80 (Dec.): 12–31.

Bigo, D. 1994. "The European Internal Security Field: Stakes and Rivalries in a Newly Developing Area of Police Intervention." In *Policing across National Boundaries*, ed. M. Anderson and M. den Boer M. London: Pinter.

———. 1996. *Polices en réseaux: l'Expérience européenne*. Paris: Presses de la Fondation Nationale des Sciences Politiques.

———. 1998. "Frontiers and Security in the European Union: The Illusion of Migration Control." In *The Frontiers of Europe*, ed. M. Anderson and E. Bort. London and Washington: Pinter.

———. 2000a. "Liaison Officers in Europe: New Actors in the European Security Field." In *Issues in transnational policing*, ed. J. W. E. Sheptycki, 67–100. London: Routledge.

———. 2000b. "When Two Become One: Internal and External Securitisations in Europe." In *International Relations Theory and the Politics of European Integration, Power, Security and Community*, ed. M. Kelstrup and M. C. Williams, 171–205. London., Routledge.

———. 2001. "Internal and External Security(ies): The Möbius Ribbon." In *Identities, Borders and Orders: Rethinking International Relations Theory*, ed. M. Albert, D. Jacobson, and Y. Lapid. Borderlines. Minneapolis: University of Minnesota Press.

———. 2003. "Le champ européen de l' (in)sécurité: Enquête et hypothèses de travail." In *Vers des périmètres de sécurité? La gestion des espaces continentaux en Amérique du Nord et en Europe*, ed. M. Fortmann, S. Roussel, and A. Macleod, 22–56. Montreal: Athéna Éditions.

Bigo, D., and E. Guild. 2003. *La mise à l'ecart des étrangers: Le visa Schengen*. Paris: L'Harmattan.

Bigo, D., and E. Guild, eds. 2005. *Controlling Frontiers: Free Movement into and within Europe*. London: Ashgate.

Bolten, J. J. 1991. "From Schengen to Dublin: The New Frontiers of Refugee Law." In *Schengen: Internationalisation of Central Chapters of the Law on Aliens, Refugees, Privacy, Security and the Police*, ed. H. Meijers et al. Utrecht: Kluwer Law and Taxation Publishers.

Bonvicini, G. 1987. "The Genscher-Colombo Plan and the 'Solemn Declaration on European Union' (1981–83)." In *The Dynamics of European Union*, ed. R. Pryce. London: Routledge.

Bort, E. 2003. "EU Enlargement—Policing the New Borders." *International Spectator* 28, no. 1: 51–68.

Boswell, C. 2003. "The 'External Dimension' of EU Immigration and Asylum Policy." *International Affairs* 79, no. 3: 619–638.

Bourdieu, P. 1998. *Practical Reason*. Stanford: Stanford University Press.

Brague, R. 1993. "Europe: Tous les chemins passent par Rome." *Esprit* (Feb.): 32–40.

Brunet-Jailly, E. 2007. *Borderlands: Comparing Border Security in North America and Europe*. Ottawa: University of Ottawa Press.

Bukovansky, M. 2002. *Legitimacy and Power Politics: The American and French Revolutions in International Political Culture*. Princeton: Princeton University Press.

Bunyan, T. 1993. "Trevi, Europol, and the New European State." In *A Handbook on the European State*, ed T. Bunyan, 15–40. London: Statewatch Publication / Unison.

Burgess, M. 2006. *State Territoriality and European Integration*. London: Routledge.

Calamia, P. 1990. "Accordi di Schengen.'" *Rivista di Cooperazione del Ministero degli Affari esteri*.

Caloz-Tschopp, M.-C., and Fontolliet, M., eds. 1994. *Europe, montrez patte blanche! Les nouvelles frontières du "laboratoire Schengen."* Geneva: Cetin.

Campbell, D. T. 1974. "Evolutionary Epistemology." In *The Philosophy of Karl Popper*, ed. P. A. Schilpp. LaSalle: Open Court Publishing Co.

Caporaso, J. A. 1996. "The European Union and Forms of State: Westphalian, Regulatory or Post-Modern?" *Journal of Common Market Studies* 34, no. 1: 29–52.

Castle, S., and Miller, M. J. 1998. *The Age of Migration: International Population Movements in the Modern World*. 2nd ed. New York: Guildford Press.

Chauviré, C. 2005. "Peirce, Popper, Abduction, and the Idea of a Logic of Discovery." *Semiotica* 153, nos. 1–4: 209–221.

Christiansen, T. and Jørgensen, K. E. 2000. "Transnational governance 'above' and 'below' the state: The changing nature of borders in the new Europe." *Regional and Federal Studies* 10, no. 2: 62–77.

Christiansen, T., K. E. Jørgensen, and A. Wiener, eds. 2001. *The Social Construction of Europe*. London: Sage.

Christiansen, T., F. Petito, and B. Tonra. 2000. "Fuzzy Politics around Fuzzy Borders: The European Union's 'Near Abroad.'" *Cooperation and Conflict* 35, no. 4 (Dec.): 389–415.

Commission of the European Communities. 2000. *The Free Movement of Persons for the Pursuit of Economic Activity in the Context of Enlargement.* Commission of the European Communities Information Note, Brussels, April 2000, mimeo.

Cooper, J., and R. H. Fazio. 1984. "A New Look at Dissonance Theory." *Advances in Experimental Social Psychology* 17: 229–245.

Corbett, R. 1992. "The Intergovernmental Conference on Political Union." *Journal of Common Market Studies* 30, no. 3: 271–298.

Curtin, D. 1993. "The Constitutional Structure of the Union: A Europe of Bits and Pieces." *Common Market Law Review* 30: 17–69.

———. 1997. *Postnational Democracy: The European Union in Search of a Political Philosophy.* The Hague and London: Kluwer Law International.

Curtin, D., and H. Meijers. 1995. "The Principle of Open Government in Schengen and the EU: Democratic Retrogression?" *Common Market Law Review* 32: 403–411.

Curzon of Kedleston, Lord. 1907. *Frontiers.* The Romanes Lecture, 1907. Oxford: Clarendon Press.

Czarniawska, B. 2004. *Narratives in Social Science Research.* London: Sage.

Dalby, S. 1991. "Critical Geopolitics: Discourse, Difference, and Dissent." *Environment and Planning D: Society and Space* 9: 261–283.

Dawkins, R. 1976. *The Selfish Gene.* Oxford: Oxford University Press.

De Zwaan, J. W. 1986. "The Single European Act: Conclusion of a Unique Document." *Common Market Law Review* 23: 747–765.

———. 1998. "Schengen and the Incorporation into the New Treaty: The Negotiating Process." In *Schengen's Final Days? The Incorporation of Schengen into the New TEU, External Borders and Information Systems,* ed. M. Den Boer, 13–24. Maastricht: European Institute of Public Administration.

Den Boer, M. 1995. "Moving between Bogus and Bona Fide: The Policing of Inclusion and Exclusion in Europe." In *Migration and European Integration: The Dynamics of Inclusion and Exclusion,* ed. R. Miles and D. Thränhardt, 92–111. London: Pinter.

———. 1996. "Justice and Home Affairs: Cooperation without Integration." In *Policy-Making in the European Union,* ed. H. Wallace and W. Wallace. 3rd ed. Oxford: Oxford University Press.

———. 2001. "The Incorporation of Schengen into the TEU: A Bridge Too Far?" In *The Treaty of Amsterdam: Challenges and Opportunities for the European Union,* ed. J. Monar and W. Wessels. London: Continuum.

Den Boer, M., ed. 1997a. *The Implementation of Schengen: First the Widening, Now the Deepening.* Maastricht: European Institute of Public Administration.

———. 1997b. *Schengen: Judicial Cooperation and Policy Coordination.* Maastricht: European Institute of Public Administration.

———. 1998. *Schengen's Final Days? The Incorporation of Schengen into the New TEU, External Borders and Information Systems.* Maastricht: European Institute of Public Administration.

———. 2000. *Schengen Still Going Strong: Evaluation and Update.* Maastricht: European Institute of Public Administration.

Den Boer, M., and L. Corrado. 1999. "For the Record or Off the Record: Comments about the Incorporation of Schengen into the EU." *European Journal of Migration and Law* 1, no. 4: 397–418.

Den Boer, M., and W. Wallace. 2000. "Justice and Home Affairs." In *Policy-Making in the*

European Union, ed. H. Wallace and W. Wallace. 3rd ed. Oxford: Oxford University Press.

Denza, E. 2002. *The Intergovernmental Pillars of the European Union*. Oxford: Oxford University Press.

Dickstein, M., ed. 1998. *The Revival of Pragmatism: New Essays on Social Thought, Law, and Culture*. Durham: Duke University Press.

Diettrich, O. 1992. "Darwin, Lamarck and the Evolution of Science and Culture." *Evolution and Cognition* 1st ser., 2, no. 3. http://www.vub.ac.be/CLEA/people/diettrich/04.pdf.

Doty, R. L. 1996. "Immigration and national identity: constructing the nation." *Review of International Studies*, 22: 235–255.

Dowding, K. 2002. "Rational Choice and Institutional Change: An Overview of Current Theories." In *Widening the European Union: The Politics of Institutional Change and Reform*, ed. B. Steuneberg. London: Routledge.

Duchêne, F. 1972. "Europe's Role in World Peace." In *Europe Tomorrow: Sixteen Europeans Look Ahead*, ed. R. Mayne, 32–47. London: Fontana.

Ehlermann, C.-D. 1987. "The Internal Market Following the Single European Act." *Common Market Law Review* 24: 361–409.

Elsen, C. 1997. "Schengen et la coopération dans le domaines de la justice et des affaires intérieurs. Besoins actuels et options futures." In *The Implementation of Schengen: First the Widening, Now the Deepening*, ed. M. Den Boer. Maastricht: European Institute of Public Administration.

———. 1999. "L'esprit et les ambitions de Tampere. Une ère nouvelle pour la coopération dans le domaine de la justice et des affaires intérieures." *Revue du marché commun et de l'Union européenne* 433 (Nov.–Dec.): 559–563.

———. 2000. "Incorporation juridique et institutionelle de Schengen dans l'UE." In *Schengen Still Going Strong: Evaluation and Update*, ed. M. Den Boer, 11–20. Maastricht: European Institute of Public Administration.

———. 2003. "Le Conseil européen de Thessalonique: un nouveau pas vers une politique commune en matière d'asile, d'immigration et de contrôle aux frontiers." *Revue du marché commun et de l'Union européenne* 471: 516–518.

Eskelinen, H., I. Liikanen, and J. Oksa, eds. 1999. *Curtains of Iron and Gold: Reconstructing Borders and Scales of Interaction*. Aldershot: Ashgate.

European Parliament. 1990. "Defining the European Community's Borders." Written question no. 2315/90 by Mr. Filippos Pierros, Mr. Patrick Cooney, Mr. Karel Pinxten, Mrs. Mary Banotti, Mr. Menelaos Hadjigeorgiou, Mr. Georgios Zavvos, Mr. John McCartin and Mr. Mihail Papayannakis to the Commission of the European Communities, 22/04/91. *Official Journal No. C* 107, p. 22.

Fairclough, N. 1992. *Discourse and Social Change*. Oxford: Polity Press.

Farago, B. 1995. "L'Europe: Empire Introuvable." *Le Debat* 83: 42–58.

Ferraris, L.V., ed. 1979. *Report on a Negotiation: Helsinki-Geneva-Helsinki, 1972–1975*. Alpen aan den Rijn: Sijthoff & Noordhoff International Publishers.

Festinger, L. 1957. *A Theory of Cognitive Dissonance*. Stanford: Stanford University Press.

Finnemore, M., and K. Sikkink. 1998. "International Norm Dynamics and Political Change." *International Organization* 52, no. 4 (Oct.): 887–917.

Fischer, Joschka. 2000. *From Confederacy to Federation. Thoughts on the Finality of European Integration*. Speech at the Humboldt University in Berlin, 12 May. Berlin: Humboldt University.

Flynn, S. 2000. "Beyond border control." *Foreign Affairs* 79, no. 6: 57–68.

Florini, A. 1996. "The Evolution of International Norms." *International Studies Quarterly* 40, no. 3: 363–389.

Flory. M. 2001. "Le couple État-territoire en droit international contemporain." *Cultures et Conflicts* 43: 252–265.

Fortescue, J. A. 1995. "First Experiences with the Implementation of the Third Pillar Provisions." In *Justice and Home Affairs in the European Union: The Development of the Third Pillar*, ed. R. Bieber and J. Monar, 19–27. Brussels: European University Press.

Foucault, Michel. 1980. "Questions on Geography." In *Power/Knowledge: Selected Interviews and Other Writings, 1972–1977*, ed. C. Gordon. New York: Pantheon.

Foucher, M. 1998. "The Geopolitics of European Frontiers.'" In *The Frontiers of Europe*, ed. M. Anderson and E. Bort, 235–250. London: Pinter.

Fridegotto, M. 1993. *L'Accordo di Schengen: Riflessi internazionali ed interni per l'Italia*. Milan: Franco Angeli.

Geddes, A. 1999. *Immigration and European Integration: Towards Fortress Europe?* Manchester: Manchester University Press.

———. 2001. "International Migration and State Sovereignty in an Integrating Europe." *International Migration* 39, no. 6: 21–42.

Geertz, C. 1973. *The Interpretation of Cultures*. New York: Basic Books.

———. 1975. "Commonsense as a Cultural System." *Antioch Review* 33: 5–26.

Gehring, T. 1998. "Die Politik des koordinierten Alleingangs." *Zeitschrift fuer Internationale Beziehungen* 5, no. 1: 43–78.

Giddens, A. 1987. *Social Theory and Modern Sociology*. Oxford: Polity Press.

———. 1976. *New Rules of Sociological Method: A Positive Critique of Interpretative Sociologies*. New York: Harper & Row.

Goudge, T. 1950. *The Thought of C. S. Peirce*. Toronto: University of Toronto Press.

Goujon, A. 2005. 'L'Europe élargie en quête d'identité: légitimation et politisation de la politique européenne de voisinage.' *Politique Européenne* 15: 137–163.

Grabbe, H. 2000. "The Sharp Edges of Europe: Extending Schengen Eastwards." *International Affairs* 76, no. 3:519–536.

Groenendijk, Kees. 2004. "Reinstatement of Controls at the Internal Borders of Europe: Why and Against Whom?" *European Law Journal* 10, no. 2: 150–170.

Groenendijk, K., E. Guild, and P. Minderhoud, eds. 2003. *In Search of Europe's Borders*. The Hague: Kluwer.

Guéhenno, J. M. 1995. *The End of the Nation-State*. Translated by Victoria Elliott. Minneapolis: University of Minnesota Press.

Guild, E. 1999a. "Adjudicating Schengen: National Judicial Control in France." *European Journal of Migration and Law* 1, no. 4: 419–439.

———. 1999b. *The Legal Framework and Social Consequences of Free Movement of Persons in the European Union*. Boston: Kluwer Law International.

———. 2001. *Moving the Borders of Europe*. [Netherlands]: Centrum Vooor Postdoctoraal Onderwijs.

———. 2003. "International Terrorism and EU Immigration, Asylum and Borders Policy: The Unexpected Victims of 11 September 2001." *European Foreign Affairs Review* 8: 331–346.

Guild, E. 2005. "What Is a Neighbour? Examining the EU Neighbourhood Policy from the Perspective of Movement of Persons." Paper presented at the Western NIS Forum for Refugee-Assisting NGOs, Yalta, 1–3 June 2005.

———. 2006. "Danger: Borders under Construction; Assessing the First Five Years of Border Policy in an Area of Freedom, Security and Justice." Challenge Network Working Paper (Brussels).

Guiraudon, V. 2001. "The EU 'garbage can': Accounting for Policy Developments in the Immigration Domain." Paper presented at the 2001 conference of the European Community Studies Association, Madison, Wisconsin, 29 May–1 June 2001.

———. 2003. "The Constitution of a European Immigration Policy Domain: A Political Sociology Approach." *Journal of European Public Policy* 10, no. 2: 263–282.

Haas, E. B. 1990. *When Knowledge Is Power: Three Models of Change in International Organizations.* Berkeley: University of California Press.

Haas, P. M., and E. B. Haas. 2002. "Pragmatic Constructivism and the Study of International Institutions." *Millennium: Journal of International Studies* 31, no. 3: 573–601.

Hailbronner, K. 1998, "European Immigration and Asylum Law under the Amsterdam Treaty." *Common Market Law Review* 35: 1047–67.

Hailbronner, K., and C. Thierry. 1997. "Schengen II and Dublin, Responsibility for Asylum Applications in Europe." *Common Market Law Review* 34: 957–989.

Häkli, J. 2001. "In the Territory of Knowledge: State-centred Discourses and the Construction of Society." *Progress in Human Geography* 25, no. 3: 403–422.

Hall, P. A. 1993. "Policy Paradigms, Social Learning and the State." *Comparative Politics* 25, no. 3: 275–296.

Ham, P. van. 2002. *Mapping European Security after Kosovo.* Manchester: Manchester University Press.

Handoll, J. 1995. *Free Movement of Persons in the EU.* Chicester: John Wiley & Sons.

Hassner P. 2001. "Fixed Borders or Moving Borderlands? A New Type of Border for a New Type of Entity." European University Institute Working Paper.

Hausman, C. 1993. *Charles S. Peirce's Evolutionary Philosophy.* New York: Cambridge University Press.

Hein, C. 2000. "Italy: Gateway to Europe, but Not the Gatekeeper?" In *Kosovo's Refugees in the European Union,* ed. J. van Selm. London: Pinter.

Herz, J. 1957. "Rise and Demise of the Territorial State." *World Politics* 9, no. 4: 473–493

———. 1968. "The Territorial State Revised: Reflections on the Future of the Nation-State." *Polity* 1, no. 1: 11–24.

Hix, S. 1994. "The Study of the European Community: The Challenge to Comparative Politics." *West European Politics* 17, no. 1: 1–30.

Hix, S., and J. Niessen. 1996. *Reconsidering European Immigration Policies. The 1996 IGC or the Reform of the Maastricht Treaty.* Brussels: Migration Policy Group.

Hodgson, G. M. 2001. "Is Social Evolution Lamarckian or Darwinian?" In *Darwinism and Evolutionary Economics,* ed. J. Laurent and John Nightingale, 87–118. Cheltenham: Edward Elgar.

Hoogenboom, T. 1991. "Free Movement of Non-EU Nationals, Schengen and Beyond." In *Schengen. Internationalisation of Central Chapters of the Law on Aliens, Refugees, Privacy, Security and the Police,* ed. H. Meijers et al. Utrecht: Kluwer Law and Taxation Publishers.

Hookway, C.J. 1985. *Peirce.* London: Routledge.

House of Lords. 1989. Select Committee on the European Communities, Session 1988–89, 22nd report. *1992, Border Control of People* (with Evidence). HL Paper 90. London: HMSO.

———. 1999. Committee on the European Communities, Session 1998–99, 19th Report. *Prospects for the Tampere Special European Council.* HP Paper 101. London: HMSO.

Houser, N. 2005. "Peirce in the 21st Century." *Transactions of the Charles S. Peirce Society* 41, no. 4: 729–739.

Hreblay, V. 1998. *Les Accords de Schengen: Origine, fonctionnement, avenir.* Brussels: Bruylant.

Hudson, V. M. 1997. *Culture and Foreign Policy.* Boulder: Lynne Ryenner Publishers.

Huysmans, J. 1995. "Migrants as a Security Problem: Dangers of 'Securitizing' Societal Issues." In *Migration and European Integration: The Dynamics of Inclusion and Exclusion,* ed. R. Miles and D. Thränhardt. London: Pinter.

———. 2000. "The European Union and the Securitization of Migration." *Journal of Common Market Studies* 38: 751–777.

Jachtenfuchs, M. 2001. "The Governance Approach to European Integration." *Journal of Common Market Studies* 39: 245–264.

Jackman, R. W., and Ross A. Miller. 1996. "A Renaissance of Political Culture?" *American Journal of Political Science* 40, no. 3: 632–659.

Jacquin-Berdal, D., A. Oros, and M. Verweij, eds. 1998. *Culture in World Politics.* London: Millennium.

Jepperson, R. L., and A. Swidler. 1994. "What Properties of Culture Should We Measure?" *Poetics* 22, no. 4 (June): 359–371.

Jileva, E. 2002. "Visa and Free Movement of Labour: The Uneven Imposition of the EU acquis on the Accession States." *Journal of Ethnic and Migration Studies* 28, no. 4 (Oct.): 683–700.

Jøergensen, K. E., ed. 1997. *Reflective Approaches to European Governance.* London: MacMillan.

Johnston, A. I. 1996. "Cultural realism and strategy in Maoist China." In *The Culture of National Security,* ed. P. J. Katzenstein. New York: Columbia University Press.

Johnston, A. I. 2001. "Treating International Institutions as Social Environments." *International Studies Quarterly* 45, no. 4 (Dec.): 487–515.

Jönsson, C., S. Tägil, and G. Törnqvist. 2000. *Organizing European Space.* London: Sage.

Joppke, C. 1998. *Challenge to the Nation State: Immigration in Western Europe and the United States.* New York: Oxford University Press.

Katzenstein, P. J., ed. 1996. *The Culture of National Security.* New York: Columbia University Press.

Keraudren, P. 1994. "Réticencs et obstacles français face à Schengen: La logique de la politique de sécurité." In *Schengen en Panne,* ed. A. Pauly. Maastricht: European Institute of Public Administration.

Krasner, S. D. 1999. *Sovereignty: Organized Hypocrisy.* Princeton: Princeton University Press.

Kuhn, T. 1962. *The Structure of Scientific Revolutions.* Chicago: University of Chicago Press.

Kuijper, P. J. 2000. "Some Legal Problems Associated with the Communitarization of Policy on Visas, Asylum and Immigration under the Amsterdam Treaty and Incorporation of the Schengen Acquis." *Common Market Law Review* 37, no. 2: 345–66.

Laffan, B. 2004. "The European Union and Its Institutions as 'Identify Builders.'" In *Transnational Identities: Becoming European in the EU,* ed. R. K. Herrmann, T. Risse, and M. B. Brewer. London: Rowman & Littlefield Publishers.

Laffey, M., and J. Weldes. 1997. "Beyond Belief: Ideas and Symbolic Technologies in the Study of International Relations." *European Journal of International Relations* 3, no. 2: 193–237.

Lahav, G. 2004. *Immigration and Politics in the New Europe: Reinventing Borders.* Cambridge: Cambridge University Press.

Lahav, G., and V. Guiraudon. 2000. "Comparative Perspectives on Border Control: Away from the Border and Outside the State." In *The Wall around the West: State Borders and*

Immigration Controls in North America and Europe, ed. P. Andreas and T. Snyder. Lanham: Rowman & Littlefield Publishers.

Lapid, Y., and F. Kratochwil. 1996. *The Return of Culture and Identity in IR Theory*. Boulder: Lynne Rienner Publishers.

———. 1977. *Progress and Its Problems: Towards a Theory of Scientific Growth*. Berkeley: University of California Press.

———. 1981. "A Problem-Solving Approach to Scientific Progress." In *Scientific Revolutions*, ed. I. Hacking. Oxford: Oxford University Press.

———. 1984. *Science and Values: The Aims of Science and Their Role in Scientific Debate*. Berkeley: University of California Press.

Lave, J., and E. Wenger. 1991. *Situated Learning: Legitimate Peripheral Participation*. Cambridge: Cambridge University Press.

Lavenex, S. 2001. "Migration and the EU's New Eastern Border: Between Realism and Liberalism." *Journal of European Public Policy* 8, no. 1: 24–42.

Lavenex, S., and E. M. Uçarer, eds. 2002. *Migration and the Externalities of European Integration*. Boulder: Lexington Books.

Leitner, H. 1997. "Reconfiguring the Spatiality of Power: The Construction of a Supranational Migration Framework for the European Union." *Political Geography* 16, no. 2: 123–143.

Lequesne, C. 1993. *Paris-Bruxelles: Comment se fait la politique européenne de la France*. Paris: Presses de la Fondation nationale des sciences politiques.

Lo Iacono, G. 1995. "La partecipazione dell'Italia all'attivita' del Gruppo di Schengen." In *Da Maastricth a Schengen*, ed. B. Nascimbene. Milan: Giuffrè.

Lodge, J. 1998a. "Intergovernmental Conferences and European Integration: Negotiating the Amsterdam Treaty." *International Negotiation* 3: 345–362.

———. 1998b. "Negotiations in the European Union: The 1996 Intergovernmental Conference." *International Negotiation* 3, no. 3: 481–505.

Lutterbeck, Derek. 2005. "Blurring the Dividing Line: The Convergence of Internal and External Security in Western Europe." *European Security* 14, no. 2: 231–253.

Maier, C. S. 2002. "Does Europe Need a Frontier? From Territorial to Redistributive Community." In *Europe Unbound: Enlarging and Reshaping the Boundaries of the European Union*, ed. J. Zielonka. London: Routledge.

Majone, G. 1994. "The Rise of the Regulatory State in Europe." *Western European Politics* 17, no. 3: 77–101.

Mann, M. 1993. "Nation-States in Europe and Other Continents: Diversifying, Developing, not Dying." *Daedalus* 112, no. 3: 115–140.

Manners, I. 2002. "Normative Power Europe: A Contradiction in Terms?" *Journal of Common Market Studies* 40, no. 2: 235–258.

Marinho, C., ed. 2000. *The Dublin Convention on Asylum: Its Essence, Implementation and Prospects*. Maastricht: European Institute of Public Administration.

McAllister, R. 1997. *From the EC to the EU: An Historical and Political Survey*. London: Routledge.

McDonagh, B. 1998. *Original Sin in a Brave New World: An Account of the Negotiation of the Treaty of Amsterdam*. Dublin: Institute of European Affairs.

McLean, I. 2003. "Two Analytical Narratives about the History of the EU." *European Union Politics* 4: 519–526.

Meijers, H., et al., eds. 1991. *Schengen. Internationalisation of Central Chapters of the Law on Aliens, Refugees, Privacy, Security and the Police*. Utrecht: Kluwer Law and Taxation Publishers.

Meinhof, U. H., ed. 2002. *Living (with) Borders. Identity Discourses on East-West Borders in Europe.* Aldershot: Ashgate.

Mény, Y. 2002. "The External and Internal, Borders of the Great Europe." *International Spectator* 27, no. 2: 19–25.

Meyer, J., et al. 1997. "World Society and the Nation State." *American Journal of Sociology* 101: 144–181.

Meyers, P. 1995. "The Commission's Approach to the Third Pillar: Political and Organizational Elements." In *Justice and Home Affairs in the European Union: The Development of the Third Pillar,* ed. R. Bieber and J. Monar. Brussels: European Interuniversity Press.

Milliken, J. 2001. "Discourse Study: Bringing Rigor to Critical Theory." In *Constructing International Relations: The Next Generation,* ed. K. M. Fierke and K. E. Jorgensen, 136–159. Armonk: M. E. Sharpe.

Milward, A. S. 2000. *The European Rescue of the Nation-state.* London and New York: Routledge.

———. 2002. *The United Kingdom and the European Community.* London: Frank Cass.

Mitsilegas, V. 2002. "The Implementation of the EU *Acquis* on Illegal Immigration by the Candidate Countries of Central and Eastern Europe: Challenges and Contradictions." *Journal of Ethnic and Migration Studies* 28, no. 5: 665–682.

———. 2003. *The European Union and Internal Security: Guardian of the People?* New York: Basingstoke.

Modelski, G. 1990. "Is World Politics Evolutionary Learning?" *International Organization* 44, no. 1: 1–24.

Modelski, G., and K. Poznanski. 1996. "Evolutionary Paradigms in the Social Sciences." *International Studies Quarterly* 40, no. 3: 315–319.

Monar, J. 1998. "Schengen and Flexibility in the Treaty of Amsterdam: Opportunities and Risks of Differentiated Integration in EU Justice and Home Affairs." In *Schengen: Judicial Cooperation and Policy Coordination,* ed. M. Den Boer. Maastricht: European Institute of Public Administration.

———. 1999. "An Emerging Regime of European Governance for Freedom, Security and Justice." *One Europe or Several?* Programme, briefing note 2/99. Falmer: Sussex European Institute.

———. 2000. "The Impact of Schengen on Justice and Home Affairs in the European Union: An Assessment on the Threshold to Its Incorporation." In *Schengen Still Going Strong,* ed. M. Den Boer, 21–35. Maastricht: European Institute of Public Administration.

———. 2001. "The Dynamics of Justice and Home Affairs: Laboratories, Driving Factors and Costs." *Journal of Common Market Studies* 39, no. 4: 747–764.

———. 2002. "Institutionalizing Freedom, Security and Justice." In *The Institutions of the European Union,* ed. J. Peterson and M. Shacleton. Oxford: Oxford University Press.

———. 2003a. "The Project of a European Border Guard: Potential, Models and Challenges." Paper presented at the workshop "Managing International and Inter-Agency Cooperation at the Border," Geneva, 13–15 March 2003, organized by the Working Group on Democratic Control of Internal Security Services (DCOIS) of the Geneva Centre for the Democratic Control of Armed Forces.

———. 2003b. "Justice and Home Affairs after the 2004 Enlargement." *International Spectator* 28, no. 1: 33–50.

———. 2004. "The EU as an International Actor in the Domain of Justice and Home Affairs." *European Foreign Affairs Review* 9: 395–415.

Monar, J., E. Bort, and G. Grasso. 2003. "The Impact of Enlargement on Justice and Home Affairs." *International Spectator* 38, no. 1: 33–80.

Monar, J., and R. Morgan, eds. 1994. *The Third Pillar of the European Union: Cooperation in the Fields of Justice and Home Affairs.* Brussels: European University Press.

Monar, J., and W. Wessels, eds. 2002. *The Treaty of Amsterdam: Challenges and Opportunities for the European Union.* London: Continuum.

Monnet, J. 1978. *Memoirs.* Translated by R. Mayne. London: Collins.

Moravcsik, A. 1998. *The Choice for Europe: Social Purpose and State Power from Messina to Maastricht.* Ithaca: Cornell University Press.

Morgan, G.. 2005. *The Idea of a European Superstate: Public Justification and European Integration.* Princeton: Princeton University Press.

Morley, D. and Robins, K. *Spaces of Identity. Global Media, Electronic Landscapes and Cultural Boundaries.* London: Routledge, 1995.

Müller, H. 1993. "The Internationalization of Principles, Norms and Rules by Governments." In *Regime Theory and International Relations,* ed. V. Rittenberger, 361–388. Oxford: Oxford University Press.

Müller-Graf, P.-G. 1994. "The Legal Basis of the Third Pillar and Its Position in the Framework of the Union Treaty." *Common Market Law Review* 31: 493–510.

———. 1995. "The Dublin Convention, Pioneer and Lesson for Third Pillar Conventions." In *Justice and Home Affairs in the European Union. The Development of the Third Pillar,* ed. R. Bieber and J. Monar. Brussels: European Interuniversity Press.

———. 1998. "Whose Responsibility Are Frontiers?" In *The Frontiers of Europe,* ed. M. Anderson and E. Bort. London and Washington: Pinter.

Murphy, A. B. 1996. "The Sovereign State System as Political-territorial Ideal: Historical and Contemporary Considerations." In *State Sovereignty as Social Construct,* ed. T. Biersteker and C. Weber. Cambridge: Cambridge University Press.

Murray, P., and Holmes L., eds. 1998. *Europe: Rethinking the Boundaries.* Aldershot: Ashgate.

Musolff, A. 2001. "The Metaphorisation of European Politics: *Movement* on the *Road* to Europe." In *Attitudes towards Europe: Language in the Unification Process,* ed. A. Musolff et al. Aldershot: Ashgate.

Nanz, K. P. 1995. "The Schengen Agreement: Preparing the Free Movement of Persons in the European Union." In *Justice and Home Affairs in the European Union. The Development of the Third Pillar,* ed. R. Bieber and J. Monar. Brussels: European Interuniversity Press.

———. 1996. "Free Movement of Persons according to the Schengen Convention and in the Framework of the European Union." In *De Schengen à Maastricht,* ed. A. Pauly. Maastricht: European Institute of Public Administration.

Nascimbene, B., ed. 1995. *Da Schengen a Maastricht: Apertura delle frontiere, cooperazione giudiziaria e di polizia.* Milan: Giuffrè.

Nelson, B., D. Roberts, and W. Veit, eds. 1992. *The Idea of Europe: Problems of National and Transnational Identity.* Oxford: Berg.

Nelson, R. R. 2004. "Evolutionary Theories of Cultural Change: An Empirical Perspective." Papers on Economics and Evolution 2004–22, Max Planck Institute of Economics, Evolutionary Economics Group.

Nelson, R. R., and S. G. Winter. 2002. "Evolutionary Theorizing in Economics." *Journal of Economic Perspectives* 16, no. 2: 23–46.

Neumann, I. B. 2002. "Returning Practice to the Linguistic Turn: The Case of Diplomacy." *Millennium: Journal of International Studies* 31, no. 3: 627–651.

Newman, D., and A. Paasi. 1998. "Fences and Neighbours in a Post-Modern World:

Rethinking Boundaries in Political Geography." *Progress in Human Geography* 22, no. 2: 186–207.

Niessen, J. 1999. "International Migration on the EU Foreign Policy Agenda." *European Journal of Migration and Law* 1, no. 4: 483–496.

Niessen, J., and F. Mochel. 1999. *EU External Relations and International Migration.* Brussels: Migration Policy Group.

Noble, John (2004). *Fortress America or Fortress North America? Law & Business Review of the Americas,* 11, nos. 3–4: 461–478.

Nye, J. 1987. "Nuclear Learning and U.S.-Soviet Security Regimes". *International Organization,* 41, no. 3: 371–402.

O'Dowd, L. 2002. "Analysing Europe's Borders." *Boundary and Security Bulletin* 9, no. 2: 67–79.

O'Dowd, L., and T. M. Wilson. 1996. "Frontiers of Sovereignty in the New Europe." In *Borders, Nations and States,* ed. L. O'Dowd and T. M. Wilson, 1–18. Aldershot: Avebury.

O'Keefe, D. 1991. "The Schengen Convention: A Suitable Model for European Integration?" *Yearbook of European Law* 11: 185–219.

———. 1992. "The Free Movement of Persons and the Single Market." *European Law Review* 17: 1–19.

———. 1994. "Non-Accession to the Schengen Convention: The Cases of the United Kingdom and Ireland." In *Schengen en panne,* ed. A. Pauly. Maastricht: European Institute of Public Administration.

———. 1995. "Recasting the Third Pillar." *Common Market Law Review* 30: 893–920.

———. 1996. "The Convention on the Crossing of the External Frontiers of the Member States." In *De Schengen à Maastricht,* ed. A. Pauly. Maastricht: European Institute of Public Administration.

Ohmae, K. 1990. *The Borderless World.* London: William Collins.

Okolski, M. 1991. "Poland across the Rio Grande." *European Journal of International Affairs* 2: 136–153.

Paasi, A. 2001. "Europe as a Social Process and Discourse. Considerations of Place, Boundaries and Identity." *European Urban and Regional Studies* 8, no. 1: 7–28.

Papademetriou, D. G. 1996. *Coming Together or Pulling Apart? The European Union's Struggle with Immigration and Asylum.* Washington, D.C.: Carnegie Endowment.

Parisi, N., and D. Rinoldi, eds. 1996. *Giustizia e affari interni nell'Unione europea.* Turin: G. Giappichelli.

Parker, Noel, ed. 2008. *The Geopolitics of Europe's Identity: Centers, Boundaries and Margins.* Houndsmill: Palgrave McMillan.

Pastor, R. 2005. "A North American Community Approach to Security," Testimony to the Senate Foreign Relations Committee, June 9, 2005. Available at http://www.cfr.org/publication/8173/north_american_community_approach_to_security.html.

Pastore, F. 1999. "Verso una politica migratoria comune? Le prospettive di applicazione del nuovo titolo IV TCE tra interessi nazionali ed interesse comune europeo." Report of the Centro Studi di Politica Internazionale, CeSPi, March, Rome.

———. 2000. "Italy Facing International Migration: Recent Policy Developments." *International Spectator* 25, no. 2: 29–40.

———. 2002a. "Aeneas' Route. Euro-Mediterranean Relations and International Migration." In *Migration and the Externalities of Integration: The Wider Impact of the Developing EU Migration Regime,* ed. S. Lavenex and E. Uçarer. Lanham: Lexington Books.

———. 2002b. "Just Another European Dream? Why Did the Communitarization of Immigration and Asylum Policies Almost Fail and How We Should Revive It." Paper presented at the international seminar for experts organized by the Cicero Foundation, "European Migration and Refugee Policy: New Developments," Rome, November 15.

Pateman, C. 1980. "The Civic Culture: A Philosophic Critique." In *The Civic Culture Revisited*, ed. Gabriel Almond, 57–102. Boston: Little, Brown.

Pauly, A., ed. 1994. *Schengen en panne*. Maastricht: European Institute of Public Administration.

———. 1996. *De Schengen à Maastricht: Voie royale et course d'obstacles*. Maastricht: European Institute of Public Administration.

Peers, S. 2000. *EU Justice and Home Affairs Law*. Harlow: Longman.

Peirce, C. S. 1998. *The Essential Writings*. Edited by Edward C. Moore. Amherst: Prometheus Books.

Perlmutter, T. 1998. "The Politics of Proximity: The Italian Response to the Albanian Crisis." *International Migration Review* 32, no. 1: 203–222.

Peterson, J., and Shackleton, M., eds. 2002. *The Institutions of the European Union*. Oxford: Oxford University Press.

Pierros, F., J. Meunier, and S. Abrams. 1999. *Bridges and Barriers. The European Union's Mediterranean Policy, 1961–1998*. Aldershot: Ashgate.

Pollet, K. 2001. "The European Union and Migratory Pressure from the Mediterranean and Central and Eastern Europe." In *The EU's Enlargement and Mediterranean Strategies: A Comparative Analysis*, ed. M. Maresceau and E. Lannon. Houndsmill: Palgrave.

Potemkina, O. I. 2002. "EU-Russia Cooperation in Justice and Home Affairs in the Context of Enlargement." IEE Document, no. 23, Institut d'Études Européennes, Université Catholique de Louvain, Louvain.

Poznanski, K. 1993. "An Interpretation of Communist Decay: The Role of Evolutionary Mechanisms." *Communist and Post-Communist Studies* 26, no. 1: 3–22.

Pryce, R. 1994. "The Treaty Negotiations." In *Maastricht and Beyond: Building the European Union*, ed. A. Duff, J. Pinder, and R. Pryce. London: Routledge.

Pryce, R., ed. 1987. *The Dynamics of European Union*. London: Routledge.

Raj, Kartik Varada. 2006. "Paradoxes on the Borders of Europe." *International Feminist Journal of Politics* 8, no. 4 (Dec.): 512–534.

Ricoeur, P. 1984. *Time and Narrative*. Chicago: University of Chicago Press.

Risse, T. 2000. "Let's Argue! Communicative Action in World Politics." *International Organization* 54 (Winter): 1–39.

———. 2001. "A European Identity? Europeanization and the Evolution of Nation-State Identities." In *Transforming Europe: Europeanization and Domestic Change*, ed. M. Cowles, J. Caporaso, J., and T. Risse, 198–216. Ithaca: Cornell University Press.

Risse-Kappen, T. 1996. "Exploring the Nature of the Beast: International Relations Theory Meet the European Union." *Journal of Common Market Studies* 34, no. 1: 53–80.

Robert, J. 1992. "Les accords de Schengen." *Revue des Affaires Européens* 1: 5–15.

Rosamond, B. 2000. *Theories of European integration*, New York: St. Martin's Press.

Rosenau J. N., and E. O. Czempiel, eds. 1992. *Governance without Government: Order and Change in World Politics*. Cambridge: Cambridge University Press.

Rosencrance, R. 1996. "The Rise of the Virtual State." *Foreign Affairs* 75, no. 4: 45–61.

Ross, M. H. 1997. "Culture and Identity in Comparative Political Analysis." In *Comparative Politics: Rationality, Culture and Structure*, ed. M. I. Lichbach and A. S. Zuckerman. Cambridge: Cambridge University Press.

Rudolph, C. 2005. "International Migration and Homeland Security: Coordination and

Collaboration in North America." *Law and Business Review of the Americas* 11, nos. 3–4: 433–459.

Ruggie, J. G. 1993. "Territoriality and Beyond: Problematizing Modernity in International Relations." *International Organization* 47, no. 1: 139–174.

Rupnik, J. 1994. "Europe's New Frontiers: Remapping Europe." *Daedalus* 123, no. 3: 91–114.

Rytövuori-Apunen, H. 2005. "Forget 'Post-Positivist' IR! The Legacy of IR Theory as the Locus for a Pragmatist Turn." *Cooperation and Conflict: Journal of the Nordic International Studies Association* 40, no. 2: 147–177.

Sanderson, Stephen K. 1990. *Social Evolutionism: A Critical History.* Cambridge: Blackwell.

Sassen, S. 1999. *Globalization and its Discontents.* New York: New Press, Saunier, G. 2001. "Prélude a la relance de l'Europe: Le couple Franco-Allemand et les projects de relance communautaire vus de l'hexagone 1981–1985." In *La couple France-Allemagne et les insitutions européennes: Une postérité pour la Plan Schuman?* ed. M.-T. Bitsch. Brussels: Établissments Émile Bruylant.

Schatzki, T. R. 2001. "Introduction: Practice theory." In *The Practice Turn in Contemporary Theory,* ed. T. R. Schatzki, K. Knorr-Cetina, and E. von Savigny E. London: Routledge.

Schatzki, T. R., K. Knorr-Cetina, and E. von Savigny, eds. 2001. *The Practice Turn in Contemporary Theory.* London: Routledge.

Schmidt, V. 1997. "Discourse and (dis)integration in Europe: The Cases of France, Germany, and Great Britain." *Daedalus* (Summer): 167–97.

Schmitter, P. 1996. "Imagining the Future of the Euro-polity with the Help of New Concepts." In *Governance in the European Union,* ed. G. Marks, F. Scharpf, P. Schmitter, and W. Streeck, 121–150. Sage: London.

Schneider, G., and M. Aspinwall, eds. 2001. *The Rules of Integration: Institutionalist Approaches to the Study of Europe.* Manchester: Manchester University Press.

Schuman, Robert. 1963. *Pour l'Europe.* Paris: Nagel.

Schutte, J. E. 1991. "Schengen: Its Meaning for the Free Movement of Persons in Europe." *Common Market Law Review* 28: 540–570.

Schutz, A. 1971. *Collected Papers II—Studies in Social Theory.* The Hague: Martinus Nijhoff.

Sciortino, G. 1998. "The Albanian Crisis: Social Panic and Italian Foreign Policy." In *Italian Politics: Mapping the Future,* ed. L. Bardi and M. Rhodes, 243–264. Boulder: Westview.

Searle, J. 1995. *The Construction of Social Reality.* New York: Free Press.

Shore, Sean. 1998. "No Fences Make Good Neighbours: The Development of the US-Canadian Security Community, 1871–1940." In *Security Communities,* ed. E. Adler and M. Barnett. Cambridge: Cambridge University Press.

Simon, H. A. 1996. *The Sciences of the Artificial.* 3rd ed. Cambridge, MA: MIT Press.

Skran, C. M. 1992. "The International Refugee Regime: The Historical and Contemporary Context of International Responses to Asylum Problems." In *Refugees and the Asylum Dilemma in the West,* ed. G. Loescher. University Park: Pennsylvania State University Press.

Slack, J. D. 1993. "The Theory and Method of Articulation in Cultural Studies." In *Stuart Hall: Critical Dialogues in Cultural Studies,* eds. D. Morley and K.-H. Chen, 113–130. London: Routledge.

Smith, M. 1996. "The European Union and a Changing Europe: Establishing the Boundaries of Order." *Journal of Common Market Studies* 34: 13–18.

Solomon, K. 1991. *Refugees in the Cold War: Towards a New International Refugee Regime in the Early Post War Era.* Lund: Lund University Press.

Somers, Margaret R. 1995. "What's Political or Cultural about Political Culture and the Public Sphere? Toward an Historical Sociology of Concept Formation." *Sociological Theory* 13, no. 2: 113–144.

Soysal, Y. N. *1994. Limits of Citizenship: Migrants and Postnational Membership in Europe.* London and Chicago: University of Chicago Press.

Spruyt, H. 1994. *The Sovereign State and Its Competitors.* Princeton: Princeton University Press.

Staples, H. 2000. "Adjudicating the Schengen Agreements in the Netherlands." *European Journal of Migration and Law* 2, no. 1: 49–83.

Stetter S. 2000. "Regulating Migration: Authority Delegation in Justice and Home Affairs." *Journal of European Public Policy* 7, no. 1: 80–103.

Steuneberg, B., ed. 2002. *Widening the European Union: The Politics of Institutional Change and Reform.* London: Routledge.

Struan, Jacobs. 2006. "Models of Scientific Community: Charles Sanders Peirce to Thomas Kuhn." *Interdisciplinary Science Reviews* 31, no. 2: 163–173.

Stubb, A. 2002. *Negotiating Flexibility in the European Union.* Houndsmill: Palgrave.

Swidler, A. 1986. "Culture in Action: Symbols and Strategies." *American Sociological Review* 51, no. 2 (Apr.): 273–286.

———. 2001. "What Anchors Cultural Practices." In *The Practice Turn in Contemporary Theory,* ed. T. R. Schatzki, K. Knorr Cetina, and E. von Savigny, 74–92. London: Routledge.

Talisse, Robert B. 2004. "Towards a Peircean *Politics* of Inquiry." *Transactions of the Charles S. Peirce Society: A Quarterly Journal in American Philosophy* 40, no. 1: 21–38.

Taschner, H. C. 1998. *Schengen.* Baden-Baden: Nomos.

Tassinari, F. 2005. "The Challenges of the European Neighbourhood Policy—A Riddle Inside an Enigma: Unwrapping the EU-Russia Strategic Partnership." *International Spectator* 40, no. 1: 45–67.

Taylor, P. J. 1994. "The State as a Container: Territoriality on the Modern World System." *Progress in Human Geography* 18: 151–162.

Thränhardt, D. 1999. "Germany's Immigration Policies and Politics." In *Mechanisms of Immigration Control: A Comparative Analysis of European Regulation Policies,* ed. G. Brochmann and T. Hammar. London: Berg.

Toffano, U. 1989. "L'accordo di Schengen o l'Europa dei fatti." *Affari Esteri* 83: 541–553.

Toje, A. 2005. "The 2003 European Security Strategy: A Critical Appraisal." *European Foreign Affairs Review* 10, no. 1: 117–134.

Tonra, B. 2001. *The Europeanisation of National Foreign Policy: Dutch, Danish, and Irish Foreign Policy in the European Union.* Aldershot: Ashgate.

Toolan, M. 1997. *Narrative: A Critical Linguistic Introduction.* London: Routledge.

Torpey, J. 1998. "Coming and Going: On the State Monopolization of the 'Legitimate Means of Movement.'" *Sociological Theory* 16, no. 3: 239–259.

———. 2000. *The Invention of the Passport: Surveillance, Citizenship and the State.* Cambridge: Cambridge University Press.

Toulmin, S. 1972. *Human Understanding.* Princeton: Princeton University Press.

Tunander, O. 1997. *Geopolitics in Post-Wall Europe: Security, Territory and Identity.* London: Thousand Oaks.

Turk, A. 1998. *Quand les policiers succèdent aux diplomates.* Rapport d'information 523 (97–8) de la Commission des lois du Sénat. Paris: Sénat.

Uçarer, E. M. 2001. "From the Sidelines to Center Stage: Sidekick No More? The European Commission in Justice and Home Affairs." *European Integration Online Papers (EIoP)* 5, no. 5: 1–20. Available at http://eiop.or.at/eiop/pdf/2001-005.pdf.

Van De Rijt, W. 1997a. "Schengen depuis le 26 Mars 1995." In *The Implementation of Schengen: First the Widening, Now the Deepening,* ed. M. Den Boer. Maastricht: European Institute of Public Administration.

———. 1997b. "Schengen et les Pays Nordiques: Aperçue de la situation actuelle." In

Schengen: Judicial Cooperation and Policy Coordination, ed. M. Den Boer. Maastricht: European Institute of Public Administration.

———. 1998. "Le fonctionnement des Institutions Schengen: 'Pragmatisme, toujours.'" In *Schengen's Final Days? The Incorporation of Schengen into the New TEU, External Borders and Information Systems*, ed. M. Den Boer. Maastricht: European Institute of Public Administration.

———. 2000. "Les initiatives bilatérales et multilatérales enter Schengen et les états (non-) membres de l'EU." In *Schengen Still Going Strong: Evaluation and Update*, ed. M. Den Boer M. Maastricht: European Institute of Public Administration.

Van Houtum, H. 2003. "Borders of Comfort: Spatial Economic Bordering Processes in the European Union." In *New Borders for a Changing Europe: Cross-border Cooperation and Governance*, ed. J. Anderson, L. O'Dowd, and T. M. Wilson. London: Franck Cass.

Veil, S. 1997. *Rapport du groupe de haut niveau sur la libre circulation des personnes*. Report presented to the European Commission on March 18, 1997. Brussels: European Commission.

Vink, M., and Meijerink, F. 2003. "Asylum Applications and Recognition Rates in EU Member States, 1982–2001: A Quantitative Analysis." *Journal of Refugee Studies* 16, no. 3: 297–315.

Vitorino, A. 2002. "New European Borders and Security Co-Operation: Promoting Trust in an Enlarged Union." In *Police and Justice Co-Operation and the New European Borders*, ed. M. Anderson J. Apap, 11–17. The Hague: Kluwer Law International.

Waever, O. 1995. "Securitization and Desecuritization." In *On Security*, ed. R. D. Lippschutz, 46–86. New York: Columbia University Press.

Waever, O. 1997. "Imperial Metaphors: Emerging European Analogies to Pre-Nation-State Imperial Systems." In *Geopolitics in Post Wall Europe: Security, Territory and Identity*, ed. O. Tunander et al. London: Sage.

Waever, O., B. Buzan, M. Kelstrup, and P. Lemaitre, P. 1993. *Identity, Migration and the New Security Agenda in Europe*. London: Pinter.

Wagner, P. 1989. "Social Science and the State in Continental Western Europe." *International Social Science Journal* 36, no. 4: 509–529.

Walker, N. 1998. "The New Frontiers of European Policing." In *The Frontiers of Europe*, ed. M. Anderson and E. Bort. London and Washington: Pinter.

———. 2002. "The Problem of Trust in an Enlarged Area of Freedom, Security and Justice: A Conceptual Analysis." In *Police and Justice Cooperation and the New European Borders*, ed. M. Anderson and J. Apap, 19–33. The Hague: Kluwer.

Walker, N., ed. 2004. *Europe's Area of Freedom, Security, and Justice*. Oxford: Oxford University Press.

Walker, R. 2000. "Europe Is Not Where It Is Supposed to Be." In *International Relations and the Politics of European Integration*, ed. Morten Kelstrup and Michael Williams, 14–32. London: Routledge.

Wallace H. 2000. "The Institutional Setting: Five Variations on a Theme." In *Policy-Making in the European Union*, ed. H. Wallace and W. Wallace. 4th ed. Oxford: Oxford University Press.

Wallace, H., and W. Wallace, eds. 2000. *Policy-Making in the European Union*. 4th ed. Oxford: Oxford University Press.

Walters, W. 2002. "Mapping Schengenland: Denaturalizing the Border." *Environment and Planning D: Society and Space* 20, no. 5: 561–580.

———. 2004. "The Frontiers of the European Union: A Geostrategic Perspective." *Geopolitics* 9, no. 2: 674–698.

Ward, Roger. 2001. "Peirce and Politics." *Philosophy and Social Criticism* 27, no. 3: 67–90.

Weber-Panariello, P. A. 1995. "The Integration of Matters of Justice and Home Affairs into Title IV of the Treaty of European Union. A Step Towards Democracy?" *European University Institute Working Paper RSC* 95(32).

Wedeen, Lisa. 2002. "Conceptualizing Culture: Possibilities for Political Science." *American Political Science Review* 96, no. 4: 713–728.

Weiss, F., and F. Wooldridge. 2002. *Free Movement of Persons within the European Community.* The Hague: Kluwer Law International.

Weldes, J., et al. 1999. *Cultures of Insecurity: States, Communities and the Production of Danger.* Minneapolis: University of Minnesota Press.

Wendt, A. 1999. *Social Theory of International Politics.* Cambridge: Cambridge University Press.

Wenger, E. 1998. *Communities of Practice: Learning, Meaning and Identity.* Cambridge: Cambridge University Press.

Wiener, A. 1998. "The Embedded *Acquis* Communautaire. Transmission Belt and Prism of New Governance." *European Law Journal* 4, no. 3: 294–315.

———. 1999. "Forging Flexibility—the British 'No' to Schengen." *European Journal of Migration and Law* 1, no. 4: 441–463.

Wiener, A., ed. 2004. *European Integration Theory.* Oxford: Oxford University Press.

Wiley, Norbert, 2006. "Peirce and the Founding of American Sociology." *Journal of Classical Sociology* 6, no. 1: 23–50.

William, D. 1996. *The Reach of Rome: A History of the Roman Imperial Frontier 1st–5th Centuries AD.* New York: St. Martin's Press.

Wilson, T. M. 1996. "Sovereignty, Identity and Borders: Political Anthropology and European Integration." In *Borders, Nations and States,* ed. L. O'Dowd and T. M. Wilson, 199–220. Aldershot: Avebury.

Wilson, T. M., and H. Donnan, eds. 1998. *Border Identities: Nation and State at International Frontiers.* Cambridge: Cambridge University Press.

Yee, A. S. 1996. "The Causal Effects of Ideas on Politics." *International Organization* 50, no. 1: 68–108.

Zacher, M. W. 1992. "The Decaying Pillars of the Westphalian Temple: Implications for International Order and Governance." In *Governance without Government,* ed. J. Rosenau and E. O. Czempiel, 58–101. Cambridge: Cambridge University Press.

Zaiotti, R. 2007. "La propagation de la sécurité: L'Europe et la schengenisation de la Politique de voisinage." *Cultures and Conflicts* 66: 61–76.

———. 2008. "Bridging Commonsense: Pragmatic Metaphors and the 'Schengen Laboratory.'" In *Metaphors of Globalization: Mirrors, Magicians, Mutinies,* ed. M. Kornprobst, N. Shah, V. Pouliot, and R. Zaiotti, 66–80. Houndmills: Palgrave.

Zielonka, J. 2001. "How the New Enlarged Borders Will Reshape the European Union." *Journal of Common Market Studies* 39, no. 3: 507–536.

Zielonka, J., ed. 2002. *Europe Unbound: Enlarging and Reshaping the Boundaries of the European Union.* London: Routledge.

Zolberg, A. 1999. "Matters of State: Theorizing Immigration Policy." In *The Handbook of International Migration: the American Experience,* ed. C. Hirschman, P. Kasinitz, and J. DeWind. New York: Russell Sage.

Zürn, M., and C. Joerges, eds. 2005. *Law and Governance in Postnational Europe: Compliance Beyond the Nation-State.* Cambridge: Cambridge University Press.